GETTING MORE OUT OF TIAA-CREF

John J. Harrigan

Hamline University

The Oak Park Press, Inc.

St. Paul, Minnesota

This book was set in 11 pt. CG Times Type and was printed and bound by
The Oak Park Press, Inc.
The cover was designed by Joan Gordon, Etc.

Printed in the United States of America

The Oak Park Press
Box 131206
St. Paul, Minnesota 55113

ISBN 0 9642568-0-0

This publication is designed to provide accurate and authoritative information in regard to
the subject matters covered. However, it is sold with the understanding that the publisher
and the author are not engaged in rendering legal, accounting, financial or other professional services. While data in this book cannot be guaranteed to be error free, it has been
obtained from public sources believed to be reliable. Investment strategies that were successful in the past cannot be guaranteed to be successful in the future.

1 2 3 4 5 6 7 8 9 10 - 99 98 97 96 95

About
the Author

John J. Harrigan is professor of political science at Hamline University in St. Paul, Minnesota. He received an M.A. degree in international relations from the University of Chicago in 1962 and a Ph.D. in political science from Georgetown University in 1970. Harrigan is author of books on urban politics, state politics, and U.S. politics. His writings on investments and retirement planning have appeared in *Academe*, *Change*, and the *Journal of the American Association of Individual Investors*.

CONTENTS

PREFACE

This book was written out of practical necessity. In the late 1980s the rules for retirement planning began to change in fundamental ways, new options were created, and like most TIAA-CREF participants I came face-to-face with choices I had never before had the luxury of making. When I started teaching, there were only two retirement choices, the fixed income based TIAA or the stock market based CREF. One of my most rewarding financial choices was to earmark all of my pension contributions to CREF. It did not seem rewarding at the time, however, because stocks immediately suffered their worst bear market since the Great Depression, and the CREF unit value dropped by 50 percent. Nevertheless, like Moliere's bourgeois gentleman who was delighted to discover that he had been speaking prose all of his life, I eventually found out that for many years I had been unwittingly practicing the renowned and lucrative investment strategy called dollar cost averaging. There were also some costly mistakes along the way. One of the worst was to panic in the wake of the 1987 market crash and switch a fourth of my CREF holdings to TIAA. TIAA's returns have declined steadily since that fateful day, while the CREF unit has more than doubled. This clarified for me what the economists meant by their term opportunity costs.

In short, it was becoming painfully clear that I lacked a systematic strategy for retirement planning that would enable me to profit from the exciting changes that were coming to TIAA-CREF. This drove me to put more effort into studying about finances, which in turn led me to the captivating world of dollar cost averaging, opportunity costs, and dozens of other intriguing concepts. That my fellow TIAA-CREF participants could benefit from these ideas was brought home to me at a Political Science conference in Chicago in 1991. While chatting with a group of friends, we began to discuss the changes taking place in TIAA-CREF. However, rather than viewing them as exciting possibilities, we saw them as confusing choices. Somebody commented that we needed a handbook to guide us through the confusion. On the long drive home the next day I mulled over the ideas that such a handbook should cover, and that was the genesis of *Getting More Out of TIAA-CREF*. It turned out to be substantially larger than the handbook that my colleagues originally wanted, but I hope that it is nevertheless useful to them and other TIAA-CREF participants.

This Book's Plan

This book offers a strategy for your retirement planning that is based on the belief that your overriding goal for retirement planning ought to be to accumulate enough capital to let you retire at the comfort level you want.

The first group of chapters in Part I offers an overview of TIAA-CREF and addresses the two costliest mistakes made by TIAA-CREF participants. These chapters urge you to open an SRA, to tailor your accumulation vehicles to your situation, and to be wary about putting too much of your money into TIAA.

Part II address the third costliest mistake made by participants. The chapters here offer low-risk strategies for accumulating and preserving your retirement assets. These are dollar cost averaging, value averaging, and strategic asset allocation.

Part III analyzes a riskier set of strategies for capital accumulation and preservation. The strategies suggested in these chapters are not appropriate for most people. Even people who can afford the capital risk entailed should follow these strategies with only a portion of their retirement assets.

Part IV addresses the fourth costliest mistake made by participants. Whereas the first three parts of the book focus on the capital accumulation phase of retirement planning, the chapters in Part IV discuss what TIAA-CREF calls the payout phase. This section analyzes the payout options that, in some ways, are even more confusing than the investment options available in the accumulation phase.

Finally, the appendices provide some useful background information. The first appendix presents a table for calculating the impact of inflation on your finances. The second gives you a table for calculating how much capital is needed to generate each $10,000 of income for stipulated time periods. The third appendix gives a table for calculating the maximum you can withdraw from each dollar of savings without exhausting your savings. The fourth appendix provides you with a systematic set of questions to put before a financial planner when he or she offers to manage your retirement savings for you.

Acknowledgements

Conducting the research for this book has helped me sort out my own thoughts about retirement planning, and I hope that this book's presentation of those thoughts is equally helpful to the reader. If so I am greatly indebted to many people who contributed to this project. First are Jeffrey Carlson and Greg Carlson who are financial planners in Minnesota. After reviewing the entire manuscript, they spent hours debating it with me and challenged me to clarify my thoughts on the annuitization choice, the financial planning profession, and many other points. I owe much to their insights. A third reviewer, who requested anonymity, saved me from making several factual errors and also influenced my perceptions of several key issues. This was invaluable. Barbara Bergstrom copy edited the manuscript. Laurie Schwab proof-read the pages. Joan Gordon designed the cover. George Redman helped me figure out how to get the book published, and Don Beimborn walked me through much of that process. This project has also benefited from many colleagues at Hamline University who have generously discussed and criticized these ideas over the years. Although this book is both sympathetic to and critical about TIAA-CREF, it does not represent the thinking of TIAA-CREF. I have neither sought endorsement from nor received endorsement from TIAA-CREF for this project. Any errors in this book are the responsibility of the author alone. Portions of the book were adapted as articles that appeared in *Academe, Change,* and the *Journal of the American Association of Individual Investors.*

While this book presents general financial strategies based on extensive research and data sources believed to be reliable, it is important for the reader to recognize that the author is not professionally engaged in financial planning or money management. Neither this book nor any other book on financial matters can adequately address the unique circumstances of each person.

There are some benefits to a book written by one who is not a professional in personal finance. The book is not only based on extensive research, but it brings a neutrality that is absent from most of the people telling you what to do with your retirement savings. Unlike the financial planner who phones, I have no desire to manage your money. Unlike

TIAA-CREF, I have no bureaucratic need to keep you bound in the system. And unlike some college employers, I have no paternalistic need to restrict your retirement choices. The pressing need that I do have, however, is the same one that you share. Figuring out how to build and preserve a comfortable retirement nest egg in a fast changing and increasingly complex world. This book presents my best thoughts on that at this time, and I hope that some of these thoughts are useful to you.

Finally, I thank my wife Sandy who shared her thoughts on portions of the manuscript and on the project.

St. Paul, Minnesota
September 1994

PART I

PRESCRIPTIONS

Part I focuses on four prescriptions for gaining financial independence through TIAA-CREF. The first is to recognize what you must do to empower yourself to gain considerable influence over the growth and preservation of your retirement nest egg. The second is to understand how TIAA-CREF fits within the universe of vehicles available to you for building a retirement fund. The third is to pay yourself first by opening a deferred compensation Supplemental Retirement Annuity. This is the single most important step that most of us can take to gain financial independence. And the fourth is to understand the advantages of CREF over TIAA during the early and mid-career accumulation years.

Chapter 1

Empower Yourself
Financially

Why a Book on TIAA-CREF?

The Teachers Insurance Annuity Association-College Retirement Equities Fund (TIAA-CREF) is the main pension plan for 1.7 million participants at more than 5,000 colleges, universities, and non-profit organizations around the country. Each of these individuals can benefit from the comprehensive information presented in this book. The contemporary forces that threaten the retirement hopes of many Americans threaten TIAA-CREF participants as well.

Despite media stories about an affluent senior citizenry, most Americans do not retire in financial comfort. The median annual income of couples aged 65 or older was only $16,975 in 1991. Subtract the average couple's Social Security benefit of $12,864, and the average couple's income from all other sources appears to have barely reached $4,100.[1] The National Center for Health Statistics painted an even grimmer picture. Its study of the finances of people who died in 1986 revealed that a majority had incomes under $15,000, and 41 percent had total assets of less than $25,000.[2]

Retirees from colleges and universities fared much better. A 1990 survey of 17,000 such retirees found that their median household income from all sources was $30,000, with retired faculty ($44,000) and administrators ($34,000) faring the best. Administrative support staff and maintenance staff did less well, with median incomes of only $23,100 and $15,800 respectively.[3]

These figures mask several considerations. Since $44,000 for faculty retirees is a median figure, half of all faculty retirees received less than $44,000 in 1990. Subtracting from that median figure a Social Security benefit of $14,000 suggests that the median income from all non-Social Security sources was only $30,000 for faculty and $20,000 for administrators. Another subtraction would have to be made for the three-fourths of respondents who reported that their household income also included other sources in addition to TIAA-CREF. Further subtractions would have to be made for those respondents who had marriage partners who also contributed to the household income. Since the survey did not put a dollar value on these figures, it is impossible to know precisely how much of the average faculty member's $44,000 came from TIAA-CREF and how much came from other sources. Finally, the 1990 survey included retirees from public pension plans and other pension plans as well as TIAA-CREF. TIAA-CREF retirees may or may not have done as well as the average retirees reported here.

Nevertheless, however one looks at the data, it is hard to believe that TIAA-CREF benefits count for more than half of the average retired faculty's household income. An earlier TIAA-CREF survey had found that TIAA-CREF annuities provided only 30 percent of annuitants' income.[4] In 1990, nearly a third of retirees said that their single biggest source of income was Social Security.[5] Only half of the faculty retirees--the category with the highest pension income--said that their pension was their largest source of income. A good guess would be that the average TIAA-CREF annual benefit for retired faculty amounted to barely $20,000. A large majority of TIAA-CREF retirees probably received even less than that.

It is important to point out that the overwhelming majority of college retirees who were surveyed felt that they had adequate finances. What is not clear from the surveys is whether the retirees' finances were adequate because of the retirees' basic TIAA-CREF pension plan, or because the retirees had exercised enough foresight to accumulate other savings and other investments. The survey respondents cited as a recurring theme the need to start effective financial planning early in one's career.[6] Those who had not planned, who had not built up other retirement savings, were not served well if they relied solely on their TIAA-CREF retirement annuities. This was especially true for support staff retirees.

Although $20,000--the upper bound of the estimated average annual TIAA-CREF benefits--is hardly a poverty-level income, it is fairly pedestrian. It does not leave much room for travel or frequent luxuries. Most TIAA-CREF retirees are learned people who spent a lifetime in a respectable profession and who made significant contributions to the education of generations of young people. How could these peoples' central pension plan leave them with such modest benefits? Equally important, how can today's professional and support staff people position themselves more advantageously for their own eventual retirement?

Planning a secure financial retirement for oneself does not promise to be a very easy task. America's economic future seems much less certain today than it has at any time since mid-twentieth century. So far in the 1990s, growth rates have been lower than they were in the 1970s or 1980s, and rapidly accelerating change in technology and the labor markets have thrown into question the ability of the American economy to provide economic security for everyone. Social Security costs and other costs associated with a growing population of elderly people will increase political pressures regarding the use of Social Security trust funds. Already, these pressures have resulted in taxing some peoples' Social Security benefits and deferring eligibility for full Social Security benefits to age 67 for people now entering the work force. Furthermore, the debt of the federal government has grown by $3 trillion over the past dozen years, and even after the deficit reduction legislation of 1993, the debt seems likely to grow by a similar amount over the next dozen years. Nobody really knows the consequences of such an increase. The economic future probably will not turn out as badly as some pessimists predict, but it is undoubtedly going to be different from past. The American economy and the global economy are moving into uncharted territory.

Sailing through those uncharted waters safely is going to require more effort on your part in the future than it has in the past. In the past, your retirement funds were divided between TIAA and CREF Stock, and TIAA-CREF decided how those funds would be invested. Today, CREF offers you seven funds, and you now have the responsibility of deciding which of those funds to use. To make reasonable decisions about the many choices you currently face, you need to empower yourself financially.

If TIAA-CREF is your central pension plan, you especially need to take maximum advantage of TIAA-CREF's various investment vehicles and options. These options give TIAA-CREF an admirable set of advantages as a retirement plan. Fully utilized, those advantages should leave no TIAA-CREF participant with a lower-than-average retirement income. Currently, most people fail to get as much out of TIAA-CREF as they could. To take full advantage of TIAA-CREF's resources you must empower yourself financially. This book aims to help you do just that.

A Sea Change in Pension Planning

In the last few years, the dramatic innovations made in TIAA-CREF have brought new confusion to our lives. These innovations are part of a nationwide sea change taking place in pension plans that is shifting the responsibility for retirement saving, planning, and investing onto the individual. Increasingly fewer corporations offer traditional, defined benefit plans in which a corporate pension fund promises to pay its retirees a specific annual income when they reach age 65.[7] So many existing corporate pension plans are underfunded that some financial writers have expressed grave concern over a potential problem that might arise if or when these pension funds fall short of keeping their promises.[8] As the problems with traditional pension plans mount, more and more corporations are moving toward TIAA-CREF-type defined contribution plans in which the individual's benefits ultimately depend upon how much he or she has saved and how well those savings have been invested.

Forcing individuals to accept more responsibility for their pension planning gives rise to two huge problems. First, too many people are saving too little.[9] Second, in contrast to the traditional plans in which professional money managers invested workers' savings, individuals today increasingly have to decide for themselves how to allocate these investments. There are now 7 CREF funds from which you can choose, plus TIAA. Allocating assets among these and other options is not an issue to which most people have given any systematic, prolonged thought. The evidence indicates that, when it comes to making these allocation decisions, individuals are much more timid than the pension fund money managers. Pension funds maintain an average of about 53 percent of their assets in equities, while individuals with tax deferred compensation plans put only about 21 percent in equities.[10] How do you learn to manage your funds correctly? asks financial columnist Jane Bryant Quinn.[11] That is the central question facing TIAA-CREF participants today.

Making Better Use of TIAA-CREF Options

TIAA-CREF participants have a critical need to educate themselves on how the changes in their pension plan affect their future. The changes in TIAA-CREF have been dramatic. Several new CREF funds were introduced. Participants can now transfer their TIAA holdings into CREF over a long period of time. Most importantly, TIAA-CREF has lost its monopoly on the retirement plans of participating institutions. Any institution using TIAA-CREF can now permit its employees to transfer CREF funds to other carriers, such as mutual fund families or mutual fund investments guided by a financial planning firm. This means that you and many of your fellow 1.7 million TIAA-CREF participants now face an array of choices that were not previously available. Used wisely, these choices will greatly enhance your financial stability.

There is a downside to these new choices, however. Because of the expansion of choices, planning for retirement now takes more effort and time than it did a few years ago. The options are sometimes confusing, and TIAA-CREF is reluctant to suggest that we make aggressive use of their various options.[12]

It is true that TIAA-CREF sends out a flood of publications each year--the quarterly *Participant*, quarterly account reports, the Annuity Benefits Report, special reports, and numerous solicitations to take out life insurance, apply for disability insurance, and open a Supplemental Retirement Annuity (SRA). What is missing from all of this is a concise and coherent strategy on how to maximize your retirement savings and preserve them once they have begun to accumulate. Because of its fiduciary responsibility, TIAA-CREF hesitates to advise participants to adopt a more aggressive strategy,[13] even when it might be in many participants' best interest. And because of its interest in keeping as many participants as possible, TIAA-CREF cannot make a reasoned calculation of the relative merits of TIAA-CREF compared to other investment vehicles that are now available to TIAA-CREF participants.

Advantages of TIAA-CREF

None of the above suggests that TIAA-CREF is a bad retirement plan. With its newly acquired options, TIAA-CREF is an excellent vehicle for accumulating retirement capital. Consider, for instance:

- You can retire any time you want and receive your TIAA-CREF benefits (although you might incur some tax penalties if you do so before age 55). In most traditional defined benefit plans you can retire only at age 65. Early retirement options almost always occur during short-term windows of opportunity that might not coincide with your best interests.

- Your employer cannot plunder or mismanage your TIAA-CREF retirement plan the way that many private employers plundered and mismanaged their company pension plans in the 1980s.

- The Supplemental Retirement Annuity (SRA) offers you one of the most lucrative accumulation plans you are likely to find.

- Because you can make extra contributions into your plan, you exercise a fair amount of control over your ultimate retirement benefits. In traditional plans, this is not possible.

- When the time comes to retire, you are offered a valuable array of options for taking your retirement income in ways that can be tailored to your own circumstances.

- In recent years TIAA-CREF has introduced new investment vehicles and new options. If that innovation continues in future years, TIAA-CREF will offer you an enviable package of choices for accumulating a substantial retirement nest egg.

- As an investment manager, TIAA-CREF has to date produced reasonable results with relatively low managerial expenses.

Common Mistakes in Using TIAA-CREF

Different people have different circumstances, and many TIAA-CREF participants are loathe to incur financial risk. However, far too many people are far too timid in using their TIAA-CREF options. This book will argue that many TIAA-CREF participants--not everyone surely, but certainly most of those who are a decade or more from retirement --ought to take a fairly aggressive investment posture. Young and mid-career people will be advised to make realistic estimates of the risk levels they can tolerate and then shift their asset mix to a level consistent with their tolerance for risk. For most people, this will probably mean becoming more aggressive in their use of TIAA-CREF. For some older participants, adjusting their investment mix to their risk level might mean becoming less aggressive with TIAA-CREF. Because of the threat of inflation, however, even older participants have to maintain some aggressiveness in their investment posture. A person could easily spend twenty or twenty-five years living on his or her retirement funds. Unless those funds were invested to compensate for the long-term impact of inflation, that person's living standard would slowly be eroded just like a river that carves out a mountain valley.

Future chapters will expand on this idea, but here are some of the most common TIAA-CREF mistakes that too many people make.

- Not enough people have opened SRAs.

- Not enough of those people who have opened SRAs put enough money into them.

- Too many people put too much of their retirement contributions into TIAA. The CREF Stock fund has substantially and consistently outperformed TIAA since CREF was started four decades ago. To bet that it will not do so again over the next four decades is to bet that the American and global economies are going to stagnate over that period. (See chap. 4.)

- The low percentage of people utilizing the CREF bond, Social Choice, Global Equities, and Money Market accounts suggests that people lack a good strategy for allocating their assets properly.

- Since 1990, TIAA-CREF plans can be combined with mutual fund families. This option offers greater opportunities for TIAA-CREF participants, but it also carries new dangers. The low percentage of TIAA-CREF participants venturing into this new arena suggests the need for guidelines to compare services and products. (See chaps. 9 and 16.)

- Some CREF participants might want to pay more attention to market trends but are unsure of how to use CREF for this. TIAA-

CREF is adamantly opposed to attempts at market timing.[14] But adventuresome participants will try to keep their investments in sync with market trends regardless of TIAA-CREF's advice. If the market is in one of its periodic bull phases, some people will see no point in standing aside while the CREF Stock fund is jumping upward. Conversely, if the market is in one of its periodic bear phases, they will see no point in riding the CREF Stock fund all the way down to the bottom. These people could benefit from an analysis of market timing. (See chaps. 10 through 13.)

Understanding Risk Management

Central to any successful retirement planning is the concept of risk management. Investment analysts have identified several different types of risk, but the most basic types for understanding successful retirement planning are capital risk and inflation risk. Focusing on only one of these to the exclusion of the other can impede your progress toward a financially secure retirement.

Capital Risk

This is the risk of losing your capital or your principal, and the heavy preference of TIAA-CREF participants for TIAA shows that they have a keen awareness of capital risk. In TIAA the returns you receive on your capital will go down if interest rates drop or if TIAA is suddenly plagued with some unsuccessful investments. But you have very little risk of losing any of the capital or principal that you have invested in TIAA. Unlike the CREF funds, TIAA does not have a unit value that fluctuates with the daily market performance of the portfolio's assets. CREF Stock fund, on the other hand, does have a unit value that fluctuates with the financial markets, and this directly exposes you to capital risk. The unit value for each CREF fund equals the total assets of the fund divided by the total number of units owned by CREF participants. The value of a CREF Stock unit has historically dropped in about one out of every four years. Each time it dropped, CREF stockholders saw their principal or capital drop accordingly.

Inflation Risk

This is the risk that inflation will erode your assets. Over the long term inflation poses a greater threat to most people than does the risk of capital loss. TIAA, as later chapters will show, is an exceedingly poor long-term hedge against inflation. The very factors that make it such an excellent protection against capital risk expose it to considerable inflation risk. It does not have a unit value that grows in price as market forces bid up the value of the assets in its portfolio. Anyone with a normal life expectancy who retires and puts all of his or her assets in TIAA can expect to see a steady erosion in lifestyle.

CREF equity accounts, by contrast, are reasonable hedges against inflation. The factors that expose them to the risk of capital loss also give it the chance to offset inflation. The CREF Stock unit value can indeed grow in price if market forces bid up the value of the underlying assets in CREF's Stock portfolio. Despite the fact that CREF Stock historically exposed investors to the capital risk of losing money every fourth year on average, it also gave them a long-term average rate of return well above the inflation rate.

Balancing Capital Risk and Inflation Risk

To protect yourself against only one of these two risks is to court disaster. The secret to protecting yourself is to determine the appropriate risk tolerance for capital loss for a person in your circumstances and then to balance your assets accordingly. This asset allocation theme will pervade many of the succeeding chapters in this book, and Chapter 8 in particular offers specific guidelines for doing this.

Conclusion

This book offers a strategy for your retirement planning that is based on the belief that your overriding goal for retirement planning ought to be to accumulate enough capital to let you retire at the comfort level you want. In sum, this book seeks to offer:

- some elementary prescriptions on how one should approach TIAA, CREF, and competing investment vehicles.

- a means for determining an appropriate level of risk for yourself.

- an analysis of three accepted and relatively low-risk ways of accumulating capital (dollar cost averaging, value averaging, and asset allocation).

- some guidelines to ponder when a sales representative suggests that you switch your funds out of TIAA-CREF and put them under his or her management.

- an analysis of the higher risk strategy of market timing and some of the professionals who attempt it.

- an assessment of critical choices you will face when you enter the so-called "payout phase."

- some final considerations on financial planners and on how your retirement plans can be affected by Medicare, taxes, and Social Security.

To make maximum use of TIAA-CREF's growing array of features and to avoid the common mistakes, it is necessary to understand how TIAA-CREF fits into the investment universe and how to make that investment universe work to your advantage. This book seeks to help foster that understanding.

Notes

1. United States Bureau of the Census, *Statistical Abstract of the United States: 1993* (Washington, D.C.: U. S. Government Printing Office, 1992), pp. 374, 458. The average monthly Social Security benefit for a male retiree and wife was $1,072. The $16,975 annual income figure was the median for all households in which the householder was over age 65.

2. See Spencer Rich, "But the Last Year Can Be Grim," *The Washington Post National Weekly*, January 11-17, 1993, p. 36.

3.   "The NACUBO/TIAA-CREF Survey of College and University Retirees," *TIAA-CREF Research Dialogues*, No. 31 (October 1991). This
was a survey of 17,000 college and university retirees, an undetermined
number of whom were TIAA-CREF participants. These results were also
summarized in *The Participant*, (February 1993): 11.

4.   *The Participant*, (February 1989): 5.

5.   "The NACUBO/TIAA-CREF Survey."

6.   Ibid., p. 11. The same theme also surfaced in a survey of TIAA-CREF
retirees conducted ten years earlier. See *The Participant* (August 1983):
3.

7.   In 1981, for example, nearly twice as many people participated in traditional pension plans (about 38 million) as in the tax-deferred 401(k) plans
(20 million). By 1992, the number of participants in 401(k) plans doubled to 40 million, while the number in traditional plans grew to only
about 39 million. See David A. Vise, "The Demise of the 'Dinosaurs'
Threatens Future Retirees," *The Washington Post National Weekly
Edition*, May 24-30, 1993, p. 20. Also see Leslie Eaton, "Nest Egg
Revolution: A Dramatic Pension Shift is Under Way," *Barron's*, July
31, 1993, p. 14.

8.   See Robert J. Samuelson's "Pension Time Bomb," *The Washington Post
National Weekly Edition*, March 15-21, 1993, p. 29. In 1991, for example, The Pension Benefit Guaranty Corporation estimated that the fifty
largest company pension plans had a collective shortfall of $24.2 billion
between assets owned and money needed to pay out benefits to which
they had committed themselves. *Investor's Business Daily*, November
20, 1992, p. 6.

9.   Much of the research for this has been sponsored by the financial community which, of course, has a vested interest in "scaring" people into
making more investments. But even discounting for this bias, the data
suggest that too many people are saving too little. A much-cited study
conducted for Merrill Lynch and Company concluded that the average
baby boomers were saving barely one third of what they needed to save
to maintain their living standard in retirement. *St. Paul Pioneer Press*,
January 28, 1993, p. 4A.

10.   *Wall Street Journal*, January 8, 1993, p. C-1.

11. Jane Bryant Quinn, "How to Bet Your Life," *Newsweek*, December 14, 1992, p. 63.

12. "Management at TIAA-CREF has long been reluctant to give unsolicited advice," said TIAA-CREF CEO John Biggs, expressing this philosophy. *The Participant* (August 1993): 9.

13. Ibid.

14. TIAA-CREF advises frankly that you are "better off with a buy-and-hold strategy." TIAA-CREF, *Guiding Your Retirement Savings* (New York: TIAA-CREF, 1992), p. 8.

Chapter 2

View TIAA-CREF as One of Many Retirement Vehicles

It is useful to view TIAA-CREF as just one of many vehicles available to you for building a retirement nest egg. Until 1988 this advice would not have made much sense, because TIAA-CREF had a monopoly on the retirement plans of most of its participating institutions, and participants had little to say about investing their funds. You had only two choices, TIAA and CREF; once you opted for TIAA, your money was stuck there forever. You also had very limited ways in which you could withdraw your money upon retirement.

Today you have many more choices, and TIAA-CREF now competes for your retirement dollar with mutual funds, brokerages, life insurance companies, and a growing army of financial planners. Since the new options are complicated, many participants will no doubt ignore them and continue to concentrate their money in TIAA, investing a somewhat smaller share in CREF Stock. Such a strategy is unlikely to lead to financial ruin. But the people who make out best in this newer, more complicated world will be those who understand the TIAA-CREF options and know how to integrate them into the broader world of other investment vehicles that are now open for your retirement dollar.

TIAA-CREF as a Defined Contribution Plan

Retirement plans are classified as either defined benefit plans or defined contribution plans. The traditional type is the *defined benefit* plan. Under this plan, over the years you and your employer make regular payments into a pension fund, and the fund guarantees you a specific benefit when you reach retirement age. Retirement age is typically defined as 65, and the guaranteed income is based on your average salary for your last few years. Most defined benefit plans are sponsored by the employer (or sometimes by large labor unions). The plan sponsor has the responsibility of ensuring that the plan is fully funded, that it has enough money to pay off all of the defined benefits. In a majority of plans these benefits are fixed and do not get adjusted upward to compensate for inflation. But about two-thirds of state university retirement systems appear to provide for a systematic inflation adjustment.[1]

Defined contribution plans like TIAA-CREF, by contrast, do not guarantee you a specific retirement benefit. Rather, you and/or your employer make regular contributions into the plan, which invests those funds into an account in your name. Your eventual retirement benefit depends on how much you have contributed over the years and on how well the plan's investments have performed. TIAA guarantees your principle plus a 3 percent return, but in fact TIAA benefit payments fluctuate with interest rates. CREF benefits fluctuate with the market performance of the CREF accounts.

It is for these reasons that your TIAA-CREF annual benefits reports cannot tell you exactly what your retirement benefits will be. Instead they tell you what your projected benefits will be under different scenarios. Your actual benefits will depend on several variables: how much you have contributed so far, how many more years you will make contributions, what your pay raises will be, how much you will contribute, which TIAA-CREF funds you own, how well those funds will perform over the years, what the life expectancy is for your age group after retirement, and how you choose to receive your payouts.

Your CREF accounts will fluctuate with the performance of the stock, bond, and interest rate markets over coming years. Because of this, CREF equity accounts have a better chance than most defined benefit plans of going up in value over the years to compensate for inflation.

In addition to being a defined contribution plan, TIAA-CREF is also a tax deferred plan. Any contributions made by you and your employer come from pretax income, which means that you pay no income tax until you withdraw them. Further, any interest or other earnings in your account also compound on a tax deferred basis. This tax deferral treatment of your contributions and the tax deferred compounding of the earnings in your account make TIAA-CREF one of the best investment accumulation vehicles you are ever likely to have. However, it is not a tax shelter or a tax avoidance plan. It only defers the taxes until the time you begin making withdrawals.

Disadvantages of the Defined Contribution Plan

At first glance it would seem that the defined contribution plan is much less desirable than the defined benefit plan. There is a fair amount of psychological insecurity in not knowing exactly how much you will receive at age 65. It would be much more reassuring to know precisely what your benefits were going to be. The defined contribution plan also requires much more planning on your part. In a defined benefit plan, the program sponsors decide how the pension funds will be invested, and you do not have to worry about that. With TIAA-CREF, by contrast, you have to pick your own investment vehicles and decide for yourself how to allocate your funds among them. Making these choices yourself is inherently more complicated than having all of the decisions taken out of your hands by the company with the defined benefit plan.

Finally, unless you maximize your voluntary contributions into TIAA-CREF, your benefit levels will probably end up being less than you would like. Most contributions are based on a percent of salary, and since most faculty work at relatively modest salaries, it usually takes extra voluntary contributions to bring one's ultimate benefit levels up to those of higher paid people in other professions.

Advantages of the TIAA-CREF Defined Contribution Plan

Weighed against these drawbacks, TIAA-CREF has several important advantages that are likely to put you ahead in the long run if you plan well and carry out your plan consistently. First, you receive immediate ownership of your TIAA-CREF accounts. Traditional plans in the private sector often require you to work many years with the same employer before you become entitled to the benefits of the plan. With TIAA-CREF your very first contribution, and all others, go directly into an account in your name and you are its legal owner. Unlike many traditional plans, your account has portability. You can carry it with you if you change jobs. If you go to another college in the TIAA-CREF system, your new employer begins making contributions where your old employer left off.

Second, your TIAA-CREF plan runs no risk of being fraudulently plundered or mismanaged by your employer, as was common among private pension plans in the 1980s. The retirees of Cannon Mills (makers of bath towels), for example, saw a 30 percent reduction in their pension checks in 1991 after the Cannon company went through several reorganizations and insured the pension fund with an insurance company that subsequently went bankrupt. Cannon Mills retirees had spent lifetimes contributing to their pension plan, and a huge portion of that money simply disappeared.[2]

Nor was this the only exploitation of a pension fund. Some companies simply underfunded their pension plans. When General Motors (GM), for example, reached an agreement with its union to make special payments to laid off workers, GM partially financed this agreement by holding down company contributions to its pension fund. It projected unrealistically short life expectancies for its workers along with unrealistically high returns on its pension fund investments.[3] By 1993, GM had a pension liability of $11.8 billion but had set aside only 77 percent of the money needed to meet those promises.[4]

In 1974 Congress created the Pension Benefit Guarantee Corporation (PBGC) to insure workers against fraudulent management or mismanagement of their pension plans. If a pension plan fails, covered workers are guaranteed up to $29,250 per year. But this guarantee itself gives corporations an incentive to underfinance their pension plans. Guarantees from PBGC mean that a company does not have to worry about its workers ending up with nothing; the company that falls into tough times can be tempted not to spend precious corporate dollars fully funding its pension plan.[5] By 1991 the PBGC identified 15,000 defined benefit plans as being underfunded by $51 billion, a sum that exceeded the assets of the PBGC.[6] Not every pension fund in the country is covered by PBGC, and workers in uncovered programs do not have the PBGC guarantees.

These pension underfunding problems cannot happen with a defined contribution plan such as TIAA-CREF. Like any pension fund, TIAA-CREF will inevitably make investment errors from time to time. However, because your account is with TIAA-CREF, your employer has no legal, financial, or physical influence over it, and there is no way that the funds in your account can be subjected to either bad judgment or fraud on the part of your employer.

Not only is it impossible for your employer to raid your TIAA-CREF account, it is also impossible for your account to be underfunded without your knowledge. TIAA-CREF sends you a quarterly statement showing exactly when deposits were made in your account. If your employer failed to make a payment, you would learn about that within three months and would, of course, have legal means to oblige the employer to pay up. There is no conceivable way that you could work for five or ten years only to discover after the fact that the funds had not been put into your account or that funds had been illegally withheld from it.

Of course, it is possible that TIAA-CREF might some day be wracked by a scandal involving fraudulent use of funds. To minimize this risk, we rely on annual audits of the books, internal mechanisms of control, the TIAA and CREF boards of directors, and on state and federal regulators to keep TIAA-CREF honest. TIAA-CREF has retained ombudsmen who can investigate a member's complaint and help bring into the open any substantiated instances of wrongdoing. As another safeguard, a participant association could be formed to serve as a watchdog on TIAA-CREF's management practices.

The TIAA-CREF Investment Vehicles

Currently TIAA-CREF offers you eight investment vehicles: the TIAA account and seven CREF accounts--a stock account, a money market account, a social choice account, a bond account, a global equities account, a growth stock account, and an equity index account. To avoid confusion with the word "account" that represents your personal monies invested in TIAA-CREF, we are going to use the term "funds" to describe the investment vehicles. Thus, for example, we will refer to the CREF Stock fund rather than the CREF Stock account as it is officially termed.

TIAA

Started by Andrew Carnegie in 1918, TIAA is the oldest of the vehicles. It grew to a $66 billion fund by 1994 and accounted for 52 percent of TIAA-CREF's combined assets of $126 billion. It clearly is the favorite accumulation vehicle of TIAA-CREF participants. Fourteen years earlier in 1980, TIAA accounted for 53 percent of combined TIAA-CREF assets. Despite the fact that every dollar in CREF Stock more than quintupled during that period and widely outperformed a dollar in TIAA, TIAA's share of the combined assets barely changed. Participants put more of their premiums into TIAA rather than CREF. In 1992, TIAA received more premium contributions than all of the CREF accounts put together.[7]

TIAA invests primarily in fixed income instruments that historically have had predictable and stable rates of return. By 1994, the bulk of these investments were in bonds and corporate loans (56 percent), mortgage loans (31 percent), and direct real estate ownership (11 percent). The fastest growing portion of this portfolio during the 1980s was direct real estate ownership, but these investments have been pared back in the 1990s. TIAA boosted its real estate investments as a means of hedging against inflation. Some of the mortgage loans also have an ownership participation feature that will enable TIAA to capture some of the buildings' profits if they occur.

TIAA promotes itself as a "safe" place for participants to put their money.[8] As evidence of its safety it cites the fact that it carries the

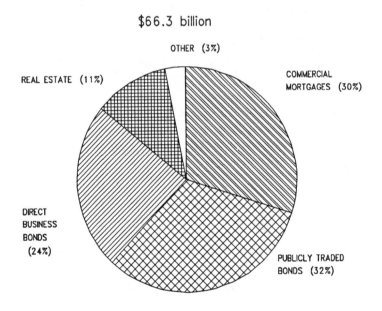

$66.3 billion

OTHER (3%)

REAL ESTATE (11%)

COMMERCIAL MORTGAGES (30%)

DIRECT BUSINESS BONDS (24%)

PUBLICLY TRADED BONDS (32%)

Figure 2-1 TIAA Investments

Source: *TIAA-CREF 1993 Annual Report*, p. 17.

highest credit ratings from the three organizations that rate insurance companies--Standard and Poors (S&P), Moodys, and A. M. Best. The company follows a policy of investing no more than 10 percent of its portfolio in below-investment-grade bonds.[9]

Some critics contend that TIAA is not as safe as it claims. They charge that TIAA's real estate portfolio is in much deeper trouble than TIAA is willing to admit.[10] Twenty-seven percent of TIAA's mortgage loans and 11 percent of its real estate investments were concentrated in California[11] whose economy and real estate market have been a shambles so far in the 1990s. Critics also contend that the main reason why TIAA receives its high safety ratings is because its guaranteed annuity dividend is lower than those of competing insurance companies and because it has a captured clientele that cannot easily transfer their holdings from TIAA to another vehicle.[12] These serious charges will be addressed in Chapter 4.

CREF Stock

This fund was established in 1952 and by 1994 it had grown to $54 billion. This made it one of the largest equity funds in the world and gave it an estimated one percent of the total value of all American stocks. Because of its huge size, CREF has little flexibility to maneuver with changing market conditions. If you lost confidence in one of your stocks, you could sell it tomorrow without having the slightest impact on the overall stock market. But CREF's portfolio is so huge that liquidating its holdings in a specific stock could easily drive down that stock's price. Consequently, except for holding a small amount of short-term cash equivalents, CREF remains fully invested at all times.

Figure 2-2 summarizes CREF Stock's holdings. Approximately two-thirds of the fund essentially acts as an index fund meant to represent the overall U. S. equity markets. An index fund is one that seeks to match the performance of some specific basket of investments. Until 1993 the S&P 500 index appeared to be the benchmark for CREF's indexing. By that year, however, it had become cumbersome to tie CREF's $54 billion portfolio to only 500 stocks. CREF announced that it was going to use the Russell 3000 index--a broader index of the 3,000 companies with the largest market value in the United States.[13] About 15 to 20 percent of CREF Stock is invested overseas, and the balance among smaller U.S. companies chosen for their investment potential.

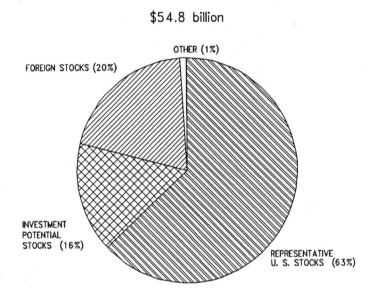

Figure 2-2 CREF Stock Investments

Source: *TIAA-CREF Annual Report: 1993*, p. 18.

In recent years CREF Stock holders have been well rewarded by this tripartite division of CREF Stock's portfolio (15-20 percent indexed to foreign markets, 63-67 percent indexed to the U. S. market, and the balance in performance stocks). Whether these indexing philosophies will work as well over the next decade remains to be seen. CREF does not really offer participants many alternative equity investments to protect themselves in case the indexing strategies lag the markets. Most large mutual fund families would supplement a large fund like CREF Stock by adding several smaller funds. The limited number of such funds is a shortcoming of CREF. Chapter 8 will suggest what some of these other fund choices could be.

CREF Money Market Fund

For decades, TIAA and CREF Stock accounts were the only options open to members. During the 1980s, this led some CREF partici-

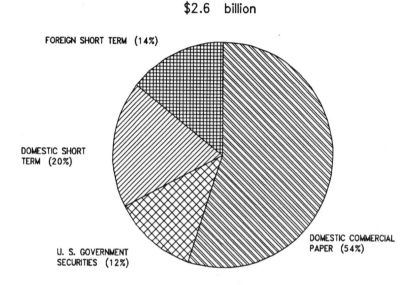

Figure 2-3 CREF Money Market Investments

Source: *TIAA-CREF Annual Report: 1993*, p. 19.

pants to complain bitterly about the lack of a money market fund and the inability to switch money back and forth between CREF and TIAA. TIAA-CREF responded to these complaints in 1988 by establishing a new money market fund that invests in treasury bills, short-term securities such as certificates of deposit, and short-term corporate loans called commercial paper.

CREF's Money Market fund differs from other money market funds you may have encountered in two key respects. The most obvious difference occurs in the method of pricing the fund. Typical money market funds maintain the net asset value of the fund at $1 per share. They do this by giving you monthly interest payments that you can either take in cash or reinvest in more money market fund shares. In contrast, the CREF money market fund reinvests its interest earnings and lets its net asset value fluctuate with the market. It started at $10 per unit in 1988 and by the end of 1993 had reached $14.22, for an annual rate of return of 6.3 percent.

A more important difference between CREF Money Market and typical money market funds lies in their investment philosophy. The average maturity of holdings in a traditional money market fund is only about fifty or sixty days, and most such funds are prohibited from holding investments with maturities longer than one year. CREF's Money Market fund seeks an average maturity of ninety days and can hold some investments with maturities of up to two years. This exposes the CREF Money Market fund to slightly more market risk than the typical money market fund, but it also enabled CREF Money Market to pay a significantly higher interest rate than typical money market funds when short-term interest rates fell dramatically during the early 1990s. In March 1994, for example, CREF Money Market paid a 3.18 percent interest rate at a time when the average money market fund paid 2.83 percent.[14] The fund held about $2.6 billion in assets by 1994.

One truly outstanding feature of CREF is that it gives you the ability to make unlimited telephone transfers between its money market fund and its other funds. Most mutual fund families also provide this benefit, but some of them put restrictions on telephone transfers to deter mutual fund timing organizations from flooding them with large orders at one time. The Twentieth Century family will not let you repurchase one of its stock funds within ninety days of selling it. Some funds impose penalties or sales charges on frequent transfers. Several families restrict the number of transfers per year into and out of their money market funds.

CREF Bond Fund

Introduced in 1990 was the CREF bond fund. By 1994 it had attracted $608 million dollars. This is a conservatively managed fund with twenty-nine percent of its holdings in government securities and government agency securities. The Bond Fund may put up to twenty percent of its holdings in "high yield" or "junk" bonds, but by 1994 these accounted for only ten percent of the Bond Fund portfolio.

CREF Social Choice Fund

This is the most misunderstood of the CREF funds. It was introduced in 1990 to provide an investment vehicle for participants who did

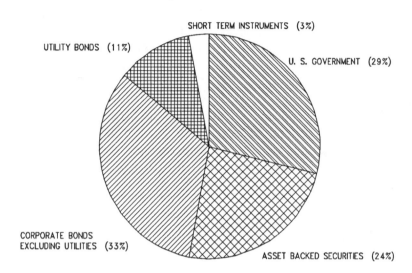

$608.4 million

SHORT TERM INSTRUMENTS (3%)

UTILITY BONDS (11%)

U. S. GOVERNMENT (29%)

CORPORATE BONDS
EXCLUDING UTILITIES (33%)

ASSET BACKED SECURITIES (24%)

Figure 2-4 CREF Bond Fund Investments

Source: *TIAA-CREF Annual Report: 1993*, p. 19.

not want their retirement funds invested in South Africa, in certain Northern Ireland companies, or in companies doing significant business in weapons, nuclear energy, alcoholic beverages, or tobacco. Accordingly, the Social Choice fund has developed investment policies to avoid these areas. In 1993 CREF responded to the changing situation in South Africa by lifting its restrictions on companies with ties to that country.

In financial terms, the Social Choice fund is a misnomer. It is essentially a balanced fund that balances its investments between stocks and bonds. CREF Social Choice had assets of $706 million by 1994 and divided those funds 61 percent in U. S. stocks, 36 percent in long term bonds, and 3 percent in money market instruments. In the long run this balanced portfolio will make the Social Choice fund less volatile than the CREF Stock fund. It will go up more slowly on stock market rallies and fall more slowly when the market declines. Over the long run, expect CREF Social Choice to lag behind CREF Stock in overall performance. Conceptually, the Social Choice fund has two bothersome aspects. First, from the perspective of socially conscious investors, the fact that the

Social Choice fund is a balanced fund means it is destined to underperform CREF Stock in bull markets. For this reason it does not offer a fair test of whether a socially conscious investment approach can match that of CREF Stock. Comparing CREF Stock to CREF Social Choice is a classic instance of comparing apples and oranges. Thus, because CREF Social Choice is a balanced fund with a heavy weighting of fixed income investments, CREF does not offer socially conscious investors a full opportunity to participate in a 100 hundred percent stock fund unless they are willing to give up a commitment to socially conscious investing.

Second, there is also a problem from the perspective of non-socially conscious investors. Because CREF's only balanced fund is the Social Choice fund, non-socially conscious investors can only invest in a balanced fund if they are willing to accept the restrictions of socially conscious investing.

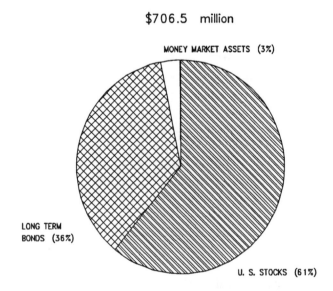

Figure 2-5 CREF Social Choice Fund Investments

Source: *TIAA-CREF Annual Report: 1993*, p. 18.

The Global Equities Fund

The fastest growing CREF fund is the Global Equities fund, started in 1992. Its plan is to invest at least 25 percent of its assets in the U.S., at least 50 percent overseas, and the balance according to its assessment of world markets. At any given moment, Global Equities could have anywhere from 50 to 75 percent invested abroad, 25 to 50 percent in the U. S., and 0 to 33 percent in bonds or fixed income instruments other than equities.[15] While this plan gives Global Equities great flexibility, it does not give CREF participants a very good picture of how their assets will in fact be invested. As of 1994, Global Equities' portfolio was 65 percent abroad, up from 53 percent only six months earlier. Japan and the Far East accounted for 41 percent of the portfolio, with Europe accounting for another 18 percent.

Some mutual fund families offer both a world fund and an international fund. The difference between them is that a world fund, like

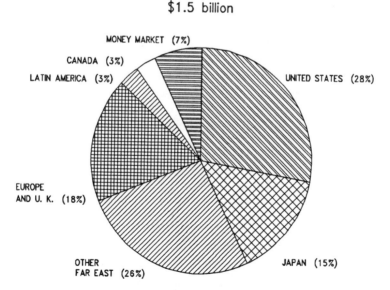

$1.5 billion

Figure 2-6   **CREF Global Equities Investments**

Source: *TIAA-CREF Annual Report: 1993*, p. 18.

CREF's Global Equities fund, invests in the U.S. as well as abroad. By contrast, a true international fund invests only in foreign markets.

The Growth and Equity Index Funds

In 1994 CREF added two new funds, a Growth fund and an Equity Index fund. The CREF Growth fund will invest in companies with high potential for growth of sales and earnings. Although it will invest in companies of all sizes, it expects to focus most of its investments on small and medium sized companies. It may invest in foreign as well as domestic stocks, but CREF has not yet indicated the ratio of foreign to domestic holdings. Although it is too early to know how this fund will perform, one would reasonably expect the Growth fund to outperform the other CREF funds over the long term. But it is important to remember that Wall Street runs in fads, and during periods when growth stocks are out of favor, the CREF Growth fund will underperform the other CREF funds. The Growth fund is also likely to be more volatile than other CREF funds in having the widest swings from overperforming the market in one year to underperforming it the next. If you can tolerate its volatility, the Growth fund will probably be a lucrative investment vehicle for some of your savings.

The new CREF Equity Index fund will be constructed to mirror the performance of the Russell 3000 Index. Again, since the fund does not yet have a track record it is impossible to know how successfully it will follow the Russell 3000. Over the long run, one would expect it to be less volatile and less lucrative than either the CREF Stock fund or the Growth fund.

Summary

Although CREF funds have performed credibly to date, they in fact reflect investment trends that worked well in the 1980s. The CREF Stock and Equity Index funds are oriented toward indexation. Most of the funds have overlapping portfolio philosophies with loosely defined and vague investment goals. This is fine if you want CREF to decide how your assets should be allocated. But it is inconsistent with much of TIAA-CREF's literature, which exhorts the individual to make his or her own decisions on allocating pension assets while leaving it up to the professionals at TIAA-CREF to exercise their stock picking and money management expertise within those parameters.[16] Many CREF participants want to play a greater role in allocating their assets. For them, the CREF options are inherently frustrating.

If you are a socially conscious investor, CREF does not offer you a stock fund. If you are not a socially conscious investor, CREF does not offer you a balanced fund. If you think that the early 1990s boom in small capitalization stocks will continue, CREF does not offer you a pure play in that area, although the new Growth fund will help. If you want international exposure but want to avoid overindexing toward Japan and the Far East, CREF does not offer you anything. If you want a pure international exposure without any U.S. stocks, CREF does not offer you anything. If you wanted to take advantage of the 1993 boom in international bull markets, imagine your disappointment when you received CREF's statement of investments for June 1993 and discovered that only 53 percent of your Global Equities portfolio was in fact invested in foreign equities.

In short, even after its recent additions of funds, CREF does not offer its participants the diversity that a large mutual fund family would offer. It is conceivable that most CREF participants do not want more options.[17] The existing ones might be confusing enough and the CREF Stock fund might suffice for them. For others, however, the CREF offerings pose important restrictions. You have been asked to assume a larger burden for allocating their assets, but the tools that CREF puts at your disposal are limited. CREF should expand its portfolio offerings to include a greater variety of funds. Chapter 8, which deals with asset allocation, will give some suggestions on what those offerings ought to be.

Finally and importantly, two-thirds of the CREF Stock fund and the entire Equity Index fund are not actively managed portfolios. They are indexed to the Russell 3,000 Index, which is a measure of the 3,000 largest American companies. Although indexation brought good returns in recent years, it is important to realize that all Wall Street trends eventually come to an end. The indexation strategies that worked so well in the 1980s may or may not work well over the coming decade. If they do end up as lucrative as they did in the past, then all is well and good. However, if they do not, CREF does not appear to have an alternative strategy ready to put in place.

Other Tax Advantaged Accumulation Vehicles

TIAA-CREF is only one out of many tax deferred investment vehicles for accumulating capital for retirement, a child's education, or any other long range goal. While there is probably no limit to the number of investment vehicles, six stand out in particular because they are broadly popular and are easy to use. In order of appropriateness for retirement planning, they are (1) The TIAA-CREF Supplemental Retirement Annuity (SRA), (2) tax deferred plans for self-employment income, (3) self directed IRAs, (4) tax deferred compensation plans separate from TIAA-CREF, (5) variable annuities and fixed annuities, and (6) Series EE Bonds.

Supplemental Retirement Annuities (SRAs)

The Supplemental Retirement Annuity (SRA) is a deferred compensation plan that supplements your TIAA-CREF retirement annuity (RA). This is an ideal capital accumulation plan for most people and is so important that Chapter 3 will be devoted exclusively to it.

Tax Deferred Plans for Self-Employment Income

Consider opening a self-employment tax deferred plan if you regularly earn income from royalty payments, consultant fees, speaking honoraria, sale of art work, or any other self-employment income source. The IRS permits you to contribute into these plans up to 20 percent of your self-employment income up to a maximum of $30,000 per year.[18]

Combined Money Purchase-Profit Sharing Plan

You can use three tax deferred options, the most likely of which is the combination money purchase-profit sharing plan or, as it is popularly called, the Keogh Plan (after the Congressman who created it). Under the money purchase portion of the plan you contribute a specific percent of your self-employment income, which must be contributed each year. Under the profit sharing portion, you may contribute from 0 to 15 percent. By combining, for example, a fixed 10 percent commitment to the money purchase plan and a flexible 0 to 15 percent commitment to the profit sharing plan, you are theoretically able to contribute up to 20 percent of your taxable self-employment income to the account.

Because of the way that the IRS makes its calculations, people are initially confused whether the maximum contribution is 20 percent or 25 percent. It is 25 percent of your self-employment income after your Keogh contribution (as the IRS calculates the maximum) or 20 percent of your self-employment income before the Keogh contribution (which is the way most people would make the calculation). If, for example, you earned $20,000 in book royalties (after subtracting your self-employment expenses), you could theoretically put 20 percent of that amount (or $4,000) into a tax deferred plan and pay taxes only on the remaining $16,000. In reality, your maximum contribution would probably be limited to about 18 percent, because you also have to subtract one-half of any self-employment Social Security tax from the $20,000 before you calculate the 20 percent figure.

This sounds much more complicated than it is. Most financial advisers, brokerage firms, credit unions, banks, or other financial institutions can quickly set up an account for you. The reporting requirements to the IRS are minimal, if you are the only person involved in your self-employment endeavor. However, if you have regular employees, the reporting becomes more complex and you probably should consult a tax adviser.

Simplified Employment Pension

As an alternative, some self-employed people choose to establish Simplified Employment Pension (SEP), which also allows you to make contributions of your taxable self-employment income into a tax deferred account set up with a financial institution. Because the SEP imposes lower maximum contributions than the Keogh Plan, however, it is not quite as attractive as the Keogh Plan.

Defined-Benefit Keogh

Finally, a third option called the defined-benefit Keogh Plan allows you to exceed the 20 percent limit. In some cases, a person can contribute 100 percent of self-employment income into the plan. You commit yourself to contributing a fixed sum into the defined-benefit plan and make an actuarial calculation to determine what your defined benefit will be when you retire. Because you need to hire a professional actuary to make the calculations and prepare the appropriate forms for the IRS, the defined-benefit Keogh has more expenses and complications than does the money purchase-profit sharing plan. Nevertheless, if the amounts involved are large enough to make it worth the extra expenses, it may be worthwhile exploring the defined-benefit Keogh.

Advantages of the Self-Employment Tax Deferred Plans

The two main advantages of these self-employment plans are that your contributions are tax deductible in the year they are made and any investment earnings in your plan are tax deferred until you begin withdrawing them. Your withdrawals are then taxed as ordinary income at whatever your income tax rate happens to be at that time. If you make any withdrawals before age 59 1/2, they will be subjected to a 10 percent penalty in addition to the tax.

The IRS also makes Keogh Plans eligible for an extra tax benefit when you take the money out. After age 59 1/2, you can withdraw the entire accumulation in a lump sum and have the lump sum averaged over five years for tax purposes. For an accumulation of $100,000, for example, this could have the effect of reducing the tax bite on your withdrawal to 15 percent. The rules for getting this favorable tax treatment, however, are quite precise, and it would be wise to consult your tax adviser to determine if you are eligible and whether it would be beneficial to you.

Finally, you gain one other important tax advantage from self-employment income (although getting this benefit does not require you to set up a tax deferred plan). You declare your self-employment income on Schedule C of your income tax return. This permits you to deduct many of your professional expenses such as subscriptions, equipment purchases, professional travel, or any professional expenses. If you claim these expenses as miscellaneous deductions on Form 1040, they are deductible only if your miscellaneous deductions exceed 2 percent of your adjusted gross income (AGI). With a $50,000 AGI, for example, you could lose the first $1,000 of these potential deductions on Form

1040. On Schedule C, by contrast, they would be fully deductible as business expenses.

When You Should Not Open a Keogh Plan

If your self-employment income is primarily book royalties, then you might have two choices for declaring this on your income tax return. If you regularly earn royalty income, the IRS requires you to declare it on Schedule C as self-employment income. However, if you publish a once-in-a-lifetime book, you might be allowed to declare the royalties on Schedule E. Using Schedule E makes you ineligible to take the tax deduction for a Keogh account, but it also exempts you from paying the Social Security self-employment tax on your royalties (which could be as high as 15.3 percent). If you set up the tax deferred account, you can take a tax deduction of up to 20 percent of your royalties, but you will be obliged to pay the Social Security tax. In 1993, a Social Security tax of 12.4 percent was levied on all incomes up to $57,600 and a Medicare tax of 2.9 percent on all incomes up to $135,000. These ceilings get adjusted upward each year with the inflation rate.

If your salary is $52,600, you only have to pay the Social Security tax on $5,000 of your royalty income. In this instance, it is probably worth filing Schedule C and paying that tax to get the benefits of the Keogh account. On the other hand, if your salary is only $37,600, the first $20,000 in royalties would be subject to the Social Security tax, which would amount to $3,060. You would have to determine whether this immediate tax was outweighed by the other tax advantages of filing a Schedule C, the long term benefits of tax deferred compounding, and the eventual increases in Social Security benefits that might come from having made a maximum contribution at this point.

For many people, tax deferral plans for self-employment income are superb vehicles for accumulating retirement capital. An excellent overview of this approach is found in the *Tax Guide for College Teachers*, published each year by the Academic Information Service.[19]

Deferred Compensation Plans Separate from Your SRA

Depending on your employer's rules, you might also be eligible to set up a 403(b) deferred compensation plan with a mutual fund, investment adviser, or a stock broker that is separate from your TIAA-CREF plan. Your contributions to this plan will necessarily be limited to the same terms that exist for your TIAA-CREF supplemental retirement annuities.

Because this is such an important option, we will spend an entire chapter (12) discussing the conditions under which it is a good idea or a bad idea to invest your retirement assets through a financial adviser rather than through TIAA-CREF.

Self Directed IRA

Until it was modified in 1986, one of the very best accumulation vehicles was the individual retirement account, or IRA, as it was more popularly called. This gave you a tax deduction for up to $2,000 contributed to an IRA account. Like other tax deferred programs, the investment earnings of your IRA also accumulate tax deferred. Since 1986, however, if you or your spouse participate in a pension plan such as TIAA-CREF, you are no longer eligible for the full $2,000 deduction unless your income is less than $40,000 for married couples or $25,000 for single people. Above those amounts, the maximum IRA contribution decreases until it drops to zero at joint incomes above $50,000 or individual incomes above $35,000.

If your income is above those ranges, you can make *non-deductible* IRA contributions. Even though that contribution will not be tax deductible, the earnings in your IRA account will be tax deferred. Many people set up a non-deductible IRA in one account and a tax deductible IRA in a separate account in the hope that they can make withdrawals from the non-deductible IRA first. This would lower the tax due on withdrawal, because the contributions had been made from after-tax dollars. The IRS, however, will not allow this. Whether you have one account or two, the IRS will prorate your withdrawals proportionate to the deductible and non-deductible amounts contributed. Thus, if you had contributed $10,000 to a non-deductible account and $10,000 to a deductible account, the IRS would treat any withdrawal as coming equally from each account, regardless of which account you actually used for making the withdrawal.

In sum, you should not make any contributions to an IRA unless you have already made the maximum contributions into your SRA and Keogh accounts. Otherwise, you are forfeiting an immediate income tax deduction. If, after making these contributions, you still have some money left over and you are eligible to make a deductible IRA contribution, that would be a reasonable investment. Before making a nondeductible IRA contribution, however, investigate the merits of using your extra funds to purchase a tax deferred annuity from an insurance company.

Tax Deferred Annuities

One popular accumulation vehicle is the tax deferred annuity (TDA) offered by most life insurance companies. Contributions to these annuities are made from *after-tax* dollars, so you do not receive a tax deduction for the initial contribution. However, earnings in the account are tax deferred, and you are not obliged to begin making withdrawals by age 70 1/2 as is true of most other tax deferred retirement plans. You can make either one time or periodic contributions.

Set up properly, you also have considerable flexibility in making withdrawals from the plan. The insurance company will let you take withdrawals in cash until your funds are exhausted, or it will offer to annuitize your account by guaranteeing you a series of monthly payments over your lifetime.

Many people use annuities as part of their estate plan. Because you can designate a beneficiary for your annuity just as you can for life insurance, your annuity will pass directly on to that beneficiary when you die without going through probate court. Many people like this feature of the tax deferred annuity because it protects their heirs from extra lawyers' fees and court costs. Some other people also use the annuity as a tax deferred accumulation vehicle for their children's college expenses. However, you need to calculate the tax consequences carefully before you do this. Withdrawing $10 or $15 thousand per year for college expenses at an age when you are already approaching your peak earning power could push you into a higher income tax bracket. Add to that an additional 10 percent penalty for cashing in if you are under age 59 1/2, and the tax costs could easily outweigh the tax deferred compounding of investment earnings.

At least three types of tax deferred annuities are available: a self directed variable annuity, a fixed annuity, and a Teachers' Personal Annuity (TPA) offered through TIAA.

Self Directed Variable Annuities

Under a variable annuity program, your contributions are invested into a package of securities that can be tailored to the amount of risk you wish to assume. High-risk annuities will be heavily invested in stocks, while low risk annuities will be heavily invested in fixed rate investments such as certificates of deposit or bonds. The performance of the variable annuity portfolios compares favorably with mutual funds of similar risk. Some annuities are self directed in that you can switch your holdings back and forth between different portfolios.[20]

Fixed Annuities

You can also purchase a fixed annuity contract from a life insurance company that will invest the funds in fixed income instruments and pay you a guaranteed amount for life or for any predetermined number of years.

Teachers' Personal Annuity (TPA)

TIAA offers the Teachers' Personal Annuity (TPA), which is essentially a fixed annuity. You may contribute any amount over $2,000 and let the funds compound tax free until you withdraw them. Based on fixed income instruments, the TIAA returns are modest, compared to long-term returns on equities. In late 1993, TIAA paid a 5.1 percent rate of return on TPA accounts. However, there are no sales charges, commissions, or early withdrawal charges (unless you withdraw before age 59 1/2). Withdrawals may be annuitized so that you are paid a guaranteed amount (see chap. 14) or taken out in cash.

Caveats

Before you sign up for one of these annuity options, several considerations need investigation. First, as in the case of non-deductible IRAs, do not put any money into a tax deferred annuity until you have reached the maximum contribution level for your TIAA-CREF SRA or other deferred compensation plan and until you are making the maximum annual contributions into a Keogh Plan. The SRA and Keogh contributions are tax deductible, while the life insurance company TDA contributions are not.

Second, do not invest into an annuity plan unless you intend to leave the funds there for at least five years. Most annuities impose surrender charges on early withdrawals. The charges usually follow a sliding scale, so that the maximum commission is charged the first year, and the charges disappear within five to seven years, depending on the plan.

Third, when it comes time to take withdrawals from the annuity, you should probably not annuitize your account. To annuitize it means accepting a contract for regular payments over your lifetime. Most annuity contracts are drawn up to the advantage of the insurance company. Unless you plan to live well beyond your life expectancy, annuitizing your contract will probably result in leaving a fair share of your principal with the insurance company rather than with your heirs. This issue of annuitizing versus cash withdrawals is so important that the better part of Chapter 13 is devoted to it.

Finally, never sign an insurance company contract before getting an independent assessment of it from a knowledgeable professional. Insurance companies have been extraordinarily imaginative at inventing fancy titles that make cash value life insurance policies appear to be tax deferred retirement plans. One of the worst scandals of this sort involved a major company whose offices in Tampa, Florida, called its salespersons "nursing representatives" and sold cash value life insurance policies to nurses under the claim that these were tax deferred retirement plans similar to TIAA-CREF's SRAs.[21] Under these insurance policies, up to half of the first year's premiums went to paying commissions to the salespersons rather than being invested. On top of this, the cash value portions of the plan were invested in low yielding fixed income instruments rather than the higher returns that the salespersons promised. Some of the policies were sold to single women with no dependents who had a limited need for life insurance but a pressing need for retirement savings. The Tampa office so successfully marketed this scheme, that the insurance company extended it to thirty-seven states. When the State of Florida finally called a halt to the scam, 18,000 Floridians were offered settlements. Nurses in other states might not be so lucky.

For most people most of the time, term insurance of the sort offered through TIAA is a much better bargain than whole life, variable life, or other cash value policies offered through commercial insurance companies. For the premium paid for a cash value policy, you can probably buy the same level of insurance through TIAA much cheaper and invest the difference in your SRA account. However, it is absolutely imperative that you invest the difference in your SRA. Otherwise, you will end up at the end of the term with no life insurance and no cash savings.

Tax Deferred Bonds

There are two types of tax deferred bonds--so-called municipal bonds and Series EE bonds of the federal government. Municipal bonds are bonds issued by states or local governments such as cities, school districts, or special local authorities. These are popular vehicles with older, rich investors in high tax brackets, because most of these bonds are very safe and the interest payments earned on the bonds are free from federal income tax and from state income taxes in the state of issuance. They can be bought individually (usually at $10,000 per bond) or through a tax exempt bond mutual fund. These bond funds enjoyed very generous tax free returns while interest rates were dropping during the early 1990s. But with the possibility of higher interest rates starting in 1994, these bond funds posed a very real possibility of incurring a significant capital loss.

A more likely accumulation vehicle for persons of more average means is the federal government's Series EE Savings Bond. You can purchase EE Savings bonds from the Federal Reserve, the U. S. Treasury, and most banks or savings and loan associations. The bonds come in denominations ranging from $50 to $10,000, and your purchase price is one-half the face value of the bond. Thus, a $1,000 bond costs you $500. There are no transaction fees. The bonds typically mature far enough into the future that they can double to their face value by maturity.

Interest on the bonds is exempt from state and local government income taxes and is allowed to compound free of any federal taxes. Interest on the Series EE bond will also be free of federal income taxes if the bonds are used to finance a child's college education and the parents' income falls below certain levels (currently ranging from $60,000 to $90,000.)[22] For people below this income range, the Series EE bond thus competes with a non-deductible IRA and a life insurance company's tax deferred annuity.

The Series EE bonds are guaranteed a respectable, if modest, rate of return if they are held for five years. They receive 85 percent of the rate for the federal government's five year Treasury notes. During the 1980s, this averaged out to a respectable 7.27 percent,[23] but the return dropped to 4 percent in 1993.[24]

The Risk-Reward Tradeoff

The tax deferred investment vehicles described above barely tap the world of investment opportunities. Some other investments are listed in Table 2-1. If you are inclined to sample some of these investments, bear in mind the general principle of the risk-reward ratio of an investment. Many investments offer greater potential returns than any of the TIAA-CREF accounts, but they are also much riskier. If you purchase currency put options on the French franc the day before France devalues its currency, you will multiply the money spent on these options by several factors in a matter of days. But if France raises rather than devalues the franc, you might lose the entire amount that you spent on this speculation.

At the other extreme, you cannot get much safer than the three-month Treasury bill. However, on the downside, the treasury bill has no growth potential, and over an extended period of time, inflation could easily outstrip the meager interest rates you earn.

Any investment, no matter what it is, ends up being a demand for a potential return in exchange for the level of risks that are being assumed. This is just as true of putting your money in TIAA as it is of speculating on cattle futures.

Table 2-1 lists several popular investments by their risk-reward ratio. The safer an investment is, the lower its potential rate of return. The higher its potential return, the riskier it is. Unless you happen to discover some extraordinary short-term market inefficiency, there are no exceptions to that rule.

Conclusion

Your plans for retirement savings should include several tax deferred accumulation vehicles. If you use your TIAA-CREF retirement

Table 2-1   **Risk and Potential Return of Investments
(Ranked from Low to High)**

Investment Vehicle	Risk Level	Potential Return
Three-month Treasury bill	Low	Low
Certificate of deposit		
Money market fund		
Government bond or bond fund		
Corporate bond or bond fund		
Zero coupon bond		
Individual stock		
Mutual fund		
Index fund		
Large company stock fund		
International stock fund		
Small company stock fund		
Commodity, stock, currency or index future	High	High

program at the core, you should also have a portfolio of other vehciles targeted exclusively for retirement income. These should be considered separate from your other savings plans, such as those for your children's education or for buying a more expensive home.

It is advisable to resort to these vehicles in the following order. First, open an SRA. Second, if you are not eligible for an SRA, open a non-TIAA-CREF deferred compensation plan with your employer. Third, if you are eligible, open a Keogh Plan or other self-employment income tax deferred plan. Fourth, fund your tax deductible IRA, if you are eligible. Only after you have exhausted all of your tax deductible contributions and only when you have money that can remain untouched for at least seven years should you consider two other vehicles. Fifth, explore a tax deferred self-directed variable annuity with a carrier other than TIAA-CREF. Be extremely careful that you are in fact buying a bona fide variable annuity and not a cash value life insurance policy masquerading as a retirement plan. Finally, open a cash account with a brokerage firm or a no-load mutual fund. Even though you will pay taxes on the earnings in this fund, it is important to have some long-term savings that are not tied up in tax deferred accounts.

Notes

1. A 1987 survey of sixty-five such plans found that forty made benefit adjustments based on the plan's performance or on some inflation indicators such as the consumer price index. Twenty-four either had no mechanism for cost-of-living adjustments or made those adjustments on an ad hoc basis. TIAA-CREF, *Summaries of Public Retirement Plans Covering Colleges and Universities* (New York: TIAA-CREF, 1987), p. 11.

2. Hearings before the U.S. Senate Committee on Banking, Housing and Urban Affairs, July, 1991. Reported in the *New York Times*, July 30, 1991, p. 1. Also see *The New York Times*, August 8, 1991, p. 1 and August 29, 1991, p. 1. *Investor's Business Daily*, December 27, 1991, pp. 1, 28.

3. Thomas G. Donlan, "A Christmas Wish: Employees Should See Retirement Incentives More Clearly," *Barron's* December 28, 1992, p. 8.

4. *Smart Money* 2, no. 3 (June 1993): 32.

5. See James H. Smallhout, "Avoiding the Next Guaranteed Bailout: Reforms for the Pension Insurance Program," *The Brookings Review* 11, no. 2 (Spring 1993): 12-15.

6. Robert Samuelson, "Pension Time Bomb," *The Washington Post National Weekly*, March 15-21, 1993, p. 29.

7. *TIAA Annual Report 1991*, pp. 28-32. TIAA received $2.231 billion in annuity premiums, while all four CREF accounts received $1.996 billion.

8. See *Special Report: TIAA Investments: A Safe Haven in Stormy Times* (New York: TIAA-CREF, March 1991).

9. *TIAA Annual Report: 1991*, p. 10.

10. Richard T. Garrigan, "TIAA's Commercial Mortgage and Real Estate Investments: The Case for Disclosure," *ACADEME* (January-February 1992): 13-17.

11. *TIAA audited Financial Statements*, December 31, 1992, pp. 12-13.

12. Gerald H. Rosen, "TIAA-CREF: Declining Returns," *ACADEME* (January-February, 1992): 8-11.

13. College Retirement Equities Fund, *Prospectus*, April 1, 1993, p. 10.

14. *Barron's*, March 7, 1994, p. MW 82.

15. College Retirement Equities Fund, *Prospectus*, May 1, 1992, pp. 16-17.

16. TIAA-CREF *Allocating Premiums: Finding the Right Balance for You* (New York: TIAA-CREF, 1991), pp. 1, 8-10.

17. In 1987 when there were no options other than TIAA and CREF Stock, 70 percent of participants surveyed said they did not want more options. Eighty percent of plan administrators expressed some concern that their employees were not sophisticated enough to handle more choices. *The Participant* (February 1988): p. 4.

18. Technically, you can contribute 25 percent of your self-employment income, but this is a misleading figure because it is based on your net income after the contribution. Consequently, it amounts to only 20 percent of your self-employment income. For example, on a $10,000 income, you can contribute $2,000. This is 25 percent of your after contribution income but only 20 percent of the original $10,000.

19. Allen Bernstein, *Tax Guide for College Teachers and Other College Personnel* (College Park, Md: 1992), pp. 236-242.

20. For a short summary of variable annuities, see Albert J. Fredman and Russ Wiles, "An Introduction to Investing in Variable Annuities," *AAII Journal* 15, no. 8 (September 1993): 9-12. Also see, Kristin Davis, "Annuities: Picking Your Way Through the Jungle," *Kiplinger's Personal Finance Magazine*, October 1994, pp. 55-63.

21. Jane Bryant Quinn, "Yes, They're Out to Get You," *Newsweek*, January 24, 1994, p. 51.

22. Paul F. Jessup, "The Purloined Investment: Series EE Bonds Make Sense," *AAII Journal* 12, no. 8 (September 1990): 11.

23. Phillip R. Daves and Robert A. Kunkel, "After the Fall: Savings Bonds Are Still Attractive Short-term," *AAII Journal* 15, no. 4 (April 1993): 11-12. For a fuller exposition on Series EE bonds, see Daves and Kunkel, "U. S. Savings Bonds: Attractive Short Term Alternatives?" *AAII Journal* 15, no. 2 (February 1993): 12-14.

24. Ibid.

Chapter 3

Open an SRA and Pay Yourself First

The most important step you can take to financial independence is to open a Supplemental Retirement Annuity (SRA). Go immediately to your institution's personnel office and fill out the forms necessary to start the plan. An SRA is the closest that most of us will ever come to finding huge sums of cash lying in the street, begging to be picked up. The SRA has been available since 1973, yet despite its advantages, barely 20 percent of TIAA-CREF participants have yet opened one. Not opening an SRA or comparable plan is the costliest mistake that a TIAA-CREF participant can make in retirement planning. It is imperative that you open your SRA as soon as possible, with whatever monthly contribution you can afford.

What Is an SRA?

As its name implies, an SRA is a supplement to the TIAA-CREF retirement annuity (RA). It is a deferred compensation plan available to employees of colleges and several other non-profit organizations. An SRA provides the best long-term savings plan that most people will ever find. Like your RA, it is labeled 403(b) by the Internal Revenue Service. It is similar to the 401(k) plans available in private industry.

When you open an SRA, you pay yourself first. Normally, you only get to save whatever money is left over after you write checks for your mortgage payment, your automobile loan payment, and all your other bills. An active SRA reverses this sequence. Your other creditors do not get paid until after your payroll-deducted savings contribution has been made. Because you pay yourself first with an SRA, it is a better savings tool than any household budgeting plan that most people are likely to adopt.

Opening an SRA is easy. You sign a payroll reduction agreement with your personnel office to withhold, for example, $200 per month from your paycheck and to contribute that money to your SRA. Because the contributions come out of your pre-tax income, however, the SRA payment will not reduce your take-home pay by the full $200. Your reduction in take-home pay can be as low as $125 if you are in the 31 percent federal tax bracket and are fortunate enough to live in a state with a high income tax.[1] At the end of a year, your SRA account has grown to $2,400 in contributions, but this has cost you only $1,500 in take-home pay. Because of these tax advantages, the SRA as a savings vehicle is superior to virtually any other savings plan that most of us can find.

The SRA is not a tax shelter; it is a tax deferred savings plan. Income taxes are deferred until you draw money out of your account. In the meantime, the earnings on your account compound tax deferred. Withdrawals before age 59 1/2 will incur a 10 percent income tax penalty. In the event of certain documented conditions, such as an early retirement forced upon you by bad health, the IRS will forgo the penalty. For most of us, however, this 10 percent penalty is advantageous, because it gives us a strong incentive to keep our retirement savings intact until the day that we retire.

The SRA also has other advantages that your regular TIAA-CREF retirement annuity (RA) does not possess. Accumulations in your SRA account will grow faster than those in your RA account, because you can contribute much more to the SRA than to your RA. Many people can contribute up to 20 percent of their salary to their SRA, but I have yet to meet an employer who would ever make such a large contribution to a worker's pension plan. Not only does your SRA contribution reduce your taxable income, but it also lowers the AGI (adjusted gross income) on your income tax return. This increases the value of deductions such as medical costs and professional expenses that are only deductible if they exceed a specific percent of your AGI. Professional expenses, for example, are deductible only if they exceed 2 percent of your AGI. Lower your AGI by $9,000 and you increase your professional expenses deduction by up to $180.

Perhaps the greatest advantages of the SRA stem from the fact that the SRA contribution is tax deductible and the earnings compound tax

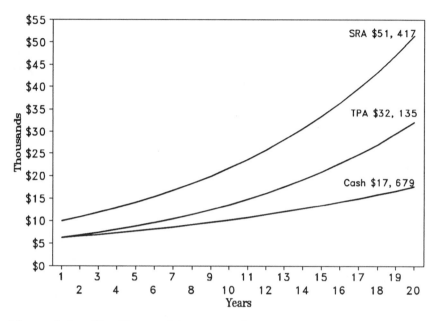

Figure 3-1   The Value of Tax Free Compounding

deferred. Figure 3-1 shows the value of this. Suppose you expect to earn an extra $10,000 this year that you plan to save for twenty years. You have three possible ways to invest this amount: (1) an SRA in which both the original $10,000 and the earnings on it are tax deferred, (2) a TIAA Teacher's Personal Annuity (TPA) in which you pay tax on the original $10,000, but the earnings compound tax deferred, or (3) a cash account in which you pay tax on both the original $10,000 and on each year's annual earnings as they occur. Note that you end up paying the taxes in any case, but the timing of their payment differs. Assume further that in each case your earnings will compound at a modest 9 percent annual rate of return, and that you are currently in a combined state-federal tax bracket of approximately 37.5 percent (31 percent federal and 9 percent state).

Figure 3-1 compares the three approaches. The SRA enables you to put the entire $10,000 to work at once and it grows to $51,417 after twenty years. Using the TPA, only the after-tax amount of $6,250 is invested initially, but the earnings compound tax deferred and after twenty years you have $32,135. The cash investment plan also allows you to put only $6,250 to work originally, and since you will have to withdraw money each year to pay taxes on the annual earnings, it grows to only $17,679. Because of its tax deductible contribution and its tax deferred compounding, the SRA gives you the best return.

Of course, since you have already paid the taxes on the cash account, you own your $17,679 without threat of further taxation, while you still have to pay taxes on withdrawals from your SRA or TPA. Let us assume a worst case scenario. You move to a high income tax state and withdraw all the money at once, which pushes you into a combined state-federal income tax bracket of 44.5 percent (39 percent federal, 9 percent state). Despite the fact that you are now paying taxes at a higher bracket than if you had paid them originally, you still end up with more after-tax money in the tax deferred accounts. After taxes, the SRA will net you $28,536 and the TPA $22,285, compared with only $17,679 for the cash account.

Note that the net after-tax result of the SRA was a whopping 61 percent greater than the cash account, while the net result of the TPA was only 26 percent greater. Part of this meager result was due to the fact that we boosted the tax bracket of the TPA from 37.5 percent to 44.5 percent. But even if the TPA was kept to the lower 37.5 percent tax bracket (which is unlikely), the net result would still have been just $22,428, only 27 percent greater than the cash account.

Clearly the huge advantage of the SRA derives from the fact that the initial investment of $10,000 comes from pre-tax dollars. If you paid the taxes first, you had only $6,250 left to invest. Over a twenty year period, the tax deferred compounding on the earnings contributed only marginally to the superior performance of the SRA. Over longer periods, of course, it would contribute more.

While Figure 3-1 shows the superiority of the SRA as an investment vehicle, it raises serious questions about the value of the TPA or any other tax deferred fixed annuity started with after-tax dollars. If over a twenty year period, the TPA will give you only 27 percent more than what you would have had in a cash investment, is it worth tying up your money for all those years? If you are thinking of a longer time span, TPA's advantage grows larger. But for shorter time periods, its advantage shrinks.

The value of the SRA is so undisputed in this example, however, that you would have to be pushed up to a 66 percent tax bracket at withdrawal time before the SRA would fail to give you a better return than the cash savings plan. Given the federal government's deficit problems, nobody can promise that you won't be pushed into a 66 percent tax bracket twenty years from now. But it does seem unlikely.

In addition to the tax deferral advantages, another advantage of the SRA is that you can borrow from it. If you need a substantial amount of cash immediately to pay for your child's college tuition or even a trip to Las Vegas, you can borrow 50 percent of the money in your SRA up to a $50,000 maximum, and TIAA-CREF will not even ask why you want the loan. You will, of course, be charged interest on these borrowings, and you must begin paying them back on a quarterly basis or the IRS will consider them taxable distributions.

Finally, you have more control over your SRA than you do over your RA. You can transfer funds from TIAA to CREF without going through the ten-year process required in your RA. Depending on when you made your contributions, you may be eligible to transfer some of your accumulations over to your IRA if you want. And, unlike the RA, you can transfer an SRA outside of the TIAA-CREF system without the approval of your employer.

Why Open Your SRA Now?

You should open your SRA today, because the cost of delay is enormous. The figure and tables below show why this is so.

Consider the hypothetical case of two professors. Professor Early Bird opens an SRA at age 30, invests $2,000 per year for eight years and then never puts in another cent. Late Riser opens an SRA in year eight and also puts in $2,000 per year. Both accounts grow at the same rate (10 percent per year in the example). Even though Early Bird stops contributing to the plan after year eight, and even though Professor Late Riser continues putting in $2,000 per year indefinitely, Professor Late Riser never catches up with Professor Early Bird. By age 60, Late Riser will have put $32,000 more into the account than Early Bird but will have about $27,000 less than Early Bird. Furthermore, the gap will grow larger each year, even if Late Riser continues making the $2,000 contribution. This assertion seems so contrary to common sense that we had better illustrate it year by year to show that it is no exaggeration. This is done in Table 3-1.

The cost of delay is even greater than suggested by Table 3-1. If you are 30 years old and have to decide between sacrificing now and making a $3,000 SRA contribution or waiting two years until age 32 to

Table 3-1   The Cost of Waiting Seven Years to Start Your SRA

Year	Early Bird Contrib- uted	Accumu- lated	Late Riser Contrib- uted	Accumu- lated	Differ- ence
1	$2,000	$2,000			
2	4,000	4,200			
3	6,000	6,620			
4	8,000	9,282			
5	10,000	12,210			
6	12,000	15,431			
7	14,000	18,974			
8	16,000	22,872	$2,000	$2,000	$20,872
9		25,159	4,000	4,200	20,959
10		27,675	6,000	6,620	21,055
20		71,781	26,000	49,045	22,736
30		186,183	48,000	159,086	27,096

start, it is tempting to think that the cost of delay is only $6,000. How-ever, you only have a finite number of years to make your contributions before 65 (or whatever age you hope to retire). The cost of delay is not the $3,000 you would have made the first year. As shown in Figure 3-2, the cost of delay is the $300,000 difference between what you would have accumulated at age 65 if you had started saving at age 30 rather than delaying it two years. Starting with $2,000 at age 30 and increasing that by 4 percent per year as your salary goes up, a 10 percent rate of return brings you $1.6 million. Starting at age 32 the same investment schedule brings you only $1.3 million.

In sum, procrastination is costly.

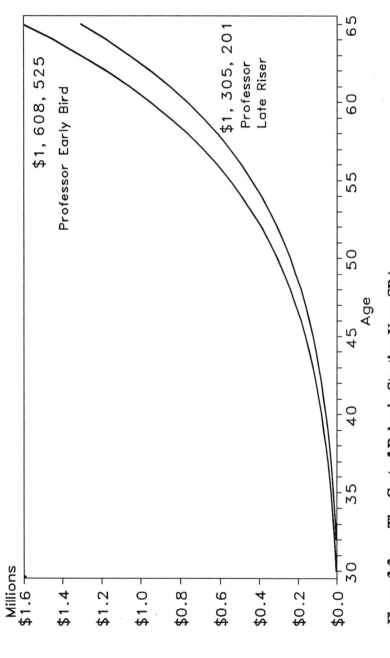

Figure 3-2   The Cost of Delay in Starting Your SRA

Raising the Money to Start an SRA

The advantages of opening an SRA immediately are all well and good, you may say, but I live on a modest academic salary and have many expenses. How can I find the money to open an SRA?

Easy!

You need to do one of four things, each of which entails a small sacrifice. We preach the value of deferred gratification to our students, and achieving the rewards of an SRA demands a little deferred gratification on our part as well.

First, start your SRA now with whatever amount you can afford, no matter how small it is. If you lack $50 per month to get yourself going, then start with $25. If you absolutely lack even $25 to start your account, then give up something until your next pay increase and use that amount to start an SRA. Simply giving up two cups of coffee per work day at forty cents per cup would easily enable you to save $25 per month. Remember, the SRA contribution is taken from your *pre-tax* income. A $25 contribution will reduce your take-home pay by only $16-$18 per month, depending on your income tax circumstances.

Second, when you receive your next pay increase, earmark half of that pay raise to increasing your SRA contributions. A 6 percent salary increase for a person earning a $35,000 salary will total $2,100 or $175 per month. You are already used to living without that money, so earmark $100 of it to your SRA, and you will barely miss it. Because it comes from pre-tax income, your salary increase will be reduced by only $65-$80 per month, depending on your income tax bracket. At the end of a year, you will have $1,200 in contributions credited to your account. If you continue increasing your SRA contributions in this manner each year, you will soon approach your maximum SRA contribution and you will be amazed at how much money has begun to accumulate in your SRA account.

True, this strategy demands some sacrifice on your part. It demands that you temporarily limit the annual increases in your standard of living. But remember, this sacrifice occurs only until you have reached your maximum SRA contribution. If you increase your monthly contribution by $200 each year, you will probably reach that level in barely three years. At $100 per month you will probably reach your maximum contribution level in six or seven years. From that point on, increasing your SRA contributions to stay at the maximum will cause only a small and negligible impact on your take-home pay.

A third way to find money for your SRA is to examine your finances for any counter-productive expenditures. There are plenty of these around. *Money* magazine in 1993 listed thirty-four different ways to cut expenditures.[2] These ranged from refinancing your mortgage to lower your monthly mortgage payment to installing a load controller to reduce your electricity bills. If *Money's* suggestions are not enough, a monthly newsletter called the *Tightwad Gazette* suggests many more.[3]

One likely possibility is that you may be paying more money for insurance than you need to pay.[4] If you have dependents, you clearly need life insurance to protect them in event you die prematurely. The best strategy for most people, most of the time, is to buy *term* life insurance from a low-cost carrier such as TIAA. Most insurance agents, however, prefer to sell cash value policies (usually called whole life, variable life, or universal life) with a savings feature built into them. These give you a smaller return on your savings than you are likely to get from CREF. In a great many instances, you would be better off cashing in your whole life insurance, taking out a lower-cost TIAA term life insurance, and putting the difference in premiums into your CREF supplemental retirement annuity.[5] In fact, as your SRA builds up, you will actually need less life insurance because your insurance needs decrease as your liquid assets increase.

Note that this plan works only if you actually invest the premium differences on a regular basis. If you fail to make these investments, you could end up in fifteen or twenty years with no cash value, no savings, and an extremely expensive term insurance renewal premium. With CREF the investment of the premium difference is very easy to do, because your investments are automatically taken from your paycheck. Also, if you replace your cash value insurance with a term policy, make sure you have your term policy in place before you cancel the cash value policy.[6]

The fourth step you can take to find money for your SRA is familiar to most of us in academia who find ways to augment our salaries. We teach summer school, receive professional development grants, talk acquisition editors into giving us advance royalties, take on temporary administrative assignments, and in some instances run businesses on the side. If you receive a $1,000 faculty development grant, put it into a separate savings or money market account and immediately increase your monthly SRA contribution by $100. This will reduce your take-home pay by $65-80 per month, and you can easily cover that shortfall by making withdrawals from the separate savings account you just opened with your faculty development grant.

Other Benefits of the SRA

If you start this strategy early in your career and follow it rigorously, three very tangible benefits will accrue to you in a very short time. First, your SRA account will eventually contain more money than your TIAA-CREF main retirement account (RA). Since you have more flexibility in tapping your SRA funds than your RA, you are accumulating a large pool of money that could be used for an emergency or any other reason.

Second, having an SRA also allows you to develop what one financial adviser called "attitude money.[7]" After a few years, you will have nearly a year's salary accumulated in your SRA. Having built up this reserve to fall back on gives most people a more positive attitude about the circumstances of their life and their job. An interesting change in perspective takes place. When you reach the point that you can pass up the summer school and the faculty development grants and suffer few financial setbacks, your entire employment circumstances seem a little more mellow than they did when you were scraping for every dollar you could get. You see your job in an entirely new light. Some people might not need a sense of financial stability. But for most of us, the psychologist Abraham Maslow[8] was probably correct. We cannot go on to meet our higher levels of human needs until our need for economic security is on the way to being met. The wonderful thing about the SRA is that it moves us solidly in the direction of gaining some economic security and independence.

A third benefit of this plan is that you can give yourself a big boost in take-home pay any time you want. If you start an SRA with a monthly contribution of $200 and increase that by $200 each year, within three years, your contributions will be $600 per month ($7,200 per year). That will reduce your take-home pay by about $450 per month. To give yourself a take-home pay increase of $450 all you have to do is discontinue the SRA contributions. Since you are used to living without that $450 per month and can see the value in adding $7,200 per year to your SRA, you will probably decide not to discontinue your contributions. But the mere knowledge that you can do so at any time sharply boosts your financial self confidence.

How Much Can I Contribute?

If this chapter has done its job, you will now want to know just how much you can contribute to your SRA each year. You can probably contribute 15-20 percent of your salary, but to get a definitive answer to that question, you need only to fill out and mail in TIAA-CREF's "Tax Deferred Annuity Questionnaire," which you can get from your benefits office.

Currently, contributions are capped at $9,500. How close your personal limit comes to that cap is a product of several factors: how many years you have contributed to TIAA-CREF, what type of institution you work for, how long you have worked there, how much your employer has contributed to your TIAA-CREF accounts, and how much you have contributed previously. Given these variables, TIAA-CREF will calculate three optional limits on contributions for the year. These are the general limit, alternative limit B, and alternative limit C. An alternative limit A is also available, but only for persons on the verge of retirement who have not maximized contributions in the past.

- General limit
  This limit is likely to permit the lowest contribution to your SRA.

- Limit B
  This limit is available for teaching institutions, churches, health organizations and welfare service agencies. It will usually allow the largest SRA contribution for members with defined contribution retirement plans who already have worked for several years for their employer and expect to continue working for some years in the future.

- Limit C
  This limit is also available for teaching institutions, churches, health organizations, and welfare service agencies. It will usually provide for the largest SRA contribution for members in state university systems with defined benefit retirement plans, persons who were just recently hired, or persons anticipating a change in employment.

If you choose the general limit, you may always switch to alternative B or C in future years, and you may switch from alternative B or C to the general limit. However, you may not switch between alternative B and alternative C; whichever alternative you choose, you must stick with that one. Under certain circumstances, you might be permitted to exceed the $9,500 cap and contribute up to $12,500.

Because these optional limits are based on complicated formulas and because there are tax penalties for exceeding your contribution, it is very important that you ask TIAA-CREF to calculate your maximum contribution before you make any increases in contributions.

Conclusion

You should open an SRA immediately. When you receive a pay raise at the start of each school year, make an increase in your SRA contributions. Eventually you will reach the maximum amount of contributions that you are legally entitled to make. If you do this with consistency over a period of time, you will very soon see your SRA accumulations grow to a level that will amaze and please you.

Notes

1.   This is based on a state income tax rate of 9 percent, not allowing for the state deductibility of federal income taxes. Eight states had a rate of at least 9 percent in 1990, but five of those allowed the deductibility of federal income taxes. United States Bureau of the Census, *Statistical Abstract of the United States: 1992* (Washington, D.C.: U. S. Government Printing Office, 1992), p. 287.

2.   Gary Belsky, "34 Ways to Cut Your Spending and Save 25% or More," *Money* (September 1993): p. 77.

3.   *Tightwad Gazette*. (R.R. 1, Box 3570; Leeds, Maine 04263; $12 annual subscription.)

4.   Sheryl Nance-Nash, "Insurance You Don't Need," *Money*, July 1993, pp. 78-79. Nance-Nash estimates that ten percent of the money people spend on insurance is not needed. She lists a dozen types of insurance to avoid.

5. For an evaluation of this strategy and other insurance issues see Kristin Davis, "Making Life Insurance Easier to Swallow," *Kiplinger's Personal Finance Magazine* (August 1993): 44-48. For an evaluation of cash value life insurance, see Peter Katt, "Cash Value Life Insurance: Separating Fact from Fiction," *AAII Journal* 15, no. 3 (March 1993): 21-23.

6. Peter Katt, "Should You Replace Your Cash Value Policy?" *AAII Journal* 15, no. 7 (August 1993): 22-24.

7. Charles Givens, *Wealth Without Risk* (New York: Simon & Schuster, 1988), p. 276.

8. Psychologist Abraham Maslow argued that there is a hierarchy of human needs. Physical security needs have to be secured before the person can devote energy to higher level needs. One step above physical security needs are economic security needs. Then come the needs for affiliation, esteem, achievement, aesthetics and self-actualization. Abraham H. Maslow, *Motivation and Personality*, 2nd ed. (Princeton, N.J.: Van Nostrand, 1970) .

Chapter 4

Favor CREF Over TIAA

If the *most* costly mistake TIAA-CREF participants make is not opening an SRA soon enough, the second most costly mistake is putting too much of their assets into TIAA rather than CREF. TIAA may be a useful annuity for some people in retirement, but it is not a very good accumulation vehicle for 30- or 40- year-old people who can look forward to many productive years of work.

This chapter will focus on TIAA from two perspectives. First, it will compare the historical returns of TIAA with those of CREF. These comparisons will show that CREF is a much more appropriate instrument for the capital accumulation phase of one's retirement planning, while some exposure to TIAA becomes more appropriate as one approaches the moment of retirement and has less room to tolerate risk. Second, the chapter will assess some common problems of TIAA that have drawn much media attention in recent years.

Since this chapter relies heavily on comparing the past performance of TIAA and the CREF Stock Fund, it is important to note the limits of such historical comparisons. The future will not necessarily unfold like the past, and a lot of money can be lost by buying an investment today simply because it went up in the past. Nevertheless, it would be a mistake to ignore history. Knowledge of conditions and developments that took place in the past is useful. There will, no doubt, be periods in the future characterized by conditions similar to those when CREF outperformed TIAA. And there will be other periods characterized by conditions similar to those when CREF lagged behind TIAA. Knowledge of these conditions and these relationships is important for making reasonable judgments about the allocation of one's assets today and in the future.

TIAA and CREF Compared

Table 4-1 presents a comparison of TIAA and CREF returns during different time spans since 1953, CREF's first full year of operation. The first row in this table shows that in the one-year periods from 1953 through 1992 CREF outperformed TIAA in 25 out of the 40 such time periods. The next seven rows show the comparisons over five year periods (for example, 1953-57, 1954-58, etc.), ten-year periods (1953-62, 1954-63, etc.), fifteen-year periods, twenty-year periods, twenty five-year periods, thirty-year periods, and one forty-year period. The first column shows the number of periods that existed within this time span. (For example, there were 36-five year periods). The second column shows the number of periods in which TIAA outperformed CREF, and the third column shows the actual time periods when TIAA outperformed CREF.

A careful scrutiny of this table and the comparative performance of TIAA and CREF leads to several observations.

CREF Has an Advantage Most of the Time

No matter which time span one observes, this table shows that CREF has outperformed TIAA most of the time, and the longer the time period, the more likely CREF was to perform better. Table 4-1 shows that CREF outperformed TIAA in all of the thirty-year periods and twenty five-year periods and in all but one of the twenty-year periods. However, it is difficult for most people to think in terms of twenty-five year or even fifteen-year periods. For this reason, the most relevant rows in Table 4-1 are probably those showing five-year and ten-year returns. Even these periods show that CREF normally has an advantage over TIAA. CREF consistently outperformed TIAA during the 1950s, the 1960s, the 1980s, and (so far) the 1990s. The only periods when TIAA outperformed CREF were those ending in the 1970s and early 1980s. As will become apparent, these were very distinctive years.

CREF Is More Volatile Than TIAA

Investing in CREF rather than TIAA brings greater rewards over the long run. But in the short-term, CREF is much more volatile than

Table 4-1   TIAA and CREF Compared: 1953 through 1992

Time Period	Number of Periods	Number of Times TIAA Outperforms CREF	Time Periods of TIAA Advantage Years Ending:
1 year	40	15	Sporadic
5 years	36	8	1970; 1973-78; 1981
10 years	31	9	1974-82
15 years	26	1	1981
20 years	21	1	1981
25 years	16	0	None
30 years	11	0	None
40 years	1	0	None

Source: Calculated from *Charting TIAA and the CREF Accounts: Winter 1992-93*, Library Series 2 (New York: TIAA-CREF, 1993), pp. 30-31, 36-37.

TIAA. TIAA has never had a losing year since the start of these comparisons in 1953, and its one year returns fluctuated within a very narrow range from a low of 2.8 percent in 1953 to a high of 13.7 percent in 1982. CREF, by contrast, has had ten losing years since 1952, and its one-year returns have ranged from a loss of 31 percent in 1974 to a gain of 48.9 percent in 1954. In the 1973-74 bear market, the CREF Stock unit lost nearly half its value.

In practical terms, this means that if you put any money into CREF Stock or the other CREF equity funds, you have to be prepared to ride out short-term periods when CREF will experience a loss. Previous experience indicates you can expect losing years to occur about 25 percent of the time.

TIAA has an Advantage in Dismal Times

If we consider closely the time periods when TIAA outperformed CREF we note that they were times of extraordinary turmoil: mostly the time periods that ended in the middle 1970s through the early 1980s. These were years, first of all, of volatile and generally rising interest rates. The returns on the federal government's three-month Treasury bill rose from an average 4.3 percent in 1967 to 7.8 percent in 1974, dropped back to 5 percent in 1976, and then rose to a whopping 14 percent in 1981.[1] Other interest rates followed a similar pattern.

Not only were interest rates volatile during these periods, so was the rate of inflation. In 1970 the Consumer Price Index (CPI) rose only 3.2 percent; four years later in 1974 it jumped 11 percent. In 1976, the CPI rate of increase dropped to 5.8 percent, then rose to double-digit increases again from 1979 through 1981 (11.3, 13.5 and 10.3 percent respectively),[2] the only time in American history that inflation rose in double digits for three years in a row. The economic misery caused by volatile interest rates and inflation was compounded by recurrent recessions. Between 1969 and 1983, there were four recessions (1969-70, 1974-75, 1980, 1981-82). Very few other fifteen-year periods in American history had seen the nation's economic performance as dismal as it was from 1968 through 1982.

Finally, these years of economic underperformance were also years of extraordinary political instability. From the retirement of President Dwight Eisenhower in 1961 to the inauguration of Ronald Reagan twenty years later, not a single president finished two full terms of office. One was assassinated. Two others (Ford and Reagan) survived attempted assassinations. One (Nixon) was forced from office to avoid impeachment and another (Johnson) left office in disgrace. Still another (Carter) was resoundingly rejected in a re-election bid. Instability at the top of the political system was matched by urban riots in the late 1960s, a disastrous war in Vietnam, vulnerability to an oil embargo in the early 1970s, inability to protect the safety of American diplomats held hostage in Iran from late 1979 through 1980, and a diminishing ability of the two major political parties to maintain control over the nation's political processes.

These, then, were the conditions from the late 1960s to the early 1980s: rising interest rates, high inflation, frequent recessions, and political instability. These conditions do not normally provide a setting for strong performance in the equity markets, and it is not surprising that the dominant equity markets did as poorly as they did during this period. This is shown in Figure 4-1. The markets showed several ups and downs during these years, but they essentially peaked in 1968 and did not permanently surpass that peak until 1982 (after adjusting for inflation).

Not all equity markets did poorly during the late 1970s, however. While the S&P 500 Index and the Dow Jones Average did poorly, small capitalization stocks performed very well. Unfortunately for CREF holders, the bulk of CREF's portfolio was necessarily concentrated on large capitalization stocks, and CREF mirrored the performance of the dominant stock averages.

Although these conditions undermined the equity markets during the 1970s, several of these factors worked to TIAA's advantage. Its big investment in fixed income instruments that are interest-rate sensitive, enabled TIAA to benefit from rising interest rates. With its exposure to real estate markets, TIAA also benefitted from the inflation of real estate prices in the 1970s. Because TIAA tended to outperform equities during periods of economic recessions, the four recessions during this period also worked to TIAA's advantage over CREF.

Early Career People Should Avoid TIAA

The trouble with knowing that TIAA performs best in dismal times is that we cannot predict with any certainty when the dismal periods will come. Fortunately, you do not need to be an economic forecaster. If you are twenty years from needing to spend your retirement funds, you can certainly ride out the short-term losses that CREF incurs periodically. Even if another dismal period like the 1970s recurs, you can probably ride that out as well.

Furthermore, as Chapter 5 will document, people in early career can utilize an investment strategy called *dollar cost averaging* to tide them through the dismal periods like the 1970s. As unbelievable as this seems, early career people using dollar cost averaging were better off in the 1970s allocating all their premiums to CREF Stock than they would have been with TIAA, even though Table 4-1 clearly shows that TIAA outperformed CREF throughout most of these years.

Finally, as a long-term savings plan, TIAA is a loser, because it barely beats the inflation rate. Although CREF's yearly performance lagged behind the inflation rate more often than TIAA (10 times compared with TIAA's 7 times), it has outperformed the CPI by a wider

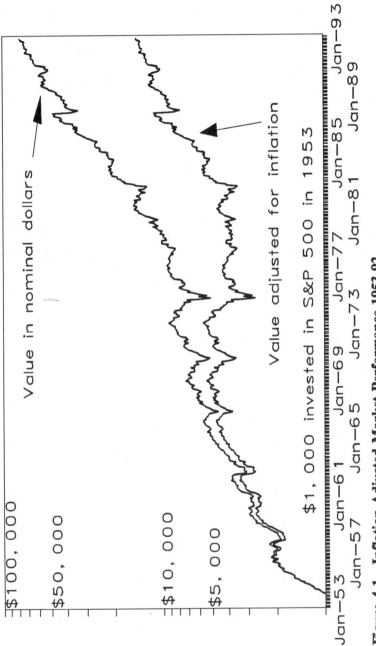

Figure 4-1   Inflation Adjusted Market Performance 1953-92

margin than TIAA. Since 1952, the purchasing power of the dollar has declined at an averaged rate of 4.1 percent per year. TIAA beat that by a margin of only 2.1 percentage points per year, while CREF beat it by a margin of 6.8 percentage points per year.[3]

Late Career People Need to Reduce Exposure to CREF Stock

A 40-year old participant in CREF has plenty of time to recover from a bear market in the CREF Stock Fund, but the same is not true for people in their sixties. In principle, the 60 year old is not as vulnerable as he or she would have been a decade ago, since teachers can no longer be forced to retire at age 65. If CREF is in a slump when you reach retirement age, you can in theory just work for another two years and wait for CREF to recover before starting your retirement withdrawals. Although a growing number of TIAA-CREF participants are indeed working beyond age 65 (from 25 percent in 1979 to 39 percent in 1991),[4] it would not be a very appealing prospect to be forced to continue working past that age only because CREF suffered one of its periodic losses on the eve of your sixty-fifth birthday. For this reason, the prudent person will reduce his or her exposure to CREF Stock Fund as retirement draws near.

Basically there are three ways to reduce your exposure to CREF. TIAA-CREF advocates that people late in their careers move 75 percent of their retirement assets into TIAA. This conservative approach gives the most psychological security. It protects you from a loss of your capital, which is critical at this age. Despite its advantages, there are some drawbacks to this approach. It is very cumbersome to switch funds out of TIAA in event that TIAA's investments fail to pan out as well as you hope. Furthermore, you may suffer what the economist call opportunity costs. In this case the opportunity cost would be losing the chance to take advantage of booms in the stock, bond, or global equities markets if those booms occurred and you had no CREF holdings.

If transferring most of your assets to TIAA is the most conservative way of coping with the market risk of CREF, the least conservative way is to try and time the market, moving funds into money market assets during bear markets and shifting them back into the CREF Stock Fund during bull markets. This risky course of action is resoundingly discouraged by most market participants[5] and economists,[6] as well as TIAA-CREF itself.[7] We will examine market timing in Part 3.

Finally, a third option to the TIAA-CREF tradeoff is to use an asset allocation strategy of dividing your assets into several asset classes that do not move together. Thus a big drop in the stock market will be compensated for by a rise in your other asset classes. Through asset allocation, you can minimize the risk of your CREF holdings without binding yourself forever into the rigidity and problems of TIAA. We will examine asset allocation strategies in Chapter 8.

Mid-career People

Individuals in mid-career should be heavily invested in CREF equity funds but should make some reduction in their exposure to equities. Ideally they should use an asset allocation strategy that is somewhat riskier than that pursued by the late career people but certainly somewhat less aggressive than that of early career people.

The Retirement Choice

Asset allocation becomes an extremely important decision when you reach the actual moment of your retirement. Once you settle on your mix of vehicles and sign up for an annuity, TIAA-CREF will no longer permit you to shift funds back and forth. Although you are not obliged to annuitize your investments, needless to say, you have to adopt a fairly conservative strategy at this point. Since you will have to live off your retirement funds, you cannot afford to see your income drop. Chapters 14 and 15 are devoted exclusively to the important decision of annuitization.

Coping with TIAA as a Captured Investment

Your retirement annuity (RA) account money in TIAA is a captured investment. Funds that you put into TIAA are stuck there for a long time. This key feature of TIAA frustrates many TIAA participants who would like to see more flexibility in TIAA and exasperates many financial planners who would like to manage your funds. However, the captured investment is an integral consequence of TIAA's investment philosophy.

TIAA's Transfer Policy

Until recently you could not take any funds out of TIAA. In the 1980s, TIAA yielded to participant pressure and permitted a one-time cash withdrawal of 10 percent upon retirement. Finally in 1991, TIAA began permitting transfers of TIAA funds to CREF, but these transfers take ten years to complete.

When you request a withdrawal of funds, you can transfer 10 percent of your TIAA holdings to CREF immediately. The balance of your withdrawal is put into a Transfer Payout Annuity. Once each year, one-tenth of the funds put into the Transfer Payout Annuity and all interest earnings over the previous year are transferred from the Transfer Payout Annuity into whichever CREF account that you designate.

TIAA's rationale for discouraging transfers is the protection of the long-term nature of its portfolio. TIAA holds many of its bonds until maturity and usually keeps its real estate investments for the long-term. If TIAA were to permit unlimited transfers, a sudden rush of withdrawals at a bad moment could force TIAA to liquidate some of its holdings at unfavorable prices. By discouraging transfers, TIAA can gain higher safety ratings for its portfolio, protect itself from making forced liquidations, and pay a higher dividend to participants than would be possible if unlimited transfers were permitted. TIAA also has a primary responsibility to pay the highest dividends possible and give a safe portfolio to participants in for the long-term. It has less responsibility to make it easy for other participants to move in and out of its investments.

These are reasonable arguments, but they are not totally persuasive. TIAA permits unlimited withdrawals from SRA accounts and does not suffer negative consequences from those withdrawals. TIAA could use its experience with withdrawals from SRA accounts to estimate what impact unlimited withdrawals would have on RA accounts. Finally, given the fiscally conservative nature of people who put their money into TIAA in the first place, it does not seem very likely that many of these people would make frequent transfers into and out of TIAA.

What TIAA Ought to Do

There could be more options available to TIAA than either the current restrictions on withdrawals in RAs or the unlimited withdrawals that exist for SRAs. Within RA accounts, a Plan A TIAA could operate under current restrictive rules on transfers, and a new Plan B TIAA could be created that would combine the unlimited transferability that exists for SRAs. To compensate for the greater risk incurred with unlimited transferability, Plan B could receive a lower interest rate than Plan A. TIAA already follows a variation of this concept in that TIAA pays a lower interest rate in SRA accounts than it pays in RA accounts.

Existing TIAA monies would stay in Plan A, but for new monies you could choose between the two plans. If you were in for the long-term and wanted the higher dividend rate, you could invest in Plan A. If you wanted unlimited transferability and were willing to accept a lower interest rate, you could invest in Plan B. Since the vast bulk of TIAA's holdings would stay in Plan A, the introduction of unlimited transferability in Plan B would pose no threat to the safety of TIAA's portfolio or the dividend rate that it pays on its investments.

While Plan B would pose no threat to the safety of TIAA, such a plan would be a very attractive option for some participants who might want to take some of their profits out of the CREF equity and bond funds. In late 1993 and much of 1994 they were deterred from doing so by lower-than-usual interest rates in the Money Market fund and reluctance to tie up their profits for ten years in TIAA. These participants would find a Plan B TIAA very attractive. It would enable them to reduce their exposure to equities or bonds, yet receive a higher interest rate than prevailed in the Money Market fund without losing control over their money for the next ten years.

An independent auditor should be contracted by TIAA to determine how much lower of an interest rate would be appropriate to have for Plan B. TIAA regularly reviews its rate anyway, and this would simply amount to an extra calculation. TIAA's historical experience with both unlimited transfers in its SRA accounts and restrictive transfers through Transfer Payout Annuities should provide an independent auditor with enough data to estimate the impact of transferability on TIAA's overall portfolio and to calculate the appropriate interest rate difference between RA accounts and the SRA accounts. SRA interest rates and Plan B interest rates could then be adjusted accordingly.

Coping with TIAA's Restrictive Transferability

Until TIAA eases its restrictions on transferability, several guidelines seem appropriate. First, especially if you are young and expect to have many working years in front of you, do not put any new money into your RA TIAA account. This is just asking TIAA to lock it up unnecessarily.

Second, in your SRA account, for those assets that you want to keep in cash equivalents, consider using TIAA rather than the Money Market fund. In SRA accounts you can make transfers from TIAA to CREF. TIAA usually pays a higher return than does the Money Market fund, but it presents you virtually no risk of capital loss. For these reasons, TIAA is a useful cash equivalent in SRA accounts.

Third, consider transferring TIAA funds in your RA account into a Transfer Payout Annuity. This will give you greater flexibility in allocating your assets between the CREF funds and TIAA. It will also allow you to use a modified dollar cost averaging (see chap. 5) as you make the annual transfer of these monies to your CREF funds. If for some reason you later on decide that you really do not want to deplete your TIAA holdings, you can always transfer CREF monies back into TIAA anytime you want. You cannot, however, transfer funds directly from the Transfer Payout Annuity itself to TIAA.

TIAA from The Critic's Viewpoint

This book has taken a critical view of two main aspects of TIAA. First, it is not as lucrative as the CREF equity accounts for long-term investment planning; second, TIAA maintains restrictive policies on transferring funds to CREF. Although the profitability of TIAA is less an issue for criticism than a reflection of the differences between equity investments and fixed income investments, TIAA has come under other criticisms that need to be examined.

Real Estate Holdings

In the early 1990s TIAA's real estate portfolio received specific criticism. A multi-year slump in commercial real estate generally posed severe problems for many banks and insurance companies. The California real estate market in particular was faltering, and by 1993 27 percent of TIAA's mortgages and 11 percent of its direct real estate investments were in that one state. TIAA-CREF's magazine, *The Participant*, periodically profiles some of TIAA's choice pieces of real estate. These invariably glowing accounts that reveal nothing about vacancy rates, the percent of ownership that is TIAA's, or the terms of such ownership partnership agreements.[9]

The dearth of such information gave critics fertile ground to sow seeds of doubt about the quality of TIAA's real estate and mortgage investments. One critic charged that as of 1990 $1.1 billion of TIAA's real estate and mortgage holdings were in default, in arrears on payments or in some other form of serious financial trouble.[10] In TIAA's defense, these amounts were barely 2 percent of TIAA's total portfolio and in any case were reported in TIAA's annual report.[11]

Risky Bond Holdings

In addition to risky real estate investments, charge critics, TIAA's bond holdings are riskier than their AAA ratings imply. As much as 15 percent of TIAA bonds are junk bonds according to this analysis, and TIAA itself concedes that half of its direct corporate loans (not rated by the rating agencies) were to such troubled companies that the loans would have carried a below-investment-quality BBB rating if they had been rated.[12] Critics also claim that TIAA is much too prone to hold its bonds to maturity rather than to take capital gains on them at appropriate times as is common among most pension funds. Buying bonds and real estate for the long-term worked well historically, but critics say this strategy is much riskier for the 1990s when markets have become more volatile.[13]

TIAA as a Safe Haven

In part because of its real estate holdings and junk bonds, critics have also charged that TIAA is not as safe a haven as it claims to be. Despite the fact that TIAA normally receives the highest safety ratings from the three major insurance rating agencies (Standard and Poors [S&P], A. M. Best, and Moody's), critics complain that these high ratings exist primarily because TIAA has two advantages that other insurance companies lack. First, TIAA makes it so difficult for participants to switch into competing forms of investment that TIAA faces no risk of a massive outflow of funds that would force untimely liquidations of its troubled real estate and mortgage holdings. Second, TIAA annuities guarantee dividend payments of only 3 percent which is lower than competing insurance companies pay, lower in fact than the inflation rate of the past forty years. Although TIAA's actual dividend payments greatly exceed the 3 percent guarantee, the guaranteed rate along with the captured clientele base were both cited in the S&P analysis of its rating for TIAA.[14] In short, critics charge that TIAA gains its high safety ratings primarily because you, the participant, are willing to settle for a sub-par guaranteed annuity dividend and because you cannot easily withdraw your funds from TIAA to search for a higher dividend elsewhere.

Assessing the Criticisms

Most of these criticisms about TIAA's investment practices surfaced in the early 1990s when the nation's commercial real estate markets were in severe difficulty. Despite these difficulties, there is no credible evidence that TIAA's financial integrity has been shaken by its limited real estate losses. TIAA still enjoys high safety ratings from rating agencies. Whether the guaranteed dividend is sub-par as critics contend is probably less relevant to TIAA annuitants than the actual dividends they receive. The actual dividend depends on the earnings on TIAA's investments, not on the guaranteed amount. In fact, TIAA still pays a reasonable, if modest, dividend in a very difficult interest rate environment.

Not surprisingly, TIAA disputes the charges that have be levied against it. Rejecting the charge that 15 percent of its bonds are junk, TIAA asserts that only 7 percent are below investment grade (BBB or lower, by the S&P rating) and only 2 percent junk.[16] More serious is the charge that TIAA's high ratings result from its low guaranteed dividends and its captured clientele. Instead of a captured clientele, TIAA sees a retirement system that plans for the long-term.[17] Because its clients are in the plan for the long-term, TIAA has the power to ride out poor market environments such as those that hit real estate in the late 1980s and early 1990s. Instead of a very low guaranteed dividend rate, TIAA sees a stable cash flow, interest rate guarantees that are prudent and dividends that are generous.[18]

The depth of TIAA's commitment to the 3 percent guarantee stems from historical experience. When the Carnegie Corporation owned TIAA's stock prior to 1952, TIAA did offer a higher guarantee of 4 percent. This had been set in the 1920s when nobody anticipated that long-term interest rates could drop below 4 percent. In the 1940s, however, long-term interest rates did indeed drop that low, causing problems for TIAA that had to be worked out. With this experience, TIAA is probably on solid ground in refusing to budge from its 3 percent guarantee. True, it is hard to imagine as of this writing in 1994 that long-term interest rates could drop below 4 percent. Only a few years ago it was hard to imagine that even money market rates could drop below 4 percent. In 1993, in fact, they dropped under 3 percent.

As to the charge that TIAA dividends do not compare favorably to S&P below investment grade bonds, TIAA prefers to compare itself to returns for other insurance companies and finds that it exceeds the averages for the industry.[18]

What is one to make of these charges? Do TIAA's high quality ratings depend on your willingness to be a captured client and your willingness to accept a low guaranteed dividend when you annuitize? The answer appears to be yes, and that is a negative from the point of view of TIAA critics. But it puts TIAA in a solid financial position, and that is a plus from TIAA's viewpoint. It is also a plus from your point of view as a participant if you can accept this proposition; a modest dividend from a solvent insurer is still preferable to a high dividend from an insurer flirting with insolvency.

The Bottom Line

So, what is the bottom line on these charges? Most of these criticisms were levied in the early 1990s when there were great fears of massive junk bond losses and a replay of the savings and loan debacle in the banking industry. Looking back on these fears from the perspective of 1994, the real estate markets no longer seem headed toward the disaster that people feared, and a great many investors, including TIAA, appear to have made significant profits on the junk bonds that they bought during those risky days. It is possible that TIAA could eventually suffer significant losses on those investments. But as of 1994, that does not look very likely, and TIAA appears to have sailed safely through a very rough period.

However, TIAA annuitants have been taking cuts in their benefit checks for the last few years. Dividends will not quickly return to the rates of old even if TIAA's critics turn out to be as off that mark as

TIAA claims and even if TIAA's investment strategies are vindicated. With the declining interest rate environment of the early 1990s, corporations have been calling in their high interest rate bonds and replacing them with lower interest rate bonds. Presumably many of the mortgages that TIAA helds were refinanced just as many Americans refinanced their home mortgages when mortgage rates dropped in the early 1990s.

This means that TIAA was doubly hit by lower rates on new investments as well as the loss of older, high-yield securities that were called in or refinanced. Nor will this situation reverse quickly when interest rates move back up. With $66 billion in assets and only about $2.5 billion in new premiums each year to invest,[25] it will take a long time for higher interest rates to become reflected in TIAA's dividend payments to annuitants. It is important to remember, however, that the declining annuity checks to participants in the early 1990s were a function of the overall decline in interest rates.

The final charge is that participants cannot know the worth of TIAA's bonds and other investments because TIAA does not mark them to the market. The downside of not marking its bonds and real estate to the market is, of course, that TIAA does not have a unit value that can grow in price as those underlying assets appreciate in value. From the point of view of TIAA, this is an unmitigated plus for the participant. Unit values that move up in price with market changes also decline in value as market prices drop. With its philosophy of holding its bonds to maturity, TIAA does not feel compelled to make daily adjustments in the market value of those holdings.[22]

The net result is that TIAA ends up being a very safe investment. It does not protect you very well from the risk of inflation, but it does protect you well from the risk of capital loss.

Conclusion

With its seven different accounts, CREF seems like a much better investment vehicle than TIAA, especially for younger participants. CREF exposes you to the risk of capital loss, but this risk diminishes if your investment horizon is long enough. TIAA exposes you to the risk of inflation, and the longer your investment horizon, the more exposed you become to the ravages of inflation.

Over the long run, the equity markets will probably outperform the fixed income markets. CREF's equity based funds will probably outperform TIAA. Equities give you a partial ownership in American industry and, to a lesser extent, foreign industries. To bet that the equity markets will not outperform the fixed income markets over the long-term is to bet that the national and world economies themselves will enter a period of prolonged stagnation of two decades or more.

Over the long run, inflation should take a greater toll on fixed income investments such as TIAA than on the CREF equity funds.

Early career people should avoid TIAA. Concentrate your investments in the CREF funds. If CREF ends up as a disappointment, you can always change your mind and switch elsewhere later. If TIAA disappoints you, however, you are stuck. It will take ten years to transfer your assets out of TIAA.

Mid-career and late career people must reduce their exposure to CREF Stock. For most people, this means developing an asset allocation strategy, and TIAA may have a role to play in this strategy. Chapter 8 will offer ideas on this issue.

Notes

1. *Statistical Abstract of the United States: 1971*, p. 445; *1984*, p. 521.

2. *Statistical Abstract of the United States: 1992*, p. 469.

3. *Statistical Abstract of the United States: 1971*, p. 333; *1992*, p. 469. *Charting TIAA and the CREF Accounts: Winter 1992-93*, Library Series 2 (New York: TIAA-CREF, 1993), pp. 30, 36.

4. A TIAA-CREF graph entitled "TIAA-CREF Annuity Income Starting Ages, 1979 to 1991," TIAA-CREF Actuarial Division, IA Master File SSN Base. Prepared by External Affairs, Policyholder and Institutional Research, July 1991. In 1979, 25.2 percent of participants beginning their annuity incomes were aged 65 or older. By 1991, this number had increased to 38.9 percent. Interestingly, the percent retiring *before* age 65 also increased from 33 percent to 40 percent over the same time frame. However, the percent retiring before 65 peaked in 1988 and has been on a downtrend since then. The percent retiring after age 65 was at an all time high in 1991.

5. For example, Peter Lynch, who is one of the most successful mutual fund managers of recent years, specifically advised people to forget

market timing. See his *One Up on Wall Street* (New York: Penguin Books, 1989), pp. 73-75.

6. See Bertrand Malkiel, *A Random Walk Down Wall Street* (New York: W. W. Norton and Company, 1990); Peter L. Bernstein, "Does Time Diversification Increase Risk or Reduce It?" *The Journal of Portfolio Management* 11, no. 4 (Summer 1985): 1.;

7. *Guiding Your Retirement Savings*, Library Series 1 (New York: TIAA-CREF, 1992), pp. 8-9.

8. *Governing TIAA and CREF: An Introduction to the TIAA and CREF Governance System* (NY: TIAA-CREF, 1991), p. 6-7.

9. See, for example, a profile of 6500 Wilshire Boulevard in Los Angeles, which makes no mention of cost, vacancy rates, terms, TIAA's ownership percent, or even whether it is a mortgage or a direct purchase. *Participant* (May 1991): 3, 6; Also see the profiles on Los Angeles' Las Colinas in *Participant* (August 1990): 3, 6 and the Minnesota's Mall of America in *Participant* (August 1992): 12-13.

10. Richard T. Garrigan, "TIAA's Commercial Mortgage and Real Estate Investments," *ACADEME* (January-February, 1992): 15.

11. *TIAA Investment Reports: 1992*, p. 14; *1993*, p. 16.

12. Maggie Mahar, "Still in an Ivory Tower: A Revisit to the College Teacher's Retirement Fund," *Barron's*, October 15, 1990, pp. 34-35.

13. Ibid., p. 35.

14. For TIAA's claim of a safe haven, see *Special Report TIAA Investments: A Safe Haven in Stormy Times* (New York: TIAA-CREF, March 1991). For criticisms of that claim, see Garrigan, "TIAA's Commercial Mortgage and Real Estate Investments," p. 14.

15. *A Safe Haven*, p. 1.

16. Gerald H. Rosen, "TIAA-CREF: Declining Returns," *ACADEME* (January-February 1992): 3.

17. Ibid., pp. 8-11.

18.   Ibid., p. 2.

19.   *TIAA Audited Financial Statements, 1993*, p. 5.

20.   For TIAA's response to this and the other criticisms, see Thomas W. Jones, "We Stand on a Record of Achievement and Security of Which We Can be Very Proud," *ACADEME* (January-February, 1992): 18 and Robert Perrin, "The TIAA Portfolio Rate of Return Continues to Out-Perform the Averages of the Life Insurance Industry Year After Year," *ACADEME* (January-February 1992): 11.

PART II

LOW-RISK STRATEGIES FOR A RETIREMENT NEST EGG

Part II focuses on three excellent strategies for building and preserving a retirement nest egg. The first two are dollar cost averaging and value averaging. They are especially lucrative strategies during the early and mid-career stages. As your retirement funds begin to accumulate, however, capital preservation becomes an increasingly important priority. The most widely recommended approach to preserving your capital while still leaving yourself open to further growth is strategic asset allocation.

Chapter 5

Start with the Magic of Dollar Cost Averaging

What is Dollar Cost Averaging?

One of the best low risk strategies for starting your retirement accumulation is to allocate 100 percent of your TIAA-CREF premiums to one or more of the CREF equity accounts such as CREF Growth, CREF Global Index, or CREF Stock. At first glance, this may hardly seem a low risk strategy, since the CREF equity accounts are much more volatile than TIAA, CREF bonds, CREF Money Market or even CREF Social Choice. Using a process called dollar cost averaging (DCA), however, greatly reduces the risk inherent to investing in the equity markets.

Dollar cost averaging is the process of investing constant dollar amounts on a regular basis into a cross section of stocks over a period of time. This occurs automatically with your contributions to CREF Stock, because your employer sends a monthly check to CREF and that check buys CREF units at their closing price on the day when it is credited to your account. If your monthly contribution is $1,000 and the CREF unit is worth $50.00 at the close of business on the day of purchase, you will purchase twenty units that day ($1,000/$50=20). When the stock market drops, the equal dollar contributions buy more CREF units. When the market rises, the equal dollar amounts buy fewer CREF units. Over any given time period, the cost per unit is averaged out so that the average dollar cost of the units is less than the highest price but higher than the lowest price. This is why it is called dollar cost averaging.

Dollar cost averaging is a tremendous tool for persons who despair of their (or anybody's) ability to predict future stock market moves. If you could predict when the market was going to drop, you would transfer all of your CREF Stock accumulations into CREF Money Market and then transfer them back to CREF Stock when the market hit bottom. Unfortunately, nobody has the ability to know when the market has hit bottom, and few people would have the courage to invest at that propitious moment even if they thought it had arrived. The beauty of dollar cost averaging (DCA) is that it lets you prosper without having to predict the market's future and without having to display extraordinary financial courage. Over any extended period of time of five or more years, it is almost impossible to lose money using the DCA approach.

Dollar Cost Averaging: A Worst Case Scenario

Sound too good to be true?

Consider the following example, which traces the CREF Stock fund through the worst bear market of its history. Between December 1972 and September 1974, the stock market suffered its second worst bear market of the twentieth century, and as Table 5-1 shows, CREF Stock dropped 49.9 percent, from $8.68 to $4.35.[1]

Assume that you were the hypothetical CREF participant shown in Table 5-1. You contributed $400 per quarter to the CREF Stock fund starting December 31, 1972, and your contributions were increased 5 percent each September to account for salary increases.

No sooner did you make your first contribution than CREF started its long steep slide of 49.9 percent over the next seven quarters. Notice that each time the unit price dropped your contribution bought increasing numbers of units, so that a large number of units went to work for you when the market started rising again. Consequently, your dollar cost averaging account returned to the break even point long before the CREF unit did. CREF did not permanently recover to its pre-crash level of $8.68 until June 1979, twenty-six quarters after the crash began. By dollar cost averaging, however, you permanently reached the break-even point sometime in the twelfth quarter, which is only five quarters after the unit bottomed out at a value of $4.35. Indeed, at the point at which you were safely in a profitable position, the CREF unit value of $6.48 was still 25 percent below what it was at the start.

Table 5-1   Dollar Cost Averaging During a Bad Market Drop

Date	CREF Unit Value	Dollars Invested $	Cumulative Amount $	CREF Units Bought	Total Units Owned	Total Value $
Dec 72	8.68	400	400	46.08	46.08	400
Mar 73	7.61	400	800	52.56	98.65	751
Jun 73	6.82	400	1,200	58.65	157.30	1,073
Sep 73	7.73	420	1,620	54.33	211.63	1,636
Dec 73	7.11	420	2,040	59.07	270.70	1,925
Mar 74	6.61	420	2,460	63.54	334.24	2,209
Jun 74	5.81	420	2,880	72.29	406.53	2,362
Sep 74	4.35	441	3,321	101.38	507.91	2,209
Dec 74	4.91	441	3,762	89.82	597.73	2,935
Mar 75	5.89	441	4,203	74.87	672.60	3,962
Jun 75	7.01	441	4,644	62.91	735.51	5,156
Sep 75	6.07	463	5,107	76.28	811.79	4,928
Dec 75	6.48	463	5,570	71.45	883.24	5,723

Source: Calculated from *Charting TIAA and the CREF Accounts: Winter 1993-1994* (New York: TIAA-CREF, 1994), pp. 50-51.

But the tremendous power of DCA is not that it allows you to make a small profit after major market declines, as shown in Table 5-1. The tremendous power of DCA is its ability to accumulate a large number of units during periods of weakness or during a trading range. This was exactly what happened for the balance of the 1970s. Anybody who allocated 100 percent of his or her premiums into CREF Stock had accumulated a large number of units with which to take advantage of the great bull market of the 1980s. In Table 5-1, those 883.24 units were bought at a total cost of $5,570 which worked out to an average cost of $6.31 per unit. By the end of 1993 the CREF unit value grew to $69.94, and the $5,570 contribution grew to $61,774.

But What if One Had
Retired on the Eve of the Bear Market?

One obvious reservation about going 100 percent into CREF Stock via a DCA strategy involves the consequence for the person who was 100 percent in CREF when he or she retired. Clearly, someone who was 100 percent in CREF Stock on December 31,1972 and who retired that day would have suffered an irreparable loss. That person's retirement income would be substantially reduced for life.

However, no prudent person would have done this. Chapter 6 will show that DCA is not a strategy to be followed blindly forever. As your assets begin to accumulate in the mid-career years, you need to make adaptations in your accumulation program. DCA may still play a role but it has to be combined with other strategies aimed at capital preservation. This becomes even more imperative as you approach the moment of retirement and of actually cashing in on TIAA-CREF benefit payments. Chapters 6 through 8 offer suggestions for doing this.

But What If We Have another Great Depression?

It is fine to show how a DCA strategy would have been profitable through the worst years of CREF, but TIAA-CREF members tend to know something about history. By now you will most certainly object that even the 50 percent market drop of 1972 through 1974 pales in comparison to that of the Great Depression. During the Depression years of 1929 to 1932, the Dow Jones Industrial Average lost 89 percent of its value. What would happen to a DCA strategy if we got another market crash on a par with that of the Great Depression?

Financial pessimists who worry about another "Great Depression" are a little like the earthquake worriers who talk of the "big one" that is going to devastate San Francisco some day. But just as San Franciscans have learned to go about daily lives not knowing when or where the big one will strike during their lifetimes, so too, we TIAA-CREF participants live with similar ignorance about the future of the economy. Nobody can guarantee that economic disaster is not around the corner. Prudent people will try to protect themselves from such disasters as best as possible, and this book shows various techniques for doing so.

But it would be equally imprudent for the today's TIAA-CREF participants to reject current opportunities simply because another Great Depression might occur some day. Most San Franciscans who love their city do not move elsewhere because the "big one" might strike someday. Nor should college personnel, who would love a comfortable retirement, avoid the equity markets because a "financial big one" might or might not be lurking around the corner.

The philosopher Santayana taught us that those who forget the past are condemned to reliving it. The follies of the past may well be relived and repeated, but they are seldom repeated the same way. A generation of people whose memories of the Great Depression led them to shun equities during the 1950s and 1960s saw their savings wiped out by the Great Inflation of the 1970s. Many of those who came to maturity during the inflationary 1970s went over their heads into real estate debt in the early 1980s only to encounter a disinflationary period in the late 1980s and early 1990s. It is important to learn from the past. But it is a mistake to try too hard to avoid the errors of our parents, for we may well make some errors that they did not make.

It is likely that dollar cost averaging would have worked very well during the Great Depression. Assume that you could have invested $100 once per quarter in the S&P 500 Index starting on September 1, 1929, the eve of the Great Crash. For the next three years, the market dropped relentlessly. By early 1932 your original investment was worth barely 14 percent of its starting value.

This is shown in Figure 5-1 where the bottom line on the right traces the S&P from its 1929 high through September 1943. As the graph shows, these 14 years saw a series of dizzying drops interrupted by aborted recoveries. The original 2 1/2 year plunge was followed by a recovery from 4 to 11 in 1933-34 which in turn was followed by a 25 percent drop in 1935. For the next two years it looked like the market was finally back on track as the S&P doubled. Then in 1937, the bottom fell out once again and the market dropped 50 percent. This was followed by another recovery that was short circuited by the growing political crisis in Europe and the outbreak of World War II. By early 1942 in the aftermath of Pearl Harbor, the S&P dropped another 40 percent leaving it barely above the level it was at almost ten years earlier when Franklin Roosevelt was first elected president.

The straight line in Figure 5-1 is a profit line that traces the dollars you would have invested during these years, and the ascending jagged line traces the value of your investment. When that line is above

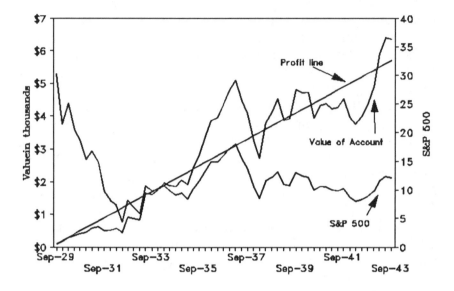

Figure 5-1   Dollar Cost Averaging in the Great Depression

the straight profit line, your account shows a profit. When below, you have a loss. With the exception of the original plunge in 1930-32 and the early World War II period, you were in the black most of the time. In fact, if dividends were factored into the graph, you would have been above the profit line almost all of the time after 1933.

As of 1943, when this graph ends, the S&P was still down 72 percent from its 1929 high, but the dollar cost average account had you sitting on a small profit. Furthermore, you had been acquiring a large number of shares in the S&P 500 at low prices. These were destined to grow handsomely when the market started to explode in the late 1940s. Even with this explosion, the market did not return to its pre-crash high until 1954, a full quarter-century after the 1929 crash. By this time your dollar cost average account grew to about $28,000, which is almost three times the $10,000 that you invested in it.

In sum, given the stock market catastrophe of the 1930s, there was no way to escape totally unhurt. But the dollar cost averaging plan, if there had been a mutual fund available, would have confined losses to a minimum, would have given you a small profit most of the time, and would have set the stage for substantial profits when the market eventually made a permanent recovery.

But What If an Unexpected Sharp Drop Hits CREF?

The sharpest stock market break in history occurred on October 19, 1987, when the market dropped 22 percent in one day. From its August peak of 336.77 to its December bottom of 223.92, the S&P 500 dropped 33.5 percent, for one of the worst four month drops ever.

Although we do not have the daily CREF Stock prices to trace the full decline of CREF Stock over this period, we do have the prices as of the end of each quarter. A person who had started a quarterly DCA investment program of $1,000 per quarter in September 1987 would have recovered to the break-even point within nine months of the crash, even though the CREF Stock unit value at that time was still 13.9 percent below what it had been at on the eve of the crash.

The Only Real Danger in Using DCA

Dollar cost averaging with CREF Stock could only turn into a disaster if you had followed this strategy for years, placed most of your assets were in CREF Stock, and encountered a market crash before you took defensive action to protect your assets. However, no prudent person would let that happen, and Chapters 6 through 8 show you how to avoid that situation.

Which CREF Accounts to Use

Of the seven CREF equity accounts, the CREF Stock, Global Equities, and Growth accounts are probably the most appropriate for dollar cost averaging. In some periods the Social Choice account will enjoy better performance than the CREF Stock account. But given the fact that CREF Social Choice is essentially a balanced fund, as discussed in Chapter 4, it is highly unlikely to outperform CREF Stock, CREF Growth, CREF Global Equities, or even CREF Equity Index over an

Table 5-2 DCA During the 1987 Market Crash

Date	CREF Unit $	CREF change Percent	Units Owned	Total Invested $	Total Value $
Sep 87	40.06		24.96	1,000	1,000
Dec 87	31.28	-21.9	56.94	2,000	1,781
Mar 88	33.52	-20.9	86.77	3,000	2,908
Jun 88	35.41	-13.9	115.02	4,000	4,072
Dec 88	35.42	-13.1	143.25	5,000	5,074
Mar 89	36.74	-9.4	170.47	6,000	6,263
Jun 89	39.11	-2.6	196.04	7,000	7,667
Sep 89	41.84	4.6	219.94	8,000	9,203

Source: Calculated from *Charting TIAA and the CREF Accounts: Winter 1993-1994* (New York: TIAA-CREF, 1994), pp. 50-51

extended time frame. Just as growth mutual funds typically outperform balanced mutual funds, the other four CREF equity funds are likely to enjoy better long-term performance than CREF Social Choice.

In comparison with the Global Equities account, the choice is not clear cut. The biggest argument for using the Global Equities fund as your dollar cost averaging vehicle is the fact that international stocks have historically outperformed the types of stocks that make up the bulk of the CREF Stock portfolio. Two-thirds of CREF Stock's portfolio has been indexed to the overall U. S. market, and those types of stocks appreciated at the rate of 9.9 percent per year from 1960 through the late 1980s. By comparison, international stocks had a 13.2 percent rate of return over that same period, and small company U. S. stocks had a 12.1 percent rate.[2] But a CREF comparison between its stock account and a hypothetically reconstructed Global Equities account for the period 1970 through 1993 showed them both appreciating at the same rate--10.5 percent per year.[3]

This is a very interesting departure from historical patterns. Historically, international stocks outperformed U.S. stocks up through

1987, but CREF Global Equities failed to outperform CREF Stock from then until 1993. Why this discrepancy? For one thing, the late 1980s and early 1990s (through 1992) were much better for the S&P 500 type stocks that make up the bulk of CREF Stock's portfolio than they were for international stocks in the Global Equities portfolio.[4]

Many financial advisers believe that the best long-term performance comes when a growth portfolio allocates about 15 percent of its assets to international stocks.[5] CREF Stock follows this policy, and that is probably one reason why CREF Stock has outperformed most mutual funds. There are other skeptics, however, who question whether foreign equities will continue to add value to one's portfolio.[6]

Even if international equities do outperform domestic stocks, performance comparisons between CREF Stock and Global Equities will be muddled by the fact that the two funds have overlapping investment philosophies. Because CREF Stock fund is usually about 15 percent invested in foreign equities, CREF Stock will reflect in part the fortunes of international stock markets. And because the Global Equities fund is at least 25 percent (currently 28 percent)[7] invested in U.S. stocks, its overseas returns are somewhat moderated by the performance of its U.S. holdings.

When putting some of your DCA monies in the CREF Global Equities fund, it is important to appreciate the currency risk involved. If the American dollar remains weak compared with the Japanese and European currencies, the Global Equities fund will get an extra boost in value, as will other dollar-denominated global funds. On the other hand, if the dollar enters a period of strength, currency conversions will act as a drag on the performance of the Global Equities fund.

A simple example will illustrate this. Suppose you bought a German stock for 1,000 Deutschmarks, at a time when each mark equaled fifty cents. The dollar cost for your German stock was, obviously, $500 (1,000 DM x $.50=$500). Assume that the stock doubles to be worth 2,000 Deutschmarks. If the dollar stays at fifty cents per Deutschmark, the dollar value of your stock has also doubled to $1,000 (2,000 DM x $.50=$1,000). If, on the other hand, the dollar strengthens to only 25 cents per Deutsch mark, the dollar value of your stock stays at $500 (2,000 DM x $.25=$500). Or, if the dollar weakens to $1.00 per mark, the dollar value of your stock quadruples (2,000 DM x $1.00=$2,000).

In short, a weak dollar gives a boost to the Global Equities fund, while a strong dollar acts as a drag on that fund. Unfortunately, it is difficult to use this knowledge in making a choice between the two funds. There are periods when the internal performance of foreign markets is so powerful that they overcome the impact of currency fluctuations. Furthermore, it is exceedingly difficult to make accurate predictions of either foreign stock markets or currency trends. Finally, CREF itself trades foreign currencies as a hedge against currency risks in its foreign investments. Because these currency contracts were not listed in CREF's financial statements,[8] it is not possible to know much about CREF's hedging operations.

However, the purpose of dollar cost averaging is to give you a long term strategy that avoids the difficult task of predicting the twists and turns of financial markets. With CREF Stock you usually have about a 15 percent foreign exposure--a portion often recommended by many investment advisers. If you wanted more foreign exposure or if you felt strongly that international markets were going to outperform the U.S. market over the next twenty years, it would not be unreasonable to put some of your CREF contributions into the Global Equities account and use both accounts as your dollar cost averaging vehicle. But the bulk of one's dollar cost averaging should probably best be done in the CREF Growth fund or the Stock fund.

Finally, the Equities Index fund is also appropriate for dollar cost averaging. In general, one would not expect an index fund to be as volatile as a growth fund or an international fund, but it is impossible to know in advance how these various CREF funds will perform. Until the Index Equity fund develops a track record, it would seem most appropriate to concentrate dollar cost averaging monies in CREF Stock, CREF Growth, and CREF Global Equities. These will probably be the most volatile CREF accounts, and volatility enhances the performance of dollar cost averaging.[9]

Conclusion

If you have just recently started your retirement savings plan and have not yet accumulated substantial funds, dollar cost averaging through one of the CREF equities funds is an admirable way to go. You are very unlikely to lose money. And over a period of ten or fifteen years, you will probably enjoy sizable returns. Unless you have some extraordinary situation that demands you limit yourself to fixed income investments, we urge you to avoid TIAA and use the CREF equity funds as your dollar cost averaging vehicle.

Notes

1. The CREF unit values cited here will not mesh with the CREF unit values that you actually had in 1972, because CREF changed its method of tabulating its unit in 1988, and the earlier units were recalculated to be consistent with the new method.

2. Gerald W. Perritt and Alan Lavine, *Diversify: The Investor's Guide to Asset Allocation Strategies* (New York: Longman Financial Services Publishing, 1990), p. 17.

3. *Charting TIAA and the CREF Accounts: Winter 1993-1994* (New York: TIAA-CREF, 1994), pp. 39, 43.

4. The annual rate of return for the S&P 500 was 15.8 percent from 1988 through 1992, but it was only 6.5 percent for international stock mutual funds. See *The Individual Investor's Guide to No-Load Mutual Funds, 12th edition 1993* (Chicago: The American Association of Individual Investors, 1993), p. 35.

5. For example, mutual fund adviser Gerald Perritt recommends keeping about 15 percent of one's assets in foreign equities. "All Weather Protection Using Asset Allocation," *AAII Journal* (July 1988): 20. Investment adviser Kenneth L. Fisher also recommends about 15 percent. "Design Your Own," *Forbes*, March 15, 1993, p. 158. William Donoghue recommends 20 percent. See "Current Allocations," *Donoghue's MoneyLetter* (April 1993), 3. Art Micheletti, a mutual fund director, also recommends 20 percent. See "Allocation Approach Seeks Lower Risk, Steady Returns: An Interview with Art Micheletti, Director of U.S. Research, BB&K Diversa Fund," *AAII Journal* (July 1988): 5.

6. See Laslo Birinyi, Jr., "Yankee, Stay Home!" *Forbes*, August 1, 1994, p. 117 and Mary Rowland, "Do World Markets Still Serve as a Hedge?" *New York Times*, July 5, 1994, p. C-12.

7. *TIAA-CREF Annual Report: 1993*, p. 18.

8. Ibid.

Chapter 6

Don't Dollar Cost Average Forever

Why Should I Stop Using DCA?

For getting started on your retirement savings program, the dollar cost averaging strategy draws widespread support from investment advisers. It has the solid endorsement of TIAA-CREF,[1] prominent academic writers such as Burton Malkiel,[2] and investment professionals. Mutual fund adviser Gerald Perritt, for example, calls it a "safe way to invest for longtime horizons of ten years or more."[3]

The only major critics of dollar cost averaging tend to be the stock pickers and market timers. Two of the most successful of these are Dan Sullivan and Martin Zweig, who consistently rank among the top investment newsletter analysts as measured by the *Hulbert Financial Digest*. And even their criticism of dollar cost averaging is muted. Zweig dislikes dollar cost averaging because it means "you buy more if a stock declines. I don't like buying on weakness."[4] This criticism, however, really is an objection to the use of dollar cost averaging with individual stocks. It is not clear if Zweig feels the same way about dollar cost averaging with mutual funds or with an annuity such as CREF. Dan Sullivan compared a dollar cost averaging system with his mutual fund timing system and found that his timing system worked better.[5] Accordingly, he urges his subscribers to dollar cost average when he has them on buy signals, switch into cash on sell signals, and then recommence dollar cost averaging in his recommended funds on the subsequent buy signals.

In sum, however, the critics of dollar cost averaging are far outnumbered by the advocates. Nonetheless, there is a catch to dollar cost averaging. Simply put, you cannot dollar cost average forever. Dollar cost averaging works best in the early and mid-career years of capital accumulation. During these years you have not yet built up enough of a nest egg that it can be greatly harmed by a sharp market drop. This is illustrated in Figure 6-1, which is constructed on dollar amounts comparable to today's. That is, the person in Figure 6-1 began in 1952 by contributing 10 percent of a $12,000 annual salary to CREF Stock in quarterly installments. Forty years later, that person's salary grew to approximately $50,000. While these would not have been typical salary levels for the period 1952 through 1976 they have the advantage of putting that period's experience in dollar terms that are easily understandable today. As Figure 6-1 shows, dollar cost averaging served this person well through some very bad stock market periods. Market drops of 20 percent or more in 1957, 1962, and 1966 appear as minor ripples on this chart. Assuming that this particular person had another ten or fifteen years to work and contribute to CREF, even the monster bear market of 1973-74 (a 49 percent drop) was surmountable. As Figure 6-1 shows, the dollar cost average contributor was back to even in less than four years. For the person who had only recently started a dollar cost averaging program, the bear market of 1973-74 was a marvelous opportunity to accumulate CREF units at a very low price.

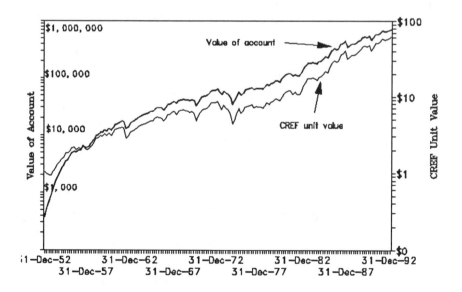

Figure 6-1   Dollar Cost Averaging in CREF 1953 through 1992

However, for anybody who had started in 1952 and planned to retire in 1974, an unprotected dollar cost average program was a disaster. The same was true for anybody else who could not afford to see their assets drop by nearly 50 percent.

As you get into mid-career, your CREF accumulations begin to mount, and each year's contributions to CREF Stock represent a smaller and smaller portion of the total accumulation. For the first ten years, the dollar cost average line grows much more rapidly than the line for the CREF unit value. Even for the next ten years the dollar cost average account outpaces the CREF unit value. From the twentieth year on, however, the slope of the two lines is virtually indistinguishable. As this happens, you run a growing risk of being harmed by a market drop, because your post-drop contributions will have less opportunity to push up your overall performance.

At what point, then, do you need to modify your dollar cost average strategy to protect yourself from this risk?

When Should I Stop Dollar Cost Averaging?

Each person has a different tolerance for risk. The closer one is to retirement or needing the money, the less risk that he or she can take. Also, the larger one's CREF accumulations and the larger the share that those CREF accumulations play in one's total assets, the less risk one can incur. Finally, psychological tolerance for risk is also important. Regardless of age, if you lose sleep at night worrying about the safety of your CREF Stock assets, then you should probably transfer some of them to a less volatile investment vehicle.

Measuring Risk as Recovery Time

With these caveats in mind, a useful way to assess the risk of continuing a DCA strategy in CREF is to examine your annual CREF contributions as a percent of your overall CREF accumulations and to estimate how long it would take the dollar cost average strategy to recover your loss of capital in the wake of a significant market drop. Obviously, the more capital you have, the more you will lose in a market drop, and the longer it will take your new contributions to make up that loss. A person with a $50,000 account (and combined RA and SRA contributions of $10,000 per year) would make up a 30 percent loss in assets in less than eighteen months, even if the CREF Stock unit stayed flat. But the person with $250,000 in assets would need six years.

Table 6-1 shows why. This table illustrates the impact of a 30 percent market drop on accounts ranging from $50,000 to $250,000 for persons making a combined $10,000 annual contribution to their retirement accounts and SRAs. Now, 30 percent market drops are not commonplace, since they have happened only three times since mid-twentieth century. But one would have to be an extraordinary Pollyanna to think that such drops will not happen again. Stock markets are volatile. When 22 percent of your CREF Stock holdings can disappear in a single day as they did on October 19, 1987, the person with substantial assets has to be concerned about capital preservation. To recover from a 30 percent loss takes a 43 percent increase in market value if no further contributions are made. Market recoveries of 43 percent are more frequent than market declines of 30 percent. There have been eight such recoveries since the mid-twentieth century. But this does not necessarily mean that one will come along just when you need it.

There are time periods in which CREF Stock can be a very dangerous holding for those with large accumulations of capital. From the end of 1965 until late 1982, the market followed a very frustrating roller coaster pattern. When the great 1980s bull market started in August 1982, the Dow Jones Industrial Average (776.92) was actually lower than it had been at its bear market *bottom* at the end of 1966 (786.41) sixteen years earlier. Extended periods like this may occur in the future as well. These will be excellent periods for accumulating capital through dollar cost averaging in CREF Stock, and they might also be excellent periods for those who can successfully time the market. But for those who have already accumulated a substantial nest egg and are nearing retirement age, these will be very dangerous periods.

Note in Table 6-1 that the smaller your contribution is as a percent of your accumulated capital, the harder it is to recover from a significant market decline. For the person who contributes $10,000 per year to CREF retirement annuities and SRA accounts and has only $50,000 accumulated, a sharp market drop is of little concern. Even if the market makes no recovery, this person returns to the break-even point within eighteen months. After one year's contributions, it takes only a 14.3 percent market recovery to gain back the person's initial $50,000. Even for the person with $100,000 in CREF Stock, a market recovery of 28.6

Table 6-1   Recovering from Market Losses

	Dollar Value of Account Prior to a 30 Percent Market Drop			
	50,000	**100,000**	**200,000**	**250,000**
$10,000 contribution as a percent of total accumulations	20%	10%	5%	4%
Years of future contributions needed to break even if no market recovery	1.5 years	3 years	6 years	7.5 years
Market recover needed to break even after 1 year if contributions continue to be made	14.3%	28.6%	35.7%	37.1%
Market recovery needed to break even after 1 year if no more contributions are made	42.9%	42.9%	42.9%	42.9%

percent would bring the person back to the break-even point within one year. This is not unlikely.

However, a person with $250,000 in CREF Stock, would need 7.5 years to get back to even in the event of a flat market. The magnitude of a 30 percent drop from $250,000 is $75,000. The magnitude of a 30 percent drop from $50,000 is only $15,000.

The message of Table 6-1 is stark. The more money you have in CREF Stock, the longer it will take you to recover from a bear market. Given the magnitude of potential losses in substantive market drops, straight dollar cost averaging makes less and less sense as one's assets begin to approach $200,000. Unless you are already independently wealthy, you cannot tolerate a potential loss of $60,000.

Many investment analysts will disagree with this statement. A potential loss is not a real loss unless you sell your equities and transfer out of the CREF Stock account. If you have the courage to ride through periodic bear markets, the market will eventually recover. This is clearly the advice of Peter Lynch, one of the most successful mutual fund managers in history. Lynch wrote, "Predicting the short term direction of the stock market is futile."[6] Even in the absence of further contributions, a 30 percent bear market will be compensated for if the subsequent bull market goes up 43 percent, which is very likely.

In theory, this sounds wonderful--if you have nerves of steel. But most of us do not. It would be a frightening prospect to see a $200,000 nest egg drop by 30 percent. The psychological pressure to take that loss rather than run the risk that it might lose another 15 or 20 percent would be irresistible for most people. Chances are that many of them would bail out of CREF Stock at the worst possible moment.

In short, dollar cost averaging will eventually present you with the problem of developing a strategy for protecting the $200,000 or $300,000 nest egg that you have built over a lifetime. While this is a nice problem to have, it is nevertheless a problem that you will have to face. You cannot afford the risk of losing 30 percent of your assets in event of a major bear market. Nor have you yet accumulated enough money that you can afford to sit on the sidelines when the next bull market comes along.

Sequential Dollar Cost Averaging

Some financial planners advise a sequential dollar cost averaging approach to protect against severe market drops. If a bull market in equities seems overextended in length or has become overvalued in terms of dividend yield or price-earnings ratios, sequential dollar cost averaging would have investors take substantial profits from their equity accounts, park the funds in a money market account, and provide for automatic monthly transfers back into the equity accounts over a two- or three-year period. This approach will cause the investors' performance to lag that of the stock funds if the bull market continues roaring along. Nevertheless, the investors will reap some of those bull market profits, because they left some assets in the equity accounts and they will be feeding new money into the equity accounts on a monthly basis. The investors' payoff will come if a bear market indeed materializes early in the period of their dollar cost averaging. Even if the bear market remains a minor one of only 15 to 20 percent, the fact of having protected a portion of their assets will give them a big boost over the buy and hold approach once the markets begin to recover.

Using sequential dollar cost averaging with TIAA-CREF would not be difficult. You simply transfer a big portion of your CREF equity accounts into the Money Market fund (or TIAA if you are using your SRA for this purpose) and then dollar cost average those monies back into your equity accounts over a twenty-four- or thirty-six-month period. At the end of that time period you are fully re-invested in equities, and, unless you are in the recovery stage from a bear market, you can start the whole process over again.

While this can be done with TIAA-CREF, it would require considerable self discipline. If you moved $100,000 out of your CREF Stock Fund into the Money Market Fund and planned to dollar cost average it back into the Stock fund over a two year period this would require you to make a telephone call each month in order to switch precisely $4,166.67 plus interest into CREF Stock. It would be far simpler if CREF would simply set up a systematic dollar cost averaging plan that enabled a computer to make the switches automatically.

TIAA-CREF could also make dollar cost averaging easier from the Transfer Payout Annuity discussed in Chapter 4. Currently, these transfers are made annually, starting one year after the Transfer Payout Annuity has been established. From a dollar cost averaging point of view, it would be more reasonable to make the transfers on a monthly basis starting one month after the CREF participant signs up for the Transfer Payout Annuity.

In theory, sequential dollar cost averaging is an admirable way to get some of the benefits of a mature bull market and protect yourself from the inevitable market collapse that follows these bull markets.

But will it work in practice?

It seems unlikely that you would lose capital by following this strategy. You would probably even outperform a buy and hold strategy in CREF Money Market or in TIAA. A buy and hold strategy simply puts a block of money into a particular investment and leaves it there for the long term. If you started the sequential dollar cost averaging at the peak of a bull market, you would substantially outperform a buy and hold strategy in CREF's equity funds.

The problem is that it is very difficult to determine just when the bull market has peaked. If your timing were atrocious and you started the sequential dollar cost averaging at the bottom of a bear market instead of the bull market peak, it still seems unlikely that you would lose money or underperform the Money Market fund. But you would clearly underperform CREF Stock.

Recent studies have suggested that you get better performance if you invest lump sums of money immediately into the equity markets rather than dollar cost average them into equities.[7] These findings do not make sequential dollar cost averaging a useless strategy. After all, once you begin approaching retirement age, capital preservation becomes increasingly important, and you have to forgo some of the risks that accompany the quest for maximum capital growth. But in addition to sequential dollar cost averaging, there are other approaches to finding the proper trade-off point between the quest for growth and capital preservation.

Conclusion

Dollar cost averaging in the CREF Stock, Growth, or CREF Global Equity Index fund will probably be a lucrative way to get started on accumulating your retirement nest egg. As your assets grow beyond $200,000, however, you need to begin protecting yourself against inevitable bear markets. One way to do this is to engage in sequential dollar cost averaging. Other strategies are offered in the chapters that follow.

TIAA-CREF could take two steps to make dollar cost averaging easier. The first would be to establish a systematic transfer plan from the Money Market fund into the other CREF funds. The second would be to establish monthly, rather than annual payments, into CREF from the Transfer Payout Annuity.

Notes

1. TIAA-CREF, *Guiding Your Retirement Savings*, Library Series (New York: TIAA-CREF, 1990), pp. 14-15 and 20-21. This booklet suggests a dollar cost averaging strategy without using that actual term.

2. Burton Malkiel, *A Random Walk Down Wall Street* (New York: W. W. Norton and Company, 1990).

3. Gerald W. Perritt and Alan Lavine, *Diversify: The Investor's Guide to Asset Allocation Strategies* (New York: Longman Financial Services Publishing, 1990), p. 163.

4. Martin Zweig, *Winning on Wall Street* (New York: Warner Books, 1990), p. 265.

5. *Chartist Mutual Fund Timer*, 49 (September 1992): 3.

6. Peter Lynch, *One Up on Wall Street* (New York: Penguin Books, 1989), p. 80.

7. Richard Williams and Peter Bacon, *Journal of Financial Planning* (1993). Using the period 1926 to 1991, they compared lump sum investments into a stock market index with dollar cost averaging the sums in over a twelve month period. In two-thirds of the cases examined, the lump sum investment produced better returns.

Chapter 7
Consider Value Averaging

Our experience with dollar cost averaging left us somewhat like Moliere's bourgeois gentleman who was delighted to discover that he had been speaking prose all his life. We CREF participants are delighted to learn that by allocating our contributions into CREF equity funds we have been practicing dollar cost averaging for years. However, just as we got used to that idea and the realization that we were on to a possible get rich slowly scheme, along comes a new proposal that promises even more miracles than dollar cost averaging. This is the idea of value averaging. If you liked the complexity of Rubik's Cube, you are going to love value averaging.

As with dollar cost averaging, value averaging seeks not to time the market tops and bottoms but to give you a reasonable way to ride out the market's roller coaster action and achieve a good return with a limited risk. It uses the same key ingredient that makes dollar cost averaging work. Over a long enough period of time, your average cost per unit of CREF Stock ends up being less than the average price per unit over the same time period. Value averaging promises an even lower average cost per unit.

Value averaging is the brain child of Michael E. Edleson, who wanted to advance the averaging concept one step further.[1] Instead of averaging the cost of units bought, Edleson has you average the *value* that your investment account must grow each period. He claims that this will enable you to end up accumulating just as much money as you plan for at less cost than you would have spent through dollar averaging. If true, value averaging would be a marvelous savings program for anyone on a limited budget which is the situation of no small number of college personnel.

Description

Under value averaging, you make an initial investment of, say, $1,000 in a mutual fund each quarter. You decide to increase the value of your fund by $1,000 each quarter. At the end of the quarter you either increase or decrease your fund holdings to reach that target value.

If the fund price declines in the quarter, you add in more than $1,000 to replace the amount that the fund lost in value. On the other hand, if the fund increases in value, you put in less than $1,000 and in some instances even take money out of the fund.

By taking some profits when the fund is going up you will end up with an even lower average cost per share than dollar cost averaging would give you. Furthermore, by adding in extra money when the fund declines in price, you end up purchasing even more shares at lower prices than you would with dollar cost averaging.

For example, suppose you set a quarterly goal of increasing your value by $1,000 each quarter. Using dollar cost averaging, you invest $1,000 into a mutual fund, but you have no control over how much your assets advance, because that is determined by the fund's performance. Under value averaging, by contrast, you will target your assets to grow to $1,000 at the end of the first quarter, $2,000 at the end of the second quarter, $3,000 at the end of the third quarter, and so forth. Edleson calls these quarterly targets the value path.

Let us say you started the plan by buying a fund at $5 per share, which would give you 200 shares for your $1,000. At the end of the quarter, the value of the fund drops to $4, giving you only $800. But your goal at the end of the quarter was to have $2,000. To amass that amount, you must own 500 shares at the current value of $4. So you buy 300 shares that quarter (which will cost $1,200) to bring your total shares up to 500 and your account's value up to $2,000. At the end of the third quarter, the fund has recovered back to $4.50 per share, giving your 500 shares a value of $2250. Your goal for this quarter is a value of $3,000, so (at $4.50 per share), you need to purchase another 166.67 shares to bring your holdings up to the $3,000 level ($4.50 per share x 666.67 shares = $3,000). These 166.67 shares will cost you only $750. Since you have been earmarking $1,000 per quarter, you put the extra $250 into a money market fund. You can then draw on this fund for those months you need to put in more than your budgeted $1,000.

Sound complicated? Well it is. Simply calculating the value path for the quarterly targets requires the use of a mind numbing formula that

Edleson provides. Without a spreadsheet or at least a financial calculator, it cannot be done.

If you can endure its complexity, value averaging will theoretically outperform dollar cost averaging, because it ends up with a lower average cost per share. In the example above, dollar cost averaging would provide an average cost per share of $4.46, but value averaging produced an average cost per share of only $4.42. Over time the gap between the value of a dollar cost averaging plan and a value averaging plan will continue to grow larger.

Michael Edleson conducted hundreds of computer simulations comparing dollar cost averaging with value averaging. Ninety percent of the time value averaging won the comparison.

Value Averaging with CREF

At first glance, it would seem impossible to use value averaging with CREF. Value averaging requires the ability to change the amount you invest every month. In CREF the amount of your RA contribution is usually fixed by your employer, and the level of your SRA contribution can be changed only once per year.[2]

With one slight modification, however, value averaging can be used with CREF. Assume for the sake of the example that you earn a $40,000 salary each year, that there is a 12 percent contribution into your CREF RA ($4,800) and that you make an extra 18 percent contribution into your SRA ($7,200). Your total contribution is $12,000 per year or $1,000 per month. Start your value averaging plan with $1,000 in your CREF Money Market account and target your CREF Stock account to grow by $3,000 each quarter. When the value averaging plan calls for you to put more than $3,000 per quarter into CREF Stock, transfer the necessary amounts from your CREF Money Market account. Conversely, when the value averaging approach calls for less than $1,000 per quarter to be invested in the CREF Stock account, transfer the necessary balance into your CREF Money Market account. Since CREF allows unlimited transfers between the two funds at no cost, your Money Market fund becomes a reserve that you can use to implement value averaging. At the end of one year, readjust your targets upward to account for inflation plus any salary increase.

A Back Test with CREF

CREF gives us forty years of Stock and Money Market fund data that we can use to back test these two strategies historically.[3] We will conduct this back test as though the CREF Money Market had been available throughout this time period and that one could have transferred back and forth between CREF Stock and CREF Money Market. Although this was not possible then, it is a reasonable condition for the back test. Transfers between the two accounts are possible today, and the point of conducting an historical back test is to examine whether a strategy possible today would have worked under CREF's historical circumstances. Although CREF's future performance will not unfold exactly as it did in the past, if one looks at long periods of time, CREF's long term rates of return fluctuate within a fairly narrow range.[4] Unless a fundamental revolution occurs in the nation's economic growth, it seems likely that future returns over long periods of time will continue to fluctuate within these narrow ranges.

For the sake of this back test, we will assume four professors, each earning approximately $53,000 per year in 1992, and all contributing 10 percent of their salary each year to CREF. The first professor's experience starts with an initial CREF contribution in December 1952 and continues contributing through December 1992. Assuming annual salary increases of slightly better than 6 percent per year, the starting salary was approximately $4,000 in 1952. The second professor's experience covers the years since 1959, the third's since 1969, and the fourth's since 1979. This gives us four distinct periods that roughly correspond to the real-life experiences of people in four different stages of their careers.

Constructing a Value Path

Our first task is to construct a value path for the first professor. Establishing this set of quarterly targets for the period 1953 through 1992 demonstrates the first complication with value averaging. The prime example used by Edleson assumes a mother who needs to reach a $100,000 goal in eighteen years to send her child to college. But the problem confronting our professors is more complicated. This mother knows that she needs $100,000 in eighteen years, but our professor has to guess at his needs a full forty years later. Financial planners are quite happy to calculate a number for us. but, knowing how complicated the world is, few of us put much weight on these precise calculations.

Given this imprecision about goals forty years into the future, we are going to set the goals at the amount that this account would have reached over each time frame if the professor had contributed 10 percent of his or her salary, if salaries were adjusted upward at the rate of 1.5% per quarter, and if the investments averaged CREF's historic performance rate of 10.8% per year from 1953-92. The ultimate goals thus become $551,215 for the period since 1952, $376,687 for the period since 1959, $203,015 since 1969, and $90,042 since 1979.

Once these goals are established, there are two ways to calculate the value paths for the quarterly targets. The first is to use Edleson's mind numbing formula, for which you need a spreadsheet or at least a financial calculator, since in the case of the first professor you need to raise one figure to its 160th exponent. The second way is simply to calculate what the value would be each quarter after a contribution of 10 percent of the professor's salary and a three month growth at CREF's historical annualized rate of 10.8 percent. You can do this with a pencil, paper, and simple calculator, but obviously it will be easier if you lay it out on a spreadsheet. Table 7-1 illustrates the results using both methods. As the table shows, there is not much difference in the results.

CREF contributions and Transfers

In the dollar cost averaging scenario, all contributions are allocated directly to CREF Stock. In the value averaging scenarios, the initial contribution is allocated to CREF Money Market, and all future contributions are allocated to CREF Stock. If the CREF Stock account balance exceeds the target value for any quarter, then enough dollars are transferred into the CREF Money Market account to bring the stock account balance down to the target. If the Stock account balance is below the target value, then enough money is transferred out of the Money Market account to bring the stock account balance up to the target value. When the Money Market account balance falls to zero, no transfers back into CREF Stock are possible. This frequently occurs during bear markets. During these periods, the stock account necessarily lags behind the target values until a sustained bull market once again drives the balance of the stock account above its target value.

Comparing the Strategies

Table 7-1 illustrates the main comparisons of dollar cost averaging with the two versions of value averaging. Several conclusions are apparent.

Positive Overall Results

In the first two time frames (1953-92 and 1960-92) value averaging ends up with substantially more money than dollar cost averaging. Furthermore, the value averaging scenarios end up with a modest amount of their money in the safety of CREF's Money Market fund. This will cause the value averaging accounts to fall more slowly than the dollar cost averaging accounts when the next bear market arrives. Value averaging will also enable them to purchase more CREF Stock units at lower cost than will be true for the dollar cost averaging scenario.

In the second two time frames (1970-92 and 1980-92) dollar cost averaging outperforms value averaging by a small margin. However, in both time frames, the value averaging accounts end up with substantial percents of their assets in the Money Market and they will undoubtedly pull ahead of the dollar cost averaging account after the next bear market.

The bottom line of Table 7-1, then, is that value averaging indeed compares favorably to dollar cost averaging. It beat dollar cost averaging handily in the first two time frames. In the second two time frames, value averaging ended up marginally behind dollar cost averaging, but because of its substantial Money Market holdings, it is well positioned to pull ahead during and after the next bear market. If that bear market does not materialize soon enough, however, the dollar cost averaging model will pull even further ahead of the value averaging model.

There is a downside to this analysis. Even though the value averaging scenarios compare favorably as of December 31, 1992, they actually trail the dollar cost averaging scenario most of the time. The professor who started value averaging in 1953, for example, was actually behind a dollar cost averaging colleague 84 percent of the time.

Whether this is a problem depends on your temperament. For those people who view life as an auto race, it probably does not matter if they are behind 84 percent of the time as long as they come in first at the end. For those people who view life as a journey, however, it would be

Table 7-1 Value Averaging with CREF Over Four Time Periods

	1953-92	1960-92	1970-92	1980-92
Straight Dollar Cost Averaging				
Ending value in $	558,722	413,108	280,443	123,380
Value Averaging with Target Values set by Edleson's Formula				
Ending value in $	577,630	434,145	276,219	118,591
Money Market balance at end	26,415	57,458	73,204	28,549
Percent of time that VA total balance exceeds that of DCA	16	21	80	25
Value Averaging with Target Values set by CREF's Historic Growth Rate				
Ending value in $	576,851	437,677	275,006	118,324
Money Market balance at end	25,635	60,990	71,991	28,282
Percent of time that VA total balance exceeds that of DCA	16	95	77	25

a little frustrating to trail another strategy 84 percent of the time just so that they could forge ahead at some precise point forty years down the road.

Modest Downside Protection

One of Edleson's claims for value averaging is that it will give you downside protection during bear markets.[4] In fact, as Table 7-2

Table 7-2   Value Averaging in Market Drops

	Percent decline in:		
	CREF Stock	**DCA**	**VA**
In the Period 1950-92			
1957	11.5%	6.2%	4.9%
1962	25.8	25.3	23.7
1966	11.9	8.4	8.4
1969-70	29.3	24.0	24.0
1973-74	49.9	45.4	45.4
1980-82	11.9	9.6	9.6
1987	21.9	21.6	19.7
1990	15.2	15.0	14.3
In the Period 1960-92			
1962	25.8	16.0	13.8
1966	11.9	5.3	5.3
1969-70	29.3	21.0	21.0

shows, both dollar cost averaging and value averaging with CREF give you some modest protection in bear markets. But the degree of protection varies greatly, depending on the time when you started your savings program. For the monstrous bear market of 1973-74, for example, the CREF unit dropped 49.9 percent from December 31, 1972, through September 30, 1974. The oldest professor got virtually no protection from this bear market through either averaging strategy, since both of them saw drops of 45.4 percent. For professors in the 1960-92 period, the market drop was reduced to 41.7 percent under dollar cost averaging and 34 percent under value averaging. Those who started the program in 1970 saw their declines reduced to about 24 percent.

In sum, however, value averaging's advantage over dollar cost averaging seems to be marginal. Of the twenty-one possible comparisons

Table 7-2   (Continued)

	Percent decline in:		
	CREF Stock	**DCA**	**VA**
In the Period 1960-92			
1973-74	49.9	41.7	34.0
1980-82	11.9	9.3	9.3
1987	21.9	21.5	17.2
1990	15.2	14.9	12.4
In the Period 1970-92			
1973-74	49.9	24.0	24.2
1980-82	11.9	8.5	8.5
1987	21.9	21.3	13.5
1990	15.2	14.7	9.8
In the Period 1980-92			
1987	21.9	20.3	11.5
1990	15.2	13.9	9.1

made in Table 7-2, the value averaging scenario declines five percentage points less than that of the dollar cost averaging scenario in only three instances. In eight of the twenty-one comparisons, the decline is exactly the same for both scenarios.

The Rip Van Winkle Effect

One limitation of using value averaging with CREF is that in all of the time frames except 1980-92, there were extended periods when the Money Market account was depleted and no transfers were possible into CREF Stock. In some instances these periods exceeded twenty years. For example, someone following Edleson's value path in the 1953 through 1992 time frame would have a depleted Money Market account from June 1966 through December 1986. Under this scenario you wake up one day to discover that for the first time in twenty years you suddenly have enough cash in your Money Market account to transfer some of it back to CREF Stock. Like Rip Van Winkle, however, you note that the world has changed greatly during those twenty years. It is highly unlikely that any reasonable person would after 20 years revert to a set of investment plans that had lain fallow all that time.

Overcoming the Rip Van Winkle Effect

It will be objected that the Rip Van Winkle effect occurs for one or both of two reasons. The first is that the target goals were too high. This could be true. The Rip Van Winkle effect is greatly reduced if the target goals are reduced. In fact, if the target growth rate is reduced from 10.8 percent per year to 90 percent of that amount, or 9.7 percent, the value average scenario beats the dollar cost average scenario by an even wider range than those shown in Table 7-1. However, there needs to be some logical reason for choosing one's ultimate goal. The 10.8 percent goal coincides with CREF Stock's historical return. Ninety percent of that amount does not logically coincide with anything.

The second reason for the Rip Van Winkle effect is that using CREF as the vehicle for value averaging makes it impossible to import cash from outside when the model requests new cash. Edleson's model is based on the assumption that there is always cash available somewhere to pump into the stock account during bear markets. With CREF, however, you cannot simply add new funds into the account any time you wanted. Your contributions to your SRA are limited to a total of $9,500 per year, beyond which you cannot legally contribute.

You could get around this problem by setting up a parallel outside account with a mutual fund family. When CREF's Money Market fund was depleted, you could put the necessary amounts into a stock mutual fund that performed similarly to CREF Stock. While this would work in principal, there would be problems making it work in practice. In prolonged bear markets, the cash infusions needed to meet the quarterly targets are so huge that few people are likely to have this much cash sitting around in a money market fund for years on end waiting to be put to work.

Conclusion

It is possible to modify value averaging so that it can be used with CREF or some other deferred annuity plan open to the use of mutual funds, such as a 403 (b) or 401 (k) plan. Based on the results in Table 7-1, value averaging also has the potential to outperform dollar cost averaging over long time frames, but its superior performance is by no means guaranteed. Value averaging also has the potential to give some modest protection against bear markets, but the downside protection is mitigated by the Rip Van Winkle effect. During the long time periods when the Money Market account is depleted, value averaging can operate essentially like a dollar cost averaging account for twenty years or more. During these periods, value averaging will not protect one from bear markets any more than dollar cost averaging will.

Value averaging seems to work best relative to dollar cost averaging in three situations. First, it is started early in a bull market so that there is time to build up the Money Market balance. Second, there need to be some bear markets during the time period that value averaging is being practiced. Otherwise, the bull market will last so long that transfers out of the stock account eventually lead the value averaging strategy to fall behind the dollar cost averaging strategy. This essentially is why the value averaging strategies failed to outperform the dollar cost averaging strategy in the last time period of Table 7-1 (1980-92). Bear markets are needed so that Money Market funds can be transferred back into the CREF Stock account and buy extra units at lower prices. Fortunately for value averaging, bear markets seem to recur with some frequency. Third, despite the need for periodic bear markets, the bears cannot last too long or be too frequent. If this happens, the Rip Van Winkle effect takes place, and the value averaging strategy begins performing like a dollar cost averaging strategy.

Notes

1. Michael E. Edleson, *Value Averaging: The Safe and Easy Strategy for Higher Investment Returns* (Chicago: International Publishing Corporation, 1991).

2. Conceivably, you could change the amount you invest in CREF Stock each month by making a monthly change in the allocation of your premiums. But a simpler way to achieve the value path goal would be to make transfers between CREF Stock and CREF Money Market.

3. *Charting TIAA and the CREF Accounts: Winter 1992-1993* (New York: TIAA-CREF, 1993), pp. 37, 41.

4. The annual rate of return for CREF Stock through 1992 from any point before 1973 varied from a low of 9.2 to a high of 11.0. During the shorter time spans since 1974 the annual rates of return are significantly higher, but these are heavily influenced by the explosive bull market of the 1980s and are very likely to revert to the norm as time passes. See *Charting TIAA and the CREF Accounts: Winter 1992-1993* (New York: TIAA-CREF, 1993), pp. 36-37.

5. Edleson, *Value Averaging*, p. 43. Edleson argues that downside protection will occur because the discipline of selling as the market peaks and buying as the market bottoms "forces you to avoid big moves into a peaked market or panic selling at the bottom."

Chapter 8

Strategic Asset Allocation

As we saw in the last chapter, value averaging is one way to respond when dollar cost averaging is no longer prudent. The more conventional approach, however, is what market professionals call strategic asset allocation.

Strategic asset allocation is another awkward financial term for an idea that you have understood intuitively most of your life. Do not put all your eggs into the same kinds of baskets. Divide your assets into different categories that respond to different market forces. The simplest example is the contrast between stocks and money market funds. Interest rate forces frequently (but not always) push these asset classes in opposite directions. Thus, rising interest rates mean that your money market fund's returns will invariably go up, while stock prices usually (but not always) go down. Conversely, declining interest rates almost always give a boost to your stock portfolio, but they reduce the income from your money market portfolio. The trick, according to asset allocators, is to divide your assets into enough different asset classes that poor performance in any one class of assets is more than offset by superior performance of other assets. The goal is to capture some of the gains of equity markets while reducing the wild price swings that characterize equities. In financial jargon, this is called reducing portfolio volatility.

The beauty of even a simple asset allocation plan can be seen by looking at a worst case scenario, the Great Depression of the 1930s. Between 1929 and 1932 stock prices plummeted almost 90 percent. Professor Marshall Blume of the Wharton School of Finance calculated that if your great grandparents had put $10 in stocks on the eve of the crash of 1929, they would not have gotten back to even until 1945, some sixteen years later. However, had they followed Blume's approach of putting $5 in stocks and $5 in bonds and then rebalancing them once a month to maintain a permanent 50-50 ratio, they would have gotten back to even by 1935, a full ten years earlier. When stock prices rose, they sold enough stocks and bought enough bonds to bring the balance back to 50-50. Conversely, when stocks declined, they sold enough bonds to rebalance.[1]

Investment professionals believe that asset allocation is much more important to your investment performance than is either market timing or your ability to select top performing stocks or mutual funds. One study of the nation's ninety-one largest pension plans concluded that only 6.4 percent of market performance was a product of either security selection or market timing. Fully 93.6 percent of performance variation resulted from decisions on whether to be in stocks, bonds, or other financial assets and what percent of the portfolio was allocated to each of those assets.[2] For example, if you had bought a portfolio of 10-15 stocks in the early 1980s and all of them turned out to be mediocre performers, you still would have done better than if you had at that time put only 10 percent of your assets into CREF Stock and the balance in TIAA.[3]

Although financial advisers agree that asset allocation is a superior investment strategy, they do not agree on the specifics of doing it. Several questions arise.

- What asset classes should you use?

- How can asset allocation be adjusted for your personal level of risk tolerance?

- How should your portfolio be divided among those asset classes?

- How frequently should you rebalance your assets?

- Should you change your division of assets as market fads change?

- Can TIAA-CREF be used effectively for strategic asset allocation?

Let us examine these issues in turn. Then we will construct a model asset allocation plan that you can tailor to your own financial situation.

Asset Classes

Professional asset allocators differ greatly on what assets they include in their asset allocation models. The Marshall Blume model cited above was very simple in that it had only two asset classes: stocks and bonds. Most asset allocators add a third, money market funds or other cash equivalents such as three-month U.S. Treasury bills or in some circumstances certificates of deposit. Other asset allocators include international bonds, gold or precious metals, real estate, and one even includes the Swiss franc. An investor could also add non-financial asset classes such as jewelry, art, and other collectibles, but these specialized areas of investment often face severe liquidity problems. Unless collectibles are an avocation, most investment advisers suggest that you buy them for aesthetic rather than for investment purposes.

Risk Tolerance
and the Allocation of Assets

Before deciding on which of these asset classes you want to include in your portfolio, estimate how much risk you can tolerate. Financial advisers usually define risk as portfolio volatility and usually the greater the potential returns of an investment, the greater the portfolio volatility. This is a fancy way of saying that putting all your assets into one high-flying mutual fund gives you a very high probability of picking up the newspaper some New Years' day to discover that your wealth has just shrunk by 20 to 30 percent over the preceding year.

Risk as Portfolio Volatility

The volatility that you would have experienced in CREF funds since their inception is shown in Table 8-1, which shows annual rates of return over two-year periods and ten year periods.[4] The stock fund and Global Equities funds are the most volatile. In the two year periods, the stock fund's annual rate of return ranged from 36.6 percent in 1953-54 to a negative 24.8 percent in 1973-74, and the annual rate of return for a hypothetical reconstruction of the Global Equities fund ranged from a 41.2 percent to a negative 20.5 percent. The Money Market fund has the

Table 8-1   Volatility of CREF Accounts

	Annual Rates of Return			
	Over Two-Year Time Periods			
	Global Equities	Stock	Bond	Money Market
Highest	41.2	36.6	19.9	14.7
Average	12.2	12.1	10.7	6.3
Lowest	-20.5	-24.8	1.6	1.4
	Over Ten-Year Time Periods			
	Global Equities	Stock	Bond	Money Market
Highest	18.8	17.7	14.1	10.1
Average	12.7	9.6	11.7	6.7
Lowest	5.7	0.7	10.4	2.5

Source: Calculated from *Charting TIAA and the CREF Accounts*, Winter 1993-94 (New York: TIAA-CREF, 1994), pp. 38-43.

lowest volatility since a hypothetical unit would have ranged from 14.7 percent in 1980-81 to a low of 1.4 percent in 1953-54. In the ten year periods of time, by contrast, CREF Stock and CREF Global Equities become much less volatile. The range between their best ten year period and their worst ten year periods is smaller than it was for the two year periods.

Over extremely long periods of time, the Stock fund substantially outperforms the Money Market fund, having grown at an annual rate of 10.9 percent for the period from 1953 through 1993, compared with a rate of only 6.1 percent for the hypothetical CREF Money Market fund. To put this difference in more graphic terms, at a money market rate of 6.1 percent, your money would take almost 13 years to double. The stock fund's 10.9 percent rate would have doubled your money in less than seven years. But to get the Stock fund's superior growth, you have to accept the risk that about one of every four years will be a losing year (ten down years in CREF's forty-one year history).

The Risk-Reward Trade-off

Most of us want the Stock fund's growth rates, but we are not willing to watch our net worth fall every four years or so. The purpose of asset allocation is to gain a better performance than the Money Market fund and at the same time reduce the gut wrenching volatility of the Stock fund. Asset allocation is simply a trade-off between risk and reward. This is shown in Table 8-2. Using two year time frames, the table compares the best, worst, and average returns for low-risk, moderate-risk, and high-risk allocation portfolios.

The low-risk portfolio allocates 20 percent of its assets to CREF Stock fund, 30 percent to the bond fund, and 50 percent to the Money Market fund. This is a very safe allocation strategy since its worst two-year return is well into positive territory, and its average rate of return handily beats the inflation rate over most two-year periods. The downside of this strategy, however, is that it does not even come close to matching the Stock fund's best returns.

By contrast, the high-risk portfolio, which is 100 percent in CREF Stock, has the highest best returns and the highest average returns for two-year periods. The downside, however, is that this portfolio brought you a whopping loss in the 1973-74 bear market. In fact, of the forty two-year periods since CREF's founding, four have shown losses, and nine have shown gains of less than 5 percent. One-third of the periods, in short, saw the high-risk strategy produce either a loss or a very meager return. This extreme volatility moderates over longer time frames. Over ten-year periods, for example, CREF never experienced a loss, and its volatility was lower, as shown in Table 8-1.

Short term volatility is the key issue in assessing your risk level. Can you tolerate the probability of going two or more years with a loss to achieve CREF's superior long-term performance? If you cannot answer yes to that question, then you should not permanently allocate 100 percent of your assets to CREF Stock or other equities.

The moderate risk portfolio presents an acceptable trade-off between the high-risk of CREF Stock and the high safety of the Money Market. By dividing its assets half in stocks and half in bonds, it manages an average two-year return that comes close to that of the high-risk

Table 8-2   **CREF Accounts and the Risk-Return Trade-Off: 1976-92**

	Levels of Return in Two Year Periods		
Levels of Risk	**Worst (%)**	**Average (%)**	**Highest (%)**
Low			
20% CREF Stock			
30% Cash			
50% CREF Bond	8.4	24.0	34.9
Moderate			
50% CREF Stock			
50% CREF Bond	3.1	29.4	51.2
High			
100% CREF Stock	-43.5	31.3	86.8

Source: Calculated from TIAA-CREF, *Charting TIAA and the CREF Accounts* (New York: TIAA-CREF, 1993), pp. 48-53.

Note: For the high-risk portfolio, worst and best returns reflect the period 1953-92, rather than the 1976-92 period reflected in the rest of the table. The 1976-92 figures for the high-risk portfolio (1.7% and 61.6%) would have shown the same pattern as those shown in the table, but they would have been extremely misleading in not showing the potential for substantial two-year losses than can occur with CREF Stock. The 1976-92 period is used for the balance of the table, because CREF does not reconstruct a hypothetical bond account return prior to 1976.

portfolio. Although its best period is not nearly as good as that of CREF Stock, its worst period does not lose you any money.

In short, Table 8-2 quantifies the risks that you have to assume to gain the higher rewards and the rewards you have to give up to gain the most safety. As we will see shortly, you are not limited to these three portfolios. You can construct a portfolio with any degree of risk that you are willing to tolerate.

Psychological and Objective Risk Tolerance

In determining your personal level of risk tolerance, two risk factors need to be considered: (1) psychological and (2) objective.

These two may not be related. You have assumed too much pyschological risk if you lose sleep at night worrying about your assets. But this sleep-easy test of psychological tolerance might or might not pass the objective test. Some 30 year olds at a 20 percent market exposure might have trouble sleeping, while some 60 year olds might sleep like babies at a 100 percent exposure. Both persons fail the objective test of risk tolerance. Judging by the fact that a majority of participants' funds are put into TIAA rather than CREF, it appears that most participants have a fairly low psychological tolerance for risk. Probably too low a level. Most of us need to train ourselves to bring our level of psychological tolerance up to our level of objective tolerance.

Objectively, risk tolerance depends mostly on how much time you have before you need your money. Any money you need next year should be kept in cash equivalents. That which is not needed for five more years can be subjected to a little more risk, and that which will not be needed for twenty years can be subjected to considerable risk.

Weighting the Asset Classes

Knowing that you should diversify your assets among different categories is one thing. However, coming up with a suitable allocation formula is much more complicated. Professional asset allocators are of little help in figuring this out since they themselves disagree on how funds should be allocated. Aggressive allocators weight their portfolios differently than do conservative allocators. For example, a listing of asset allocation mutual funds showed that the percentage allocated to stocks varied from a low of 2 percent for one fund to a high of 79 percent for another.[5]

A logical starting point would be to examine how market professionals allocate their assets. Mutual fund advisor Gerald W. Perritt did this and estimated that the world-wide distribution of all non-real estate wealth was 15 percent in cash equivalents, 30 percent in bonds, and 55 percent in equities.[6] Instead of looking at world-wide distribution of assets, investment adviser Kenneth L. Fisher examined the holdings of pension funds and found them to be 14 percent in cash equivalents, 32 percent in bonds, and 54 percent in stocks.[7] Based on these two investigations, you would be pretty much in the mainstream for retirement funds if you weighted your portfolio 15 percent cash, 30 percent bonds, and 55 percent stocks.

This scheme, however, neglects two other asset categories. Some advisers think that gold funds or precious metal funds ought to comprise about 5 percent of any substantial portfolio.[8] These funds performed terribly during the 1980s, but they could easily spike upward if hyperinflation were to occur over the next decade. If that were to happen, of course, you would need something to spike upward, because hyperinflation would devastate the bond portion of your portfolio. It would not treat your TIAA or stock accounts very kindly either. So the case for gold is that it is an insurance policy against hyperinflation. During the market crash of 1973-74, for example, when stocks tumbled nearly 50 percent, gold mining stocks soared 170 percent.[9]

Much the same case is made for real estate. It, too, was a terrible market performer in the 1980s, but real estate advocates like to recall the quip of Will Rogers, "Buy land; they aren't making any more of it." Since 1926, the average annual return on real estate has outpaced inflation, bonds, cash equivalents, and most categories of stocks.[10] But real estate, like most hard assets, performed terribly in the 1980s. Some market analysts think that investment trends will reverse in the late 1990s. Paper assets like stocks and bonds will deflate while hard assets like precious metals and real estate will inflate.

Nobody can predict the future, but if these arguments make sense to you, it would be appropriate to allocate about 5 percent of your assets to a precious metals fund or a real estate investment trust and let it sit there--just in case. You will not make any money on them if the market trends of the past decade-and-a-half prevail. You might even lose money. But you also might offset some losses in your stock and bond holdings if existing investment trends reverse themselves or if inflation does rear its ugly head once more.

Weighting by Age and Risk Level

How do you decide how much weight to give each of these asset classes in your allocation formula? For most investment advisers, the key to this issue is the amount of time you have remaining before you are likely to need the assets. Kenneth L. Fisher, for example, puts 20 year olds 90 percent in stocks and then scales back stock exposure each year until at age 80 they are only 10 percent in stocks.[11] What do you do with the funds taken out of stocks? Up to age forty Fischer puts them in bonds. After age forty, for each cutback in stocks, one-half goes to bonds and the other half to a money market account. Thus, when you reach age 65, Fischer would have you 30 percent in stocks, 53 percent in bonds, and 17 percent in the money market.

Some other investment advisers argue against holding any bonds.[12] From the early 1980s through 1993, bonds enjoyed a rip-roaring bull market as interest rates declined. With interest rates unlikely to decline over the next few years, these critics urge that you avoid bonds and split those funds instead between the money market and high-dividend stocks. We, however, will follow the traditional practice of including bonds in the asset allocation.

Age and Risk Tolerance

Why is age so key to risk tolerance? Younger people with normal life expectancies can tolerate more financial risk because they have more years of working life to recover when they suffer a financial setback. If you are an able bodied person under age 40 with an average life expectancy, adequate life insurance, and an emergency savings fund, you can probably afford the risk of being 100 percent in stocks. At 60 you cannot afford that risk because you will need to withdraw some of that money soon, and there isn't time to rebuild your assets if a major bear market erupts. However, if you are 60 and have an average life expectancy, you also cannot afford to be entirely out of the equity markets, because you could easily live for another quarter century. Over that time span you need some equity exposure to combat the corrosive effects of inflation.

By age 80, life expectancy is much lower and this makes inflation much less of a threat to your assets. So unless you have a much younger spouse or someone else who depends on your assets for their livelihood, it would be wise to reduce stock exposure to 10 percent and put the balance in securities that pay high interest rates.

There is, however, one very important caveat. While age is generally the chief determinant of one's objective level of risk tolerance, there are other considerations that cannot be ignored. If four other persons depend on you for their livelihood, you cannot tolerate as much risk as someone with no dependents. If you own $2 million you can tolerate a 50 percent loss more easily than someone who with only $200 thousand. Obviously, if you are 40 years old and a major portion of your portfolio is for your children's college education that starts only two years from now, you cannot tolerate as much risk in those funds as your friends who do not plan to send their children to college. So, while age is the chief factor in assessing one's objective level of risk tolerance, each person must make this assessment according to the circumstances of his or her own life.

Weighting by Age

Given that the younger person should be mostly in stocks and the older person mostly out of stocks, how do we quantify these different risk levels by age? Starting with Kenneth L. Fisher's recommendations described above, we can modify them to correspond to a person's life stages. This is shown in Table 8-3.

This table is a good starting point for quantifying your risk tolerance. All you need to do is divide your assets as shown in Table 8-3, depending on your life stage. Note how dramatically your stock exposure should drop after age 50.

If moving through five different portfolios strikes you as too many changes, you can easily adapt it to just three portfolios: aggressive risk, moderate risk, and low-risk. Just work with the portfolios for early career, late career, and late retirement. Of, if you want to change allocations more frequently, you can easily extrapolate for the ages in between those shown in Table 8-3.

Finally, the allocation model in Table 8-3 attempts to quantify objective risk. Everybody must still tailor it to fit their own psychological level of risk. For example, the allocations for age 40 in Table 8-3 rest on the assumption that the person will not lose much sleep during those periodic bear markets that will reduce his or her assets. However, some 40 year olds might want an even lower risk level. They can do that by adopting the less risky portfolio of the late career stage or something in between. Table 8-3 offers some prudent benchmarks for each age category that you can use to help establish your own comfort levels.

What Stocks to Use for the Equity Portfolio

What stocks, mutual funds, or CREF funds should one use for the equity portion of his or her portfolio? Most market professionals currently agree that some foreign stocks should be included and that the

Table 8-3   Allocation of Financial Assets by Career Stage

Career Stage	Percentage Invested in			Annual Percentage Rate of Return Using		
	Cash	Fixed Assets	Stocks	TIAA-CREF[1]	Big Stocks[2]	Small Stocks[3]
Early Career (to age 40)	0	0	100	10.8	11.1	12.4
Mid-Career (to age 55)	0	20	80	9.9	10.0	11.1
Late Career (to age 65)	15	35	50	8.5	8.4	9.1
Early Retirement (to age 75)	25	45	30	7.6	7.3	7.7
Late Retirement (after age 75)	45	55	10	7.3	6.8	7.0

[1]   Data is for TIAA-CREF 1953-1992. Stock date is CREF Stock, cash data is CREF Money Market, and fixed asset data is TIAA.

[2]   Series B data is from Ibbotson Associates for the period 1953-1990. Stock data is for large companies similar to the S&P 500 companies.

[3]   Series C data is from Ibbotson Associates for the period 1953-1990. Stock data is for small companies.

Sources: TIAA-CREF, *Charting TIAA and the CREF Accounts* (New York: TIAA-CREF, 1993), pp. 48-53'; Ibbotson Associates, *Stocks, Bonds, Bills and Inflation: 1991 Yearbook* (Chicago: Institutional Property Consultants, 1992).

domestic stocks should include large, mid-sized, and small companies, with some attempt to diversify between growth stocks and value stocks. Unfortunately, however, money managers do not have precise definitions of these terms. The size of a company is usually measured by its market capitalization--the number of shares in existence times the price of each share. A mutual fund, for example, can be considered a large stock fund if its average market capitalization exceeds $5 billion, and it can be considered a small stock fund if its average capitalization is less than $1 billion.[13] Mid-cap funds are those in between. A growth stock is one with rapidly growing earnings that are not dependent on a particular phase of the business cycle. Value stocks, by contrast, are usually viewed as ones whose market value is less than the value of the total assets of the company. The stock market runs in fads, but there is no way to know in advance whether next year's fad is going to reward or punish the holders of small company growth stocks. By dividing your equities among these four different types of U.S. stocks you participate in virtually all bull markets and are somewhat protected when the fads shift from one type of stock to another.

The profitability of including small company stocks among your equities can be seen in the annual rates of return columns of Table 8-3. For the highly aggressive all-stock portfolio, CREF Stock returned 10.8 percent per year since 1952. Large company stocks did somewhat better by returning 11.1 percent. But a portfolio divided between large and small companies grew at a 12.4 percent rate of return.

Probably the easiest way to see how your mutual funds fit these categories of size and style is to check them out in the Morningstar guide to mutual funds, which can be found in most sizable libraries. Morningstar presents a handy graph for each fund that shows whether its portfolio is predominantly small-cap, large-cap, or a blend of the two. It also indicates whether the portfolio is predominantly in growth stocks, value stocks, or a blend of the two.

Just as market professionals do not agree on a precise definition for small-cap, mid-cap, and large-cap stocks, they also do not agree on how you should divide your assets between value stocks and growth stocks. One investment adviser urges a very precise distribution of 15 percent foreign, 38 percent large company growth, 31 percent large company value, 8 percent small company growth, and 8 percent small company value.[14] This precise distribution would be impossible to maintain with TIAA-CREF. It would be much easier to find mutual funds that fit into those categories.

If you are just getting started and the equity portion of your portfolio is only $10 or $15 thousand, you might not want to spread that small amount of money among several mutual funds. It would be reasonable to concentrate about 15 percent in an international fund and divide the balance between a growth fund and a value fund. As your equities start approaching $100,000, however, you may want to establish a more systematic allocation strategy. Investment professionals are not unanimous on what that allocation should be, but you would certainly be in the mainstream if you divided you equity assets as follows:

15 percent   one international fund

45 percent   three growth funds or aggressive growth funds (including one large company fund, one mid-capitalization fund, and one small-capitalization fund)

40 percent   two value funds or a high income stock fund (including one large company fund and one small- or mid-capitalization fund).

This distribution will give approximately equal weighting to each of the six individual funds in your portfolio, and six funds is not too many for you to track. You probably do not want to track them daily. But it is a good idea to check them quarterly or least annually to see that the distributions between them have not gotten grossly out of balance and to ensure that one of them has not greatly underperformed other funds in its category.

As long as your funds keep pace with other funds in their categories, it is not a good idea to trade them frequently in the hopes of finding the very best performer. You do, however, want to weed out the funds that greatly underperform their category. For example, suppose you chose a small company growth fund and after a year discovered that the fund lost five percent in value over the previous year while comparable small company funds averaged a five percent gain. Unless there was an apparent non-recurring reason for this underperformance, it probably would be a good idea to replace that fund with a different small company fund that was in the top half or top quarter of its category.

Rebalancing the Asset Classes

Having settled on an asset allocation that leaves you comfortable, how frequently should you rebalance your portfolio? Let us assume you are in the late-career risk bracket and have $100,000 that you have divided according to the guidelines in Table 8-3: $50,000 is in equities, $35,000 in bonds, and $15,000 in a money market account. A wild bull market has driven up your stocks so that you now have $80,000 in stocks, $40,000 in bonds, and $15,000 in the Money Market for a total portfolio of $135,000. When should you rebalance your portfolio so that it is back to its ideal allocation of 50 percent, 35 percent, and 15 percent?

The easiest method is to rebalance once every year or at most once every six months.[15] Market cycles, however, are not congruent with the calendar, so a second approach would have you rebalance when the stock portion gets above or below its target allocation by a given percent. Fifteen or twenty percentage points would be a reasonable number. This not only keeps your portfolio balanced, but it also forces you to begin selling your stocks as bull markets move up to their peak and to begin buying them back as stock prices drop. This has the effect of reducing your equity exposure as bull markets get overextended and march toward their peaks. Conversely it increases your equity exposure as bear markets wind down and the stage is set for the next bull market to begin.

Tactical Asset Allocation

What you want to resist is the temptation to adjust your allocations according to your expectations of where the stock market is headed. If you think the market is headed up you will be tempted to overweight the stock portion of your portfolio. On the other hand, if you think the market is headed down, you will be tempted to sell stocks and increase your exposure to fixed income securities. Investment professionals call this tactical asset allocation, to distinguish it from the strategic, or passive, allocation that we have been discussing.

Tactical asset allocation of this sort is in reality a form of market timing. However, as Chapter 10 will discuss, it is very difficult to time the market's direction with any consistent success. If you want to use an asset allocation scheme, you probably should not try to combine it with market predictions or market timing.

Asset Allocation and
Sequential Dollar Cost Averaging

Slightly different from tactical asset allocation is the tactic of combining strategic asset allocation with sequential dollar cost averaging. If the stock markets have been in a multi-year extended phase, the process of strategic asset allocation automatically has you take some of your stock profits off the table. But a decision rule for putting those profits back into equities gets triggered only if a market decline erodes the value of your remaining equities. Some financial planners will urge you to take even more profits off the table after extended market rises and use the tactic of dollar cost average to put them back into stocks over a two- or three-year period. This differs from tactical asset allocation, because you are not waiting for the market to drop so you can reinvest as a lump sum.

As Chapter 5 discussed, the jury is still out on whether sequential dollar cost averaging is a lucrative strategy. It does not seem likely that you will lose money under this strategy, and if it worked, your profits would be measurably better than they would have been under a strict strategic asset allocation plan. If it did not work, however, your returns would be somewhat diluted.

Using TIAA-CREF for Asset Allocation

With TIAA-CREF the strategic asset allocation model outlined here cannot be followed precisely. Several features of TIAA-CREF inhibit any systematic plan for strategic asset allocation. These features involve rebalancing, accessibility to funds, and overlapping investment philosophies between funds.

Rebalancing

Rebalancing, as we saw, is the practice of periodically bringing the percent of assets in each asset class back to its target percentage. This is especially difficult to do with TIAA-CREF. In fact, once you have retired and converted to a retirement annuity it is impossible. CREF does not allow you to shift funds between accounts once your annuity years have begun. Whatever allocation formula you select at the moment of annuitizing is the formula you are stuck with for the rest of your life, even though that violates the fundamental concept of risk management that your level of risk tolerance varies with age. As Table 8-3 illustrated, your ideal asset allocation at age 65 is quite different from what it is at age 80.

TIAA makes asset allocation especially difficult. You can transfer only 10 percent of your holdings out of TIAA each year. If you were using TIAA as part of your allocation formula and the time came to rebalance, you simply could not use TIAA for that purpose. To transfer out of TIAA, you apply for a Transfer Payout Annuity. One-tenth of that annuity plus interest then gets transferred into your CREF account each year for the next 10 years, whether or not the rebalancing in a given year calls for funds to be withdrawn from TIAA. In theory, you could set up a different Transfer Payout Annuity each time you needed to rebalance your accounts. But after a half dozen years of this you would have so many different transfer payout annuity contracts that keeping track of them would become inherently confusing. As a practical matter, TIAA's transfer procedures are unworkable for rebalancing your strategic allocation plan.

The only place where TIAA works well as part of a strategic asset allocation plan is in your SRA. In SRA accounts, you can shift funds at will between CREF and TIAA. Furthermore, since your TIAA poses virtually no risk of capital loss, at times it has an advantage over bond funds that do indeed pose such a risk.

Inaccessible CREF Funds

There are also serious difficulties in using CREF for strategic asset allocation. Not all CREF participants have access to all CREF funds in their retirement annuity accounts. Some institutions do not permit their employees to own the CREF Bond, Social Choice, Growth, Equities Index, or Global Equities funds in their RA accounts. Although this is not CREF's fault, it is nevertheless a hindrance for the participants involved.

CREF will not permit its bond fund be used when you annuitize your account. CREF's rationale for this policy stems from a fear that retirees do not understand the risk inherent in bonds. Bonds carry an image of safety that stocks do not. Not realizing that bonds suffer periodic bear markets, some retirees might overweight their portfolios with bonds and then sue CREF for allowing them to do so when the eventual setback occurs.[16]   Notwithstanding CREF's concerns for its fiduciary responsibilities, virtually all asset allocators advocate some bond exposure for people over age 65. CREF's refusal to let its bond account be used as an annuity does a disservice to CREF participants.   CREF should eliminate this restriction.

Overlapping Investment Philosophies

One of the most serious roadblocks to asset allocation stems from the fact that CREF only has one equity fund distinct enough to fit neatly into the categories recommended above.   CREF Stock fund holds 15-20 percent of its assets in international funds, indexes two-thirds of its assets to the Russell 3,000 index, and puts the balance in stocks that it thinks will perform well.   The Social Choice fund also lacks a true investment focus.   It is in reality a balanced fund, since its portfolio is divided between stocks and bonds.   For the foreign portion of one's asset allocation, the Global Equities fund is not totally appropriate, since at least 25 percent of its funds will be always be invested in the U.S. market, and at the height of the booming international markets in mid-1993, only 53 percent of its assets were actually invested in foreign equities.[17] In fact, Global Equities' foreign equity holdings can vary from 50 percent to 75 percent. Given this wide range, you have no way to know how much exposure to foreign equities you will have over the coming year or two if you put your money in the Global Equities fund. The CREF Bond fund has a distinct enough portfolio philosophy to be an appropriate vehicle for asset allocation.   But, as noted, it becomes unavailable if you decide to annuitize your CREF holdings.

The CREF Growth fund is the only equity fund that would fit neatly into an allocation scheme based on growth stocks, foreign stocks, and value stocks. But even it does not specify what percent of its holdings will be international or how it will divide its portfolio among large-cap, mid-cap, and small-cap stocks.   The Equity Index fund would be appropriate if you wanted part of your portfolio to match the overall U.S. market.

Finally, *no* CREF fund breaks down its holdings according to the discrete investment categories most asset allocators advise using. If you adopt the three category scheme we discussed earlier[18]   there is no way for you to know which or what percent of CREF Stocks were picked to fit which category. Even if we use CREF Stock's own allocation scheme (foreign, indexed, and investment potential stocks), it is not clear which stocks in the portfolio listing were chosen for their investment potential and which ones were part of the indexed portion. In sum, whether you use your own asset allocation categories or the one's described in the TIAA and CREF prospectuses, it is impossible to figure out which investments fit into which categories.

The net result of this is that it becomes virtually impossible to put together a combination of TIAA and CREF funds to duplicate any of the asset allocation formulas shown in Table 8-3. If you hold TIAA, dividing its mix of assets into the allocation formulas is a mathematically daunting task.

If you do not have any TIAA holdings and have not yet opened an annuity contract, you could easily use CREF's Bond and Money Market funds to match up with their portion of the allocation formula you choose. But the stock portion of the formula would present a serious problem. You would most likely put your equity holdings into CREF Stock, which is two-thirds indexed to the overall U.S. market. This would not be a disaster, of course, but there are substantial reasons why many CREF participants would prefer not to be indexed so heavily to the overall U.S. market. Young participants might prefer to be more heavily weighted in small company stocks. Older participants might prefer to be more heavily weighted in stable, high-dividend utility stocks. Many participants might fear that the old indexing strategy that worked so well in the 1980s is out of tune with the future.

If you did not want to put your U.S. stocks into the CREF Stock fund you could put them into the CREF Social Choice fund which is about 60 percent weighted to stocks. But the investment philosophy (as distinct from its social choice philosophy) of this fund is not articulated by CREF. Consequently, you have no way to know how your Social Choice stocks are invested, unless you want to pore through the financial assets statements with a calculator in hand and a collection of S&P stock reports at your side so you can figure it out for yourself.

A Sample Asset Allocation Using TIAA-CREF

Surely, it will be argued, the situation is not so dire. Even if one cannot use TIAA-CREF to construct a portfolio that fits precisely into

Table 8-4   Asset Allocation with TIAA-CREF

	Allocation of Assets in Dollars and Percents			
	Before the Market Drops	After the Market Drops	After Rebalance	Transfers Needed to Rebalance
TIAA	60,600 (54.5)	63,024 (63.3)	54,242	-8,782
CREF Stock	46,960 (42.3)	32,872 (33.0)	42,033	9,161
Money Market	2,600 (2.3)	2,704 (2.7)	2,327	-377
Bond	453 (.4)	471 (.5)	405	-66
Social Choice	344 (.3)	287 (.3)	308	21
Global Equity	222 (.2)	157 (.2)	199	42
Total	111,179 (100.0)	99,514 (100.0	99,514	

some financial wizard's asset allocation strategy, the fact remains that anyone will be widely diversified if they simply hold a cross section of TIAA-CREF funds. By switching between CREF funds, anybody can adequately rebalance their portfolios periodically.

Let us explore this possibility by looking at a hypothetical participant, Professor Average, who owned exactly one-millionth of TIAA-CREF's portfolio (approximately $111,179 in 1992) and allocated those holdings exactly as TIAA-CREF did. That is $60,600 is in TIAA, $46,960 in CREF Stock, $222 in Global Equities, $343 in Social Choice, $452 in the bond fund, and $2,600 in the Money Market fund.[19] Over the following year, all the assets except the stock assets appreciate by 4 percent. But a powerful bear market knocks all of the stock holdings down 30 percent, and it is time to rebalance the assets. Can this be done?

On the surface, there is no problem. Table 8-4 tells the story. The left-hand column shows how Professor Average's assets were originally divided. The next two columns show how the assets are divided after the 30 percent stock market decline and after the rebalancing. The last column shows what transfers will be needed to rebalance the funds back to their original targets.

The asset allocation in this example did precisely what it was supposed to do. In the midst of a significant 30 percent bear market, this portfolio declined only 10.5 percent. If it can be rebalanced back to its original distribution of assets, the portfolio will be admirably positioned to take advantage of the next bull market.

The problem comes in the rebalancing. To rebalance, Professor Average needs to make the transfers shown in the right hand column of Table 8-4. The amounts of money to be transferred between the Bond, Global Equities, Money Market, and Social Choice accounts are so piddling that nobody would bother to pick up the phone to make the transfers. However, a substantial amount of money needs to be withdrawn from TIAA and deposited in the CREF Stock fund. As was explained earlier, there is no way to do this in an RA account. Only 10 percent of a TIAA account can be transferred each year, and since Professor Average only has $60,600 in the TIAA account, it is impossible to transfer the $8,782 needed to rebalance the portfolio this year.

Using Mutual Funds and CREF

Although TIAA-CREF makes it very difficult to practice strategic asset allocation, those difficulties can be eased by combining TIAA-CREF with mutual funds (or other equity investments).

Mutual Funds with CREF

To illustrate how this can be done, let us take the case of Professor Average one step further. Assume, as we did earlier, that the Average family owns exactly one-millionth of TIAA-CREF's total portfolio ($111,179) which is divided proportionately to TIAA-CREF's overall holdings. This makes their two largest holdings TIAA at $60,600 and CREF Stock at $46,960. Assume further that the Averages are both 60 years old and, after reading this chapter, they decide to allocate their

Table 8-5 Asset Allocation with TIAA-CREF and Mutual Funds

	Target Allocation	TIAA-CREF	Mutual Funds
Fixed Income Securities	(35%)		
TIAA-CREF TPA		54,540	
Bonds		0	19,373
Total Fixed Income	73,913	54,540	19,373
Money Market Funds	(15%)		
Total Money Market	31,677	31,677	0
Stock Funds	(50%)		
Growth (45%)	47,515	24,962	22,553
Value (40%)	42,236	0	42,236
International (15%)	15,838	0	15,838
Total Stock Funds	105,589	24,962	77,627
Totals	211,179	111,179	100,000

assets in accord with the recommendations made in Table 8-3. In addition to Professor Average's TIAA-CREF holdings of $111,179, their retirement holdings also include $100,000 in IRAs, Keogh accounts, and other accounts, giving them a total accumulation of $211,179.

Is it possible to divide this up according to the 15 percent cash, 35 percent bonds, and 50 percent stocks ratio suggested for 60 year olds in Table 8-3? (p. 123) Had these funds all been invested in TIAA-CREF and had the Average's followed the typical pattern of keeping more than half their assets in TIAA, it would, as we have seen, be extremely difficult if not impossible to make this allocation.

Making the allocation is possible, however, if we include the Average family's mutual funds in our calculations and if we make a conceptual adjustment to the allocation strategy. This adjustment is to consider both bonds and TIAA as fixed income assets and use the fixed income assets as our investment category in place of bonds. This is not a totally satisfactory adjustment. TIAA does not offer the long-term possibility of capital growth that bonds offer. But at least it permits the

Averages to establish an asset allocation plan that includes their TIAA funds.

Carrying out the allocation is a five step process. The first task is for the Averages to decide on their target allocation. Being 60 years old, they decide to use Table 8-3's Late Career allocation model by putting 35 percent of their total retirement savings in fixed assets, 15 percent in cash equivalents or money market funds, and 50 percent in stocks. This comes out as shown in Column 1 of Table 8-5 to $73,913 in fixed income securities, $31,677 in money market funds, and $105,589 in stock funds.

The second step is to transfer 10 percent of their $60,600 TIAA holdings to CREF and the balance of $54,540 to a Transfer Payout Annuity (TPA). Using the TPA instead of TIAA has important advantages for the Averages. While in the TPA their funds will earn the same interest as they would in TIAA, but the TPA will give them greater flexibility than TIAA in making future allocations. Also, on the anniversary dates of setting up the TPA, the Averages will receive a notification of that year's transfer from the TPA into CREF, and that notice will remind them to conduct their annual rebalancing.

The third step is to allocate their CREF assets among the seven CREF funds. They need some criteria to use for choosing from among the funds, so they use the priority rankings given below and decide to put $31,677 in CREF Money Market and $24,962 in CREF Growth. To follow this ranking, you would put your full target allocation into the top ranked fund before you would put any monies into a lower ranked fund.

CREF Fund	Rationale
Money Market	Pays a higher interest rate than most commercial money market funds.
Growth	A pure growth stock fund divided among low-cap, mid-cap, and large-cap stocks.
Bond	A pure bond fund.
Social Choice	A balanced fund with about one-third of its holdings in bonds. Would be useful if more bond exposure were needed.

Global Equities Investment philosophy overlaps with CREF Stock and probably Equity Index. Impossible to know the degree of international exposure at any given moment. Many pure international funds are available in the market place.

CREF Stock A good choice if this were your only CREF fund. But investment philosophy overlaps with Global Equities and Equity Index. Calculating what portions of CREF Stock fit the growth, value, and international criteria would be mathematically daunting.

Equity Index Good choice if you favor indexing all or part of your portfolio to the overall U.S. market.

The fourth step is to calculate the allocation of the mutual fund portion of the Average's portfolio. They do this by subtracting the figures in the TIAA-CREF column from those in the Target Allocation column. This shows them that they need to put $19,373 in a bond fund, $22,553 in a large-cap or mid-cap growth fund, $15,838 in an international stock fund, and $42,236 divided equally among three value funds or high-income equity funds.

The fifth and final step is to rebalance their allocations on the anniversary date of the TPA.

Mutual Funds in Place of TIAA-CREF

Even though Table 8-5 shows that asset allocation can be practiced by combining TIAA-CREF with mutual funds, the process is cumbersome. You have to go outside TIAA-CREF to find value funds and pure international funds. And if you have large amounts tied up in TIAA, it will take several years for the Transfer Payout Annuity to bring your fixed assets down to their target level. Someone who was really serious about following a coherent asset allocation strategy would find it a lot simpler to begin transferring his or her TIAA holdings to CREF where they could be transferred to a large mutual fund family. Any large mutual fund family would have a broader selection of funds that would fit more appropriately than CREF's into the threefold category outlined for this model. Several families provide guidance on how to match up their specific funds with your allocation priorities.[20]

However, deciding to transfer out of CREF is a major decision, and Chapter 9 will discuss the pros and cons of making such transfers. It would be better for everybody concerned if CREF would respond by making asset allocation easier rather than encouraging people to transfer out to mutual funds.

Some Guidelines on Mutual Funds

If you do use mutual funds as a supplement to your TIAA-CREF plans, it is important to develop some guidelines. The number of funds has proliferated to more than 5,000, versus only about 1,700 stocks on the New York Stock Exchange. As the number of funds has increased so has the difficulty of choosing from among them. Most investment professionals recommend that you buy no-load funds or invest through a discount broker willing to sell no load funds. Choose funds that have low fees, charge no front-end or back-end loads and that do not have an annual maintenance fee. Unless you invest through a discount broker, choose a fund family that has generous telephone switching policies so you can rebalance at least once per year.

Even following these guidelines either you will have to invest considerable energy into studying funds so that you can make intelligent choices or find an investment adviser you can trust to help you do this. Chapter 16 explores the issue of finding an investment adviser.

How TIAA-CREF Could Facilitate Strategic Asset Allocation

If asset allocation is indeed as valuable an investment strategy as current research suggests, then TIAA-CREF is not serving its participants well. In terms of asset allocation, TIAA-CREF seems to have the worst of two worlds. Even with its new additions, TIAA-CREF does not have the right kinds of funds for TIAA-CREF participants to conduct their own asset allocation. Nor does it have an asset allocation fund that follows an allocation strategy coherent enough to relieve participants of the burden of doing so for themselves. If TIAA-CREF were a mutual fund family without a captured audience, it would have a great deal of trouble gaining those customers seriously concerned about asset allocation.

To remedy this shortcoming, TIAA-CREF should take the following five steps.

Step 1: Facilitate Transfers from TIAA

It will be impossible to include TIAA in a rigorous asset allocation plan unless it becomes easier to transfer assets between TIAA and CREF. TIAA has resisted making such transfers easier on the grounds that the potential for a massive outflow of funds would compromise the long term nature of TIAA investments. As Chapter 4 argued, this is not a very persuasive argument. The majority of TIAA participants are financially cautious people who are highly unlikely to exit TIAA in droves.

A solution to this problem would be to create a Plan B TIAA as argued in Chapter 4. New monies put into Plan B would be eligible for unlimited transfer to CREF. This would greatly improve the ability of participants to use strategic asset allocation. And, as Chapter 4 argued, it would not pose any threat to the stability of TIAA's portfolio.

Step 2: Create Several New Discrete Portfolio Funds

This step addresses the needs of those participants who want to take personal charge of their asset allocation decisions. CREF should create several new funds that correspond to some generally accepted categories of asset allocation. Each fund should concentrate on a discrete asset category. At a minimum these should include:

- an international equity fund
- an international bond fund
- a U.S. large company growth stock fund
- a U.S. small and midcap growth stock fund
- a U.S. maximum capital appreciation fund
- a U.S. large company value stock fund
- a U.S. small and midcap value stock fund
- a hard assets fund of precious metals and real estate

- a dividend oriented equity fund or a utilities fund
- a social choice equities fund

These funds would differ significantly from the sector funds currently proliferating among mutual fund families. Given that the purpose of the funds would be for strategic asset allocation, CREF would not be pushing the funds as "hot" funds and hence would not attract people jumping onto last year's investment bandwagon.

Because these funds would be set up for the purpose of facilitating true asset allocation, the amount of switching back and forth would be minimal. Participants would be switching primarily to rebalance their total portfolios.

Step 3: Create a New Asset Allocation Fund

This fund would be designed for those TIAA-CREF participants who do not want the responsibility of making their own asset allocation decisions and prefer leaving those decisions to CREF. The fund would have five separate portfolios that would correspond to the portfolios shown in Table 8-3 (p. 123). The late-career portfolio, for example, would contain 50 percent equities, 35 percent bonds, and 15 percent money market instruments. The portfolio would not select its own stocks and bonds. Rather it would simply divide its assets among the discrete funds outlined above in step 2.

The other four asset allocation portfolios would range from a highly aggressive early career portfolio to a highly conservative late retirement portfolio. The composition of these would be as outlined in Table 8-3.

This creation of a set of asset allocation portfolios to invest in other CREF funds is not a revolutionary idea. It has already been pioneered by the Fidelity and T. Rowe Price families of mutual funds.[21]

Step 4: Permit the Use of the CREF Bond Fund by Annuitizers

Upon retirement, TIAA-CREF offers you the option of annuitizing your accounts. This means that TIAA-CREF will offer you (and your spouse) a monthly payment for life so that you do not have to worry about outliving your retirement savings. The soundness of this idea will be addressed in Chapter 13. One distinctly bad feature of annuitizing under TIAA-CREF is that you cannot use the CREF Bond fund if you annuitize. Almost all financial planners advise some bond exposure in an asset allocation plan. As a fixed income plan, most people view TIAA as a substitute for bonds. It is certainly less volatile than CREF Bond and does not expose you to the risk of capital loss that is present in the CREF Bond fund. But it also does not give you opportunities for capital growth that exist in the Bond fund. For these reasons, CREF should make its Bond fund available for annuitants.

Step 5: Permit Annual Rebalancing of TIAA-CREF Annuities

For those do make the decision to annuitize, TIAA-CREF has another fundamental flaw. Once you annuitize your accounts, you can no longer switch assets back and forth between the CREF funds. This violates two of the most important provisions of asset allocation. First, it makes it impossible to make your allocation more conservative as you get older and your risk tolerance decreases. Second, it makes it impossible for you to rebalance your portfolio after a big market move has thrown the portfolio out of balance. Other insurance companies have self directed annuities that give annuitants flexibility to shift funds between portfolios,[22] and TIAA-CREF should also give its participants that flexibility.

Conclusion

If your assets have grown to $200,000, pure dollar cost averaging can no longer protect you from the threat of a significant capital loss. You need a strategy to reduce your market risk. Current conventional wisdom promotes strategic asset allocation as an ideal way to do this. Current research also suggests that such strategies would have performed well historically.

In setting up your strategic asset allocation plan, it will be useful to keep some guidelines in mind.

- First, determine what risk level you will use, keeping in mind both the risk of capital loss and the risk of inflation. Any distribution of your assets exposes you to some level of risk, even if you do nothing and leave the entire decision up to TIAA-CREF. By setting your own risk level, you empower yourself to take charge of your own financial security.

- Second, chose an asset allocation formula that is comfortable psychologically and is appropriate for your age and objective level of risk tolerance. Use Tables 8-1 and 8-2 to gain a feel for the risk-reward ratios of the CREF funds. Use Table 8-3 to develop some guidelines on adjusting your equity exposure to your level of risk tolerance.

- Third, using CREF funds or no-load mutual funds, allocate your overall retirement assets according to the risk level you have decided to assume. To the extent that you use mutual funds, keep in mind the guidelines discussed earlier.

- Fourth, rebalance your portfolio once per year. If you want to be more aggressive, you can rebalance any time that the stock portion of your portfolio is more than 15 percent away from its target value.

- Fifth, resist the temptation to engage in tactical asset allocation in which you change your formula in accord with your predictions for the market. If you want to time the market, then read Section 3 of this book and good luck. The secret of asset allocation is that you don't have to time the market or even be a great stock picker to get good growth and reduce risk.

Notes

1. Jane Bryant Quinn, *Newsweek*, August 31, 1987, p. 47.

2. Gary Brinson, Randolph Head, and Gilbert Beebower, "The Relative Importance of Asset Allocation," *Financial Analysts Journal* (October 1987).

3. Maria Crawford Scott, "Asset Allocation Among the Three Major Categories," *AAII Journal* (April 1993): 13-17.

4. These calculations on CREF account returns are drawn from data presented in *Charting TIAA and the CREF Accounts: Winter 1992-1993* (New York: TIAA-CREF, 1993). Data for the CREF Stock fund are based on CREF's actual performance since 1952. Recent data for the other funds are taken from their actual performance since inception, but the historical data is based on CREF's estimated reconstructions of how those funds would have performed historically. These hypothetical reconstructions extend back to 1953 for the Money Market account, 1976 for the bond market account, and 1970 for the Global Equities account.

5. *The Individual Investor's Guide to No-Load Mutual Funds*, 12th ed. (Chicago: The American Association of Individual Investors, 1993), p. 604.

6. Gerald W. Perritt, "'All-Weather' Protection Using Asset Allocation," *AAII Journal* (July 1988): 18-21.

7. Kenneth L. Fisher, "Design Your Own," *Forbes*, March 15, 1993, p. 158.

8. Gerald Perritt, for example, suggests that 10 percent should be kept in gold. "All-Weather Protection,", p. 20.

9. Gerald W. Perritt and Alan Lavine, *Diversify: The Investor's Guide to Asset Allocation Strategies* (New York: Longman Financial Services Publishing, 1990), p. 44.

10. Ibbotson Associates, *Stocks Bonds, Bills and Inflation: 1991 Yearbook* (Chicago: Institutional Property Consultants, 1992).

11. Fisher, "Design Your Own," p. 158.

12. Jerry Edgerton, "Who Needs Bonds? Probably Not You," *Money*, September 1994, pp. 120-124.

13. *Morningstar Mutual Fund Sourcebook: Volume I, Equity Mutual Funds, 1994* (Chicago: Morningstar, Inc., 1994), p. A29.

14. Fisher, "Design Your Own," p. 158.

15. See John Markese, "Asset Allocation Strategies: Portfolio Balancing Acts," *AAII Journal* 12, no. 6 (July 1990): 31-34.

16. This was a TIAA-CREF representative's response when the author asked why CREF Bond fund cannot be used in annuitized accounts. TIAA-CREF Lifestages Seminar. May 25, 1993. Minneapolis, Minnesota.

17. CREF Unaudited Financial Statements, June 30, 1993.

18. These are international funds, U.S. growth funds and U.S. value funds.

19. *The Participant* (April 1993): 4, 12, 14, 16.

20. The Fidelity, T. Rowe Price, and Stein Roe families offer such services. See *Investor's Business Daily*, April 29, 1993, p. 25; June 18, 1993, p. 21.

21. Ibid.

22. See Albert J. Fredman and Russ Wiles, "An Introduction to Investing in Variable Annuities," *AAII Journal* 15, no. 8 (September 1993): 9-12. Also see Kristin Davis, "Annuities: Picking Your Way Through the Jungle," *Kiplinger's Personal Finance Magazine*, October 1994, pp. 55-63.

PART III

HIGHER RISK STRATEGIES FOR RETIREMENT SAVINGS

Part II focused on three low-risk strategies for capital accumulation: dollar cost averaging, value averaging, and strategic asset allocation. These, of course, are not the only investment strategies available to TIAA-CREF participants. The third section of this book examines the merits of three higher-risk strategies for managing your financial affairs: following the advice of a professional market timer, creating your own market timing strategy, and shifting your assets out of TIAA-CREF to a mutual fund or a financial planner. The arguments for and against trying to time the market are explored in Chapter 9. Chapter 10 shows how the advice of professional market timing services could be applied to CREF or to a portfolio of mutual funds. Chapter 11 constructs and backtests three different timing strategies. And the merits of switching your TIAA-CREF assets to the care of a financial planner are evaluated in Chapter 12.

Chapter 9

Market Timing as a Strategy for Asset Management

It would be a rare CREF participant who did not feel the urge now and then to nail down some CREF Stock profits and to transfer some of those funds to the safety of the money market account, hoping to buy back into CREF Stock at a lower price later on. Do not do it, is the advice of conventional wisdom. According to most financial experts, the riskiest thing you can do with your CREF accounts is to try and time market cycles. Try moving into equity accounts when the stock market booms and retreating to the safety of the money market when things start to fall apart and you are more likely than not to end up doing just the opposite. So say the experts.

The lure of trying to time the market is understandable enough, because the profits would be enormous if you could pull it off. If you could buy into each bull market within 15 percent of the bottom, sell within 10 percent of the top, and not get whipsawed in between, you could no doubt afford to quit teaching at an early age and devote the most productive years of your life to your favorite research project, writing a novel, or doing whatever you pleased. But the lure of market timing is dangerous. Were you to have the opposite experience of consistently selling near the bottom of the bull markets and buying back in at the tops, you could look forward to grading blue books until age 85.

The Allure of Market Timing

The allure of market timing stems from the assumptions that there are patterns to human behavior, that those patterns can be identified, and that they can be quantified precisely enough to give you an edge in dealing with the markets. Certainly no one would question the first two assumptions, that patterns exist in human behavior and that they can be identified. Human behavior is not random. We stake our lives on that assumption every time we cross an intersection fully confident that those automobiles hurtling toward us at forty miles per hour will stop for no reason other than a light has turned red. Entire industries thrive on identifying patterns of human behavior: Las Vegas casinos, Madison Avenue advertisers, and a cadre of election consultants, to name just three. (Well, we didn't say that all these enterprises were desirable).

Stock market technicians look at the nation's securities markets and see patterns at work there as well. If we would only pay attention to their charts and computer signals, they say, we could achieve that dream of all stock players--buying low and selling high.

But can it be done? First, let us examine the formidable argument against the market timers. Then let us weigh these arguments against the allure of market timing .

The Case against Timing the Market

The roster of investment professionals opposed to trying to time the market is legion. TIAA-CREF frankly advises that you are "better off with a buy-and-hold strategy."[1] Peter L. Bernstein reported in the *Journal of Portfolio Management* that even the best market timers barely beat the market itself.[2] John Bogle, head of the Vanguard mutual fund family observed, "In 30 years in this business, I do not know anybody who has done it successfully and consistently, nor anybody who *knows* anybody who has done it successfully and consistently. Indeed, my impression is that trying to do market timing is likely, not only *not* to add value to your investment program, but to be counterproductive."[3] Perhaps the most successful mutual fund manager in recent history, Peter Lynch, also advised against market timing. Lynch noted, "Predicting the short term direction of the stock market is futile."[4] The dean of stock analysis, Benjamin Graham, counseled that "There is no basis either in logic or in experience for assuming that any average investor can anticipate market movements more successfully than the general public of which he is himself a part."[5] Finally, the great economist and gifted investor John Maynard Keynes, wrote, "We have not proved able to take much advantage of a general systematic movement out of and into ordinary shares as a whole at different phases of the trade cycle. . . . As a result of these experiences I am clear that the idea of wholesale shifts is for various reasons impracticable and indeed undesirable."[6]

These impressive warnings come from impressive sources. On what is the case against market timing based? Six arguments stand out.

Random Regularities

The first charge against market timing asserts that many seeming market regularities are nothing more than random events. To demonstrate this principle, Burton Malkiel has his students each flip a coin, and he uses the coin flips to generate plausible charts of stock market action.[7] If heads, the stock goes up half a point; if tails, it drops half a point. The notion that such an exercise could actually reproduce a plausible looking stock chart pattern seemed so bizarre that it deserved to be tested. So we used a table of random numbers to generate 104 price changes for a hypothetical stock starting at a price of $50. This represents two years worth of weekly data. Each odd random number produced a drop of

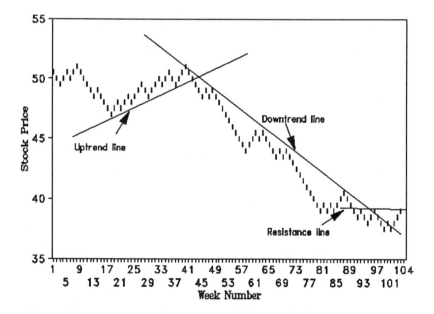

Figure 9-1   A Random Price Movement of a Stock

fifty cents, and each even number a gain of fifty cents. Figure 9-1 shows the unnerving results, a stock price chart that resembles three very common patterns of technical analysis. Using standard charting procedures, a stock market technician would most likely conclude that in the forty-first week a sell signal was given when the uptrend line was broken. In the final weeks, the stage was set for an upside breakout when the price not only broke through the downtrend line, but also reached the resistance level. Were the next closing price to be on the upside, this would clearly signal many market technicians that this stock was posed for a strong upward move.[8]

But these patterns, which the chartist would identify so confidently, are nothing more than a succession of randomly picked numbers. The absurdity of seeing patterns in random events leads skeptics such as Malkiel to conclude that "past movements in stock prices cannot be used to foretell future movements."[9]

Not only are price patterns random events, say the critics, but so are the results of market forecasters. Some market forecasters may have more success than others over a short period of time, but such success is statistically irrelevant. One would expect that to happen, just as one would expect a no-hitter to be pitched in major league baseball every year or two. If enough pitchers start enough games, over enough years, there is a precise statistical probability that somebody will eventually pitch a no-hitter. But you could lose a lot of money betting on which particular pitcher would hurl that no-hitter, even if you had put your money on Nolan Ryan who threw seven of them.

The same thing is true of market forecasters. It is statistically inevitable that some market forecasters will have beaten the market this past year or even over the past five years. However, to identify in advance the one person who will beat the market over the next ten- or fifteen-year period is about as probable as identifying in advance the pitcher who will end up throwing two or three no-hitters over his career.

In short, many patterns that appear to be regularities are not regularities at all. They can be easily explained by statistical probability.

Explosive Market Moves

One of the things that makes market timing so difficult is that so much of the market's advance takes place in short, explosive moves. The bull market advance of 1991-94, for example, saw the S&P 500 advance

55 percent. Nearly half of that occurred in just three months. From January 9, 1991 through April 17 the S&P 500 shot up 25 percent. If you missed that explosive burst, you picked up only a 23 percent gain over the next three years.[10]

Nor does the 1991-94 bull market appear to be unique. Robert H. Jeffrey tabulated the movements of the S&P 500 through every quarter from 1926 through 1982, 228 quarters in all. A mere fourteen quarters, only 6 percent of the total, accounted for all of the market's returns above and beyond the inflation rate. Take out those fourteen quarters and the real returns after inflation were zero.[11]

Another pair of researchers conducted a comparable study using months instead of quarters. If you had missed the 50 best months from 1926 through 1987, you would have missed all the gain in the S&P 500. The average return for all other 694 months was zero. The entire 62-year gain was produced in only 6.7 percent of the months.[12]

Of course, timers reply that this is not an even handed research method. If you are going to take out the fifty best months, you should also take out the fifty worst months. Gary Schilling concluded that if you were out of the market for the fifty worst months from 1946 through 1991, you boosted your annual rate of return from 11.4 percent to 19.9 percent. On the basis of this, Shilling concluded that it is worth timing if it can get you to avoid the worst of the bear markets.[13] Timing, from this perspective becomes a measure of risk avoidance. You do not hope to outperform bull markets but to cut your losses early in the bear markets.

The Upward Bias of the Market

A correlary of the explosive market thesis is an argument based on the fact that the stock market has a long-time upward bias. Since its inception through 1993, the CREF Stock unit moved upward in 115 quarters and downward in only 51 quarters. Any random time spent out of CREF Stock had better than a two-to-one chance of missing an upward movement. Given those odds, a timing system has to have a very high success rate to beat a simple buy and hold strategy. One researcher put this needed success rate as high as 80 percent. To be right on 80 percent of your market calls would be an extraordinary achievement. From this perspective, the odds are against you if you stay out of the market. You miss out more through opportunity losses from being out of bull phases than you make up by being out of bear phases.[14]

Profit Erosion through Taxes

Unless market timing is done in a tax deferred account, the tax bite on market transactions is very likely to eat up most of the extra profits gained through timing. *The Hulbert Financial Digest* examined twenty-nine timing systems that showed an overall profit from 1987 through 1991. After taxes were taken into consideration, only one of these beat a buy-and-hold approach.[15]

The Psychological Difficulty of Timing

Timing the market successfully requires extraordinary self discipline. For example, a timing strategy that has you make purchases after the market has fallen 15-20 percent is very difficult to follow. Indeed, at those times, the normal impulse is to sell whatever you have left at those times and wait for things to improve a little before you get back in. Although such impulses might be normal, a study of such panic selling found that in the overwhelming majority of cases investors would have been better off three years later if they had resisted the urge to unload their equities after sharp market downturns.[16]

If you adopt a timing strategy, it may call on you to buy into what looks like a sinking market or sell into a strong market. It is very hard to do this just because some abstract timing system tells you to do so. But you must make those trades if your trading strategy is going to work. If you have isolated a trading strategy that worked in the past, you have to carry out all the trades to make that system work in the present. You cannot just pick and choose to follow the ones that feel comfortable. The trouble in following this dictum, though, is that you know that any system can give false signals, that any system can fall out of sync with changing market conditions and no longer work. There are going to be times when knowing this magnifies the difficulty of following your strategy.

In short, no matter what trading system you adopt, the psychological pressure not to follow it faithfully is enormous. Following a timing strategy is psychologically very difficult to do.

Compounding these psychological problems is the possibility that you might miss some critical signals. You might be so busy with meetings on one of the trading days that you simply forget to call CREF to make the transfers you had planned. Or, if you are following the advice of a market advisor, you might fail to call your advisor's hot line on the day a critical signal is given. Worse yet, your timing advisor might put out a special signal that you do not learn about until it is too late. These scenarios are not as farfetched as they seem. One advisory service announced a special sell signal on its telephone hot line on Thursday, October 15, 1987, just in time for subscribers to sell before the market dropped 22 percent the following Monday. Unfortunately, most subscribers did not know that there would be a hot line update that Thursday, so they never got the word.[17]

The Poor Record of Market Timers

Even if you are convinced that there are nonrandom regularities to be exploited, that you have a timing strategy capable of catching enough of the explosive upbursts of the market, and that you have the self-discipline to follow a systematic strategy, there is still one more important problem with market timing. Judging from the evidence compiled by *The Hulbert Financial Digest*, most market timers fail to beat the market most of the time. Of ninety-two timing portfolios Hulbert examined from 1990 through 1992, only twenty-six beat a buy-and-hold approach.[18] Hulbert's longer-term analysis of market timers is even less encouraging. For the five-year period ending in 1992, only six of the sixty-five timing portfolios followed by Hulbert beat the return of the S&P 500. Only three out of twenty-one beat it over the ten year period. And only one out of the sixteen tracked beat it over a twelve-and-one-half-year period. Interestingly, the lone performer that beat the market over the longest time period failed to beat it over the more recent three year, five year, and year time periods, indicating that most of its sterling long term performance was garnered 11 to 12 years ago.

In addition to the newsletter writers, the other oft-cited measure of the inability of investment professionals to time the market is the amount of cash that mutual fund managers hold. If they are loaded up with a lot of cash, this is generally interpreted as a sign that they are negative on the market. If they hold very little cash, this is a sign that they are positive on the market. If you overlay a graph of those cash holdings with a price graph of the stock market, a nice relationship emerges. The more bearish they are, the more likely the market is to go up. There are two ways to interpret this. Burton Malkiel takes it as evidence that the pros themselves are incapable of timing the market.[19] Norman Fosback uses it as evidence of a contrary indicator. If you think that the pros are wrong at the extremes, then that is the time to buy.[20] Fosback, incidentally, is one of the few market timers to perform fairly well by Hulbert's yardsticks.

Some Other Timing Problems

There are some other timing problems as well. Most timing strategies are based on mechanistic trading systems. To follow them religiously is to forego extraordinary opportunities that pop up from time to time. For example, most trend following systems would have had you sell the market after its 22 percent drop on Black Monday in October 1987, and not buy back into the market until it had already recovered 15 or 20 percent.

Another problem is that market fads change often. You constantly run the risk that a timing strategy that worked well under one set of market circumstances will no longer work when the fads change. Even if your strategy gets you out of the market before a crash, you still have to get in afterwards. Timing systems that get you out before the crash are frequently not very good at getting you back into the market in time for the next bull phase.

Even if your system works most of the time, it only takes one big mistake to bring a serious erosion of your capital. And your probability of error is increased by the fact that not all trading systems give clear signals about what to do. For example, one of the oldest timing strategies is the Dow theory originally developed by *Wall Street Journal* editors Charles H. Dow and William P. Hamilton. At least two newsletters follow the Dow theory today, and they have completely different records of market performance.[21]

If there is one book to read before you venturing into try developing a market timing strategy, it is Burton G. Malkiel's entertaining and informative *A Random Walk Down Wall Street*.[22] Malkiel does not deny the existence of patterns and regularities in the markets. Indeed, he claims to have made some money from them. But with wit and insight, he tells a tale of repeated financial foolishness from the tulip bulb mania of 17th century Holland to the nifty fifty craze of the 1970s. He also gives you plenty of warning against indulging in the fancy of short-term market timing.

The Case for Market Timing

Market timers would quibble with such evidence. Much of the argument against timing is based on studies that do not directly measure market timing strategies. Rather they measure market performance under hypothetical conditions that few timing systems try to emulate. This is especially true of studies that show what happens when market timers miss the fifty best months or quarters. At the very least, measuring only the fifty best periods is not a direct test of market timing. It is highly unlikely that any timing system could capture all of the best periods and avoid all of the worst. However, it does seem plausible that a timing strategy could capture enough of the best quarters and avoid enough of the worst quarters to beat a buy-and-hold strategy.

In the face of the arguments against market timing, there are only two things that can be said in favor of it. First, some timing strategies have consistently beaten a buy-and-hold strategy in historical back tests over reasonably long periods of time. These results emerge without massaging the data. It is also possible to identify the types of markets under which certain timing strategies work best and the market conditions under which they work the poorest.

Second, if these timing strategies do in fact work over the long term, they have the potential to produce enormous profits. Even a small improvement over a buy-and-hold strategy leads to an enormous difference over time. If you were to accumulate $110,000 by age 45, CREF's historic 10.9 percent rate of return would multiply that to approximately $281,000 years later. Increase the rate of return by only two percentage points to 12.9 percent and the result is approximately $336,000, a difference of $55,000. Let that money sit for another ten years until the normal retirement age of 65, and the difference between the two rates of return grows to $340,000.

How likely is it that a timing strategy could have added two percentage points to CREF's historic rate of return? This will be explored in coming chapters.

CREF as a Timing Vehicle

If market timing is possible, is CREF an appropriate timing vehicle? Traditional advisers would say no. As the equity core of your retirement savings, CREF should not be exposed to the risks of market timing. If CREF is your only financial asset, it would be wise to follow this traditional advice. However, as Chapter 2 pointed out, CREF is increasingly becoming simply another tax deferred asset that fits into one's overall holdings--IRAs, Keoghs, 403b plans, stock accounts, mutual fund accounts, real estate, certificates of deposit, and other assets. If you are fortunate enough to have accumulated other assets in some of these other investment vehicles and you want to indulge in market timing, then it seems reasonable to consider CREF along with your other investment vehicles in determining which ones are the most appropriate for market timing.

CREF gives you some big advantages as a timing vehicle. With CREF you can make an unlimited number of easy, cost-free transfers of money from one fund to another. This is not true of some stock brokers or mutual fund families. When you make transfers to the CREF Money Market account, your funds go to work in that account immediately, and they go to work in a money market account that has tended to pay a higher interest rate than the average money market mutual fund. With some brokerage firms you do not get a good money market rate and the funds are not immediately deposited. Also, since CREF is a tax deferred account, you do not have to worry about taxes draining your profits away from your trading strategy. You pay the taxes only when you make withdrawals from CREF.

The drawbacks of CREF as a trading vehicle exist mostly for those people who want to assume more risk in the hopes of gaining a greater overall return. CREF does not have a high-performance capital appreciation fund, so CREF funds will rise less in bullish markets than will high-performance mutual funds and fall less in bearish markets. A trading strategy that successfully keeps you in most of the bullish phase and out of most of the bearish phase might do better with performance-oriented no-load mutual funds than with the CREF funds or with mutual funds indexed to the overall market. The performance-oriented person will also be able to use margin in trading no-load mutual funds in a non-tax deferred brokerage account, whereas that is not possible with CREF. Margin is the practice of borrowing stock so you can earn a greater return on your investment. For example, with $50,000 in a margin account, you can buy $100,000 worth of mutual funds. If the market goes up, the person who buys funds on margin will earn twice as much as the one who did not use margin. But he or she will also lose twice as much if the market goes down.

Conclusions

Although the weight of the argument falls against trying to time the market, market timing could produce huge rewards if one could do it successfully. These potential huge rewards give market timing a powerful allure to some people. The following guidelines may assist those investors who choose to try this potentially lucrative, potentially perilous approach.

- Market timing is very risky business, and most people should not try it. Nevertheless, those who attempt it should benefit from the background information provided in the next few chapters.

- CREF has both advantages and disadvantages as a timing vehicle.

- Submit only a small portion of your assets to market timing.

- If you submit any portion of your RA or SRA to market timing, make sure that you have an equal amount of money set aside in some other tax deferred account (such as an IRA or a KEOGH) that will serve as your retirement reserve in event your timing system goes awry and you lose the funds you exposed to timing.

- The biggest advantage of CREF as a timing vehicle is the fact that it permits unlimited, cost-free transfers of funds between the CREF accounts. This makes CREF a less expensive trading vehicle than many other vehicles you can find.

- As a timing vehicle, CREF has two disadvantages. The first disadvantage is that CREF does not have a high-performance, high-volatility fund that most mutual fund families offer. Such funds typically outperform bull markets and thus add financial gains to a successful timing system. Second, you cannot use the leverage of margin with CREF, whereas you can use margin while trading mutual funds through discount brokers.

- The most successful market timers focus on reducing risk and portfolio volatility. They reduce the amount of time spent in the market, and they aim to avoid the lion's share of periodic bear markets. If they can avoid the brunt of bear markets, they think they will come out ahead even if they lag in bull markets.

Notes

1. TIAA-CREF, *Guiding Your Retirement Savings* (New York: TIAA-CREF, 1992), p. 8.

2. Peter L. Bernstein, "Does Time Diversification Increase Risk or Reduce It?" *The Journal of Portfolio Management* 11, no. 4 (Summer 1988): 1.

3. Quoted in Burton G. Malkiel, *A Random Walk Down Wall Street* (New York: W. W. Norton & Company, 1990), p. 178.

4. Peter Lynch, *One Up on Wall Street* (New York: Penguin Books, 1989), p. 80. Lynch directed the Fidelity Magellan Fund from the middle 1970s through the late 1980s when it was the number-one performer among mutual funds.

5. Quoted in Gerald W. Perritt and Alan Lavine, *Diversify: The Investor's Guide to Asset Allocation Strategies* (New York: Longman Financial Services, 1990), p. 190.

6. Quoted in Malkiel, *A Random Walk Down Wall Street*, p. 180.

7. Ibid., pp. 135-38.

8. This is precisely the interpretation suggested in Curtis M. Arnold and Dan Rahfeldt, *Timing the Market: How to Profit in Bull and Bear Markets With Technical Analysis* (Chicago: Probus Publishing, 1986), pp. 22-23, 58-61.

9. Malkiel, *Random Walk*, p. 133.

10. This calculates the bull market as of its February 2, 1994 peak. A move of 25.3 percent occurred from the S&P 500 low of 311.49 on January 9, 1991 to its April 17 level of 390.45. From that level to its February 2, 1993 peak of 482.00, the S&P 500 moved another 23.4 percent. The overall move was 54.7 percent.

11. Robert H. Jeffrey, "Putting Market Timing to the Test: Is It Worth the Risk," *AAII Journal* 7, no. 8 (September 1985). Also "The Folly of Stock Market Timing," *Harvard Business Review* (July-August, 1984).

12. P. R. Chandy and William Reichensein, "Timing Strategies and the Risk of Missing Bull Markets," *AAII Journal* (August 1991).

13. A. Gary Schilling, "Exits and Entrances," *Forbes*, September 16, 1991.

14. Gerald W. Perritt, "Mutual Fund Timing: Is It Worth the Trouble?" *AAII Journal* 9, no. 2 (February 1987): 23.

15. Mark Hulbert, "Market Timing Strategies: Taxes Are a Drag," *AAII Journal* 14, no. 7 (August 1992): 18-20.

16. John A. Vann, "The Costs of Panic-Selling in Stock Market Investing," *AAII Journal* 13, no. 3 (March 1991): 14-15.

17. Mark Hulbert, "Timing the Moving Averages: How Good Is the Performance?" *AAII Journal* 12, no. 2 (February 1990): 25-27.

18. *The Hulbert Financial Digest* (January, 1993):

19. Malkiel, *A Random Walk Down Wall Street*, p. 179.

20. Norman G. Fosback, *Stock Market Logic: A Sophisticated Approach to Profits on Wall Street* (Fort Lauderdale, Fla: The Institute for Econometric Research, Inc., 1992), pp. 80-84.

21. These are the *Dow Theory Letters* and *Dow Theory Forecasts*. For performance ratings of each see Mark Hulbert, *The Hulbert Guide to Financial Newsletters* (New York: New York Institute of Finance, 1991), pp. 1-115.

22. Malkiel, *A Random Walk Down Wall Street*.

Chapter 10

Professional Timing Strategies

Introduction

If you decide to risk a small portion of your portfolio trying to time the market, where do you go for reliable advice? A reasonable place to start is to review the work of investment advisers who themselves use an understandable strategy and whose recommendations could easily be applied to CREF or to your other investment holdings.

Recent years have seen a troubling proliferation of timing advisory services. Most of the more than one hundred timing portfolios tracked by *The Hulbert Financial Digest*, have been started within the last few years. This proliferation of advisory services is distressing for several reasons. Perhaps a dozen different timing strategies can consistently beat the market, but it seems highly unlikely that one hundred of them can. Too many people are offering timing advice, and they cannot all be equally good. There are probably some charlatans in the business. Certainly a substantial number of advisors make exaggerated claims about their strategies and use carefully selected statistics to tout their services, and it is very difficult to tell the successful from the unsuccessful. If you subscribe to a timing service on the basis of its advertised claims, you are just as likely to end up with a bad one as a good one.

So what is a person to do? Several important tactics will help in your search. First, distinguish between different timing strategies so that you can choose ones that make some logical sense to you. This chapter will help by outlining some key ideas on timing. Second, examine the range of timing services that appear to have been successful in recent years. This chapter will indicate some of these services, but a more thorough source is *Timer's Digest*[1] or *The Hulbert Financial Guide to Investment Newsletters*.[2] If your library does not own these publications, have it order them. They will give you a wealth of useful data, including information on how to obtain copies of newsletters that look interesting. Finally, develop a set of guidelines for assessing a timing service before you begin following its recommendations.

This chapter then intends to identify timing strategies and newsletters that follow those strategies. The ones that we identify may not necessarily be the best, but they use a coherent enough strategy that it can be followed with CREF.

Timing Strategies

This chapter examines four common timing strategies, identifies a newsletter that advocates each strategy, and asks several questions about strategies and the newsletters. What does the strategy aim to do? How good has the sample newsletter been in following the strategy? How easy is the strategy to use, and how honest is the newsletter in its claims? How would the strategy have worked historically with CREF, as best we can judge? Under what types of market conditions does this strategy work best, and under what conditions does it falter?

The four strategies to be examined are the (1) trend following, (2) interest rate, (3) valuation, and (4) seasonality strategies.

Trend Following Strategies

The Aim of Trend Following

The aim of trend following, in the colorful terms of market guru Martin Zweig, is "Don't fight the tape!"[3] The "tape" refers to the old ticker tapes that were used to transmit stock prices around the country in the early twentieth century. Market tycoons such as Joseph P. Kennedy had them in their offices, and the movies gave us the image of frantic speculators fingering miles of ticker tape strewn across the floor. Today you can enjoy that same frantic experience--minus the mounds of paper-- by watching the bottom of your television screen when you tune into CNBC Business News during the day time. Beside the ticker symbol for each company (General Electric, for example, is GE) you will see the last price at which that company's stock changed hands and the number of shares that were traded.

"Don't fight the tape" means don't fight the trend. Trend followers have a Newtonian confidence that a trend set in motion will stay in motion until something happens to stop it. You make money by being in the market when the tape says that the trend is rising and getting out when the trend turns down. Don't buy until the market is on its way up, and don't sell until it is on its way down. The trend is your friend, say trend watchers. Follow the trend and you will do okay.

Of course, to follow the trend, you have to be able to identify it, and that is the hard part. There are various devices for trend identification, but the most common one is probably the moving average, and the most commonly used moving average is probably the 200 day one.[4] It is not the optimal one to use, but it may be the most convenient one to examine, since the 200 day moving average for several key indexes is graphed regularly in the *Investors's Business Daily*.

To calculate a moving average for CREF Stock, for example, you add up all of the unit values for the previous 200 trading days and divide that total by 200 to get the average unit value. After today's close you simply add today's closing price to the total and subtract the first day's unit value. Divide the new total by 200 to get the updated moving average. As each day passes the average price literally moves forward and can be graphed over time.

There are many ways to interpret the moving average. The most common way views the market as bullish if the current price is above the moving average and the moving average is sloping upward, as it is in Figure 10-1 from early 1991. Conversely, if today's closing price is below the moving average and the graphed curve is sloping downward, the market trend is down. Thus, the first few weeks of Figure 10-1 show that CREF still had not yet come out of the 1990 bear market and the new bull market had not yet been confirmed. The word "confirmed" becomes very important in this context. The moving average does not predict a market change; it only confirms the market change at some point after it actually took place.

A Sample Newsletter

Different trend followers use different techniques to identify the trend, and a fairly successful one has been Dan Sullivan's *The Chartist Mutual Fund Timer* (CMFT).[5] According to *The Hulbert Financial Di-*

gest the CMFT increased 57.5 percent over the three years ending 1992, compared with a return of only 35.9 percent for the S&P 500 and a return of only 30.6 percent for CREF Stock.[6] A substantial portion of Sullivan's superior return came from selecting good performing mutual funds, rather than from his timing. Nevertheless, the timing system itself beat the market over this period. Hulbert calculates that even if you had limited yourself to trading a market index, the CMFT would have beaten a buy-and-hold strategy, returning 39.7 percent, compared 35.9 percent for the buy-and-hold.

Sullivan's system would be very easy to use with CREF. You simply buy a CREF equities fund when he gives a buy signal and transfer back to the money market or bond fund on his sell signals. Keeping the graph in Figure 10-1 in mind, however, it is important to note that any trend-following system will get you into the bull market after CREF Stock has already turned up and, depending on the system, it might temporarily move you out of the market during its rise. Because of this, any trend-following system used with CREF is likely to lag the performance of CREF Stock on the way up. At some point, however, CREF is going to fall into a bear market. And it is then that Sullivan's trend-

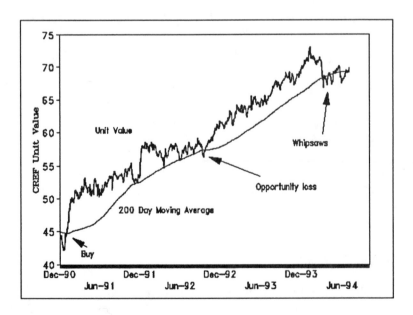

Figure 10-1   200 Day Moving Average of CREF Stock

following system will save you money--if it works. Since it is designed to get you out of the bear market early, it preserves your capital, so that you put more money to work during the next up trend than you would if you rode out the bear market. Over a succession of two or three market cycles, a good trend-following system aims to keep you ahead of a buy-and-hold strategy. Whether Sullivan's is that good, of course, is what you would be betting on if you followed it.

The *Chartist Mutual Fund Timer* also receives high marks for forthrightness. Sullivan put $100,000 of his own money into trading with this system in 1988, and he reproduces his actual brokerage account statement in each newsletter so that you can see the current status of the account. Additionally, he states his willingness to send the records of all previous trades to any subscribers who request them. Since the CMFT uses a real cash account and displays the account statement on the front page of his newsletter, he has little room to fudge the results.

How Trend Following Works

Sullivan uses what he calls "momentum" to identify long-term trends. He does not define how he measures momentum, but he apparently uses a combination of moving averages involving the Russell 2000 index (an index of small company stocks) and one of the major indexes (probably the S&P 500). By monitoring the performance of both small and large company stocks, he hopes to have a better measure of market trends than he would if he were limited to one index.

Sullivan tracks the performance of about one hundred aggressive mutual funds from the bottom of each bear market until his momentum indictor generates a buy signal. He then urges you to buy the funds that advanced the most during that period. He calls these high relative strength funds. Like a true Newtonian, he theorizes that the funds set in motion the most forcefully at the beginning of a bull market will continue to be the strongest performers throughout the bull market.

When his momentum indicators look especially strong, Sullivan also urges you to buy mutual funds on margin. This allows you to borrow enough money from your broker to buy twice as many shares as you ordinarily could. If you have $10,000 in your account, the use of margin enables you to buy $20,000 worth of funds. If your funds rise by 30 percent, you earn $6,000 profit instead of the $3,000 profit you would have earned on the $10,000. The broker charges you a monthly interest

Interest Rate Strategies

If trend followers have a Newtonian belief that a market trend set in motion will stay in motion until stopped by some event, that pivotal event is more likely to be a change in interest rates than anything else. At least that's what one group of strategists believe.

"Don't Fight the Fed"[8] is the slogan of interest rate watchers. The "Fed" is the Federal Reserve Board that is charged by Congress with regulating short-term interest rates, the availability of credit, and the amount of money in circulation. These collectively influence the monetary environment. And "Don't Fight the Fed" is short-hand for the principle of buying into the stock markets when the monetary environment is favorable and selling the markets when it become unfavorable.

The most visible measure of the monetary environment is the course of short-term interest rates. These rates include the money market rate that you receive on your money market accounts, the Three Month Treasury Bill rate (simply called the T-Bill) that the U.S. Treasury pays for its short-term borrowings, the discount rate that the Federal Reserve Bank charges to the nation's commercial banks, the federal funds rate that banks charge each other for overnight loans, and the prime rate that banks charge their best customers. When these rates make sustained moves up, stocks often (but not always) go down. When the rates come down after having been high, stocks almost always go up.

Whether this variation is cause and effect or something else at work is difficult to know. But Figure 10-2 shows the undisputable relationship between short-term interest rate changes and stock prices. This graph is based on the simplest of interest rate strategies, changes in the direction of the discount rate. Buy signals in Figure 10-2 are triggered the first time that the Federal Reserve Board lowers the discount rate after it had previously been going up. Sell signals are triggered the first time that the Fed raises the discount rate after it had previously been going down. As the graph makes clear, anyone who had followed this simple strategy over the past twenty years would have done well. It gave only thirteen buy signals, and each one produced market gains.

The Aim of Interest Rate Watchers

Given their belief in the power of interest rate changes to drive the market, interest rate watchers have a straightforward goal. They warn you to stay out of the stock markets when the monetary environment is bad and to get back into the markets when the monetary environment improves.

Why should short-term interest rates affect the stock market? Analysts point to three reasons. First, interest rates have a big impact on the economy and the course of the economy has a big impact on the stock markets. Rising interest rates usually mean a tighter monetary environment that will make it more difficult to borrow money to expand businesses, build houses, or buy automobiles. As investors see the monetary environment tighten, they anticipate that corporate profits will eventually decline. Since they also think that corporate profits drive the stock markets, they anticipate that stock prices will decline. Consequently they sell.

The second reason for the monetary environment's effect on stock prices is that monetary conditions influence the amount of money that can go into the nation's financial markets. We saw a classic case of this in the wake of the late 1980s banking crisis and the 1990 recession. Fearful of a possible banking collapse, the Fed moved dramatically to lower short-term interest rates and boost the nation's money supply. A

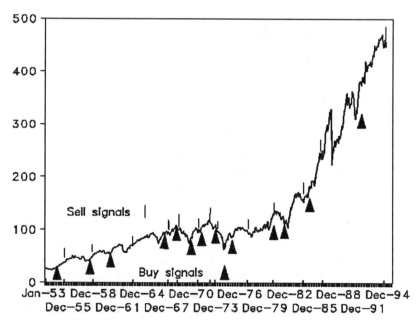

Figure 10-2   Discount Rate Changes and the S&P 500 Index

huge amount of money poured into the nation's banks in 1991 and 1992, but for a variety of reasons little of that money was lent for the purpose of business expansion and job creation. Much of it found its way into the nation's stock and bond markets. This was wonderful for you if you owned the CREF Stock, because you got a nice boost to your net worth. But it did not do very much for your children or your students if they had just graduated and were out looking for work in what was a fairly stagnant job market.

You saw visible evidence of the third reason why interest rates influence the stock markets when the interest on your CREF Money Market account dropped from about 7.5 percent at the end of 1990 to barely 3 percent three years later. Since 3 percent was less than the inflation rate, people were actually losing money by keeping it in the money market. They had to find a more lucrative place for their investments, and by the millions they turned to mutual funds, the stock market and variable annuities.

A Sample Newsletter

Interest rate watchers abound, and some of the most successful of them use elaborate statistical models that regress several variables to generate trading signals. One of the most straightforward interest rate watchers is William E. Donoghue, who tracks the interest rates paid by the money market funds around the country and distributes his findings to most metropolitan newspapers. This is an extremely valuable service. While reading your morning paper at breakfast you can see how your particular money market fund compares with all the others. You can also examine the average weekly rate for all money market funds, and this is a useful measure of trends in short-term interest rates.

Donoghue publishes a monthly newsletter called *Moneyletter* in which he gives advice on asset allocation, mutual fund selection, and market timing. Like the *Chartist Mutual Fund Timer*, Donoghue's signals are easily adaptable to CREF. On a buy signal you buy one of the CREF equity funds, and on the sell signal you move 100 percent into the safety of the money market. This timing signal has generally been successful since its start. From 1990 through 1992, a 48.2 percent gain was achieved by using the timing signal together with the mutual funds recommended by Donoghue. Use of the timing signal alone produced a 37.5 percent gain. This compares favorably to the gain of 35.9 percent for the S&P 500 and 30.6 percent for CREF Stock over the same peri-od.[9] Donoghue's advice scores above average on the forthrightness criteria, but not as highly as the CMFT. He is not above hyping his newsletter with hyperbolic overstatement that is characteristic of most investment newsletters.[10] Mark Hulbert's *Hulbert Financial Digest* has also complained that Donoghue has exaggerated his ratings in Hulbert's rankings of newsletter performance.[11] Donoghue's performance claims are verifiable, however, and they generally tend to be in line with the results published by Hulbert.

How the Interest Rate Strategy Works

Donaghue's signal system is elegant in its simplicity. He bases it on a 25-week exponential moving average of the average weekly interest rate of all the money market funds he tracks. When the current week's interest rate drops below that of the 25-week moving average, a buy signal is generated. A sell signal comes when the current interest rate rises above the moving average. The exponential moving average dif-fers from the simple moving average discussed earlier in one key re-spect. The exponential moving average is weighted so that the most recent week counts for more than any of the previous weeks. This ap-peals to many moving average advocates, because it lets your timing system be influenced more by what is happening today than by what happened half a year ago.

How the Strategy Would Have Performed

Since Donoghue does not publish the precise buy-and-sell dates that were generated historically by his signal system, it is not possible to reconstruct his performance with any precision. However, results de-rived from constructing our own exponential 25-week moving average and back testing it do not match those claimed by Donoghue. This prob-ably occurred because there are different ways to construct an exponen-tial moving average and we may not have used the same formula that he used.[12] Nevertheless *The Hulbert Financial Digest* finds that the Dono-ghue signal beat the market for the one- and three-year periods ending in 1992.

Like the trend-following strategy, Donoghue's interest rate strategy performed better when used with aggressive mutual funds than it did when used with a market index such as the S&P 500, which would be closer to CREF's experience. Donoghue's method of fund selection is not as clearly explained as is Sullivan's in the *Chartist Mutual Fund Timer* so it would be more difficult to replicate Donoghue's strategy on your own.

Advantages and Pitfalls

The biggest advantage of the interest rate strategy comes when the stock market appears to move dramatically in response to interest rate changes. The most explosive example of this can be seen in Figure 10-2, with the bull market that ran from 1984 through August 1987. A discount rate buy signal would have gotten you in as close to the bottom as any reasonable person could hope for, and a sell signal would have gotten you out within 7 percent of the peak. Not a shabby achievement. Donoghue's signal also would have gotten you out before the great crash of 1987.

Sometimes, however, the market is out of sync with interest rate trends, and that is when this strategy experiences its pitfalls. In Figure 10-2, for example, the discount rate model would have kept you on the side-lines during a modest market rise from 1978 through early 1980 and through the explosive market rebound in 1988 and 1989. This was not the worst of all worlds. The model eventually got you back into the market at a respectable price in both cases, and you were earning a decent money market return in the meantime. But most investors would have found it very difficult psychologically to sit on the sidelines while the equity markets seemed to be exploding without them.

In summary, an interest rate strategy makes a lot of intuitive sense. The graph of the discount rate strategy in Figure 10-2 suggests that it would have enjoyed good historical performance, and the advice of Donoghue's *Money Letter* yielded positive results.

Valuation Strategies

A third investment strategy is to buy undervalued assets in the hopes that they will soar in price after other investors realize their true value. It is difficult, but not impossible, to apply this strategy to a broad collection of stocks such as CREF. At times the markets are grossly overvalued, and when that happens there is not much profit potential left in the market. At other times--usually at the end of devastating bear markets--stocks become grossly undervalued, and the profit potential is enormous.

The Aim of Valuation Strategies

The aim of a valuation strategy is simply to find a benchmark for determining when the market is over- or under-valued. When it is un-dervalued you buy; when overvalued you sell. There are several ways to measure valuation, but one of the simplest and easiest to follow is to keep your eye on the dividend yield of the S&P 500, which is published every week in *Barron's*. The yield of a stock is the dividends per share divided by the price, and it is expressed in percentages. Thus the divi-dend yield of the S&P is the sum of the dividends of the 500 S&P stocks divided by the S&P 500 index price.

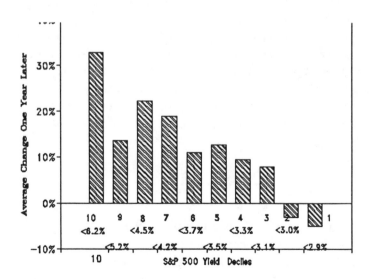

Figure 10-3   Dividend Yields and Change in CREF Stock

Figure 10-3 shows the range of dividend yields divided into deciles for the end of each quarter during the period from 1953 through June 1994. Only 10 percent of the time was the dividend lower than 2.9 percent, and all quarters with yields lower than that amount fall within the first decile (the lowest tenth). At the other extreme, the tenth decile (the highest tenth), consists of those quarters in which the yields exceeded 5.2 percent. Half of the time the yield was 3.66 percent or less.

As Figure 10-3 shows, there is a very powerful relationship between the dividend yield of the S&P and the future prices of CREF Stock. When yields were in the lowest decile, a unit of CREF Stock dropped an average of 5 percent in value over the subsequent 12 months. At the other extreme, when yields were in the highest decile, CREF Stock rose an average of 32.8 percent over the following year. Buying CREF Stock when yields were low and stock prices overvalued led to sub par performance in the short run.

Not only did buying CREF Stock at low yields produce sub-par results over the short-term, but you also were not able to count on the long run to bail you out. After 10 years, CREF units bought in the lowest decile of yields appreciated an average of only 49.5 percent, but those bought at the highest decile rose 341.4 percent.

Following these observations, the aim of valuation strategists is obvious. Lighten up on your stock holdings as yields drop close to or below 3 percent. Load up on stocks as yields rise to or above 4 percent. Other measures of market value could be used in addition to dividend yields. The two most common are price-to-book-value ratios and price-to-earnings-ratios. These ratios as well as the dividend yields are easy to follow because they are published weekly for both the Dow Jones Averages and the Standard and Poors 500 index in the financial weekly *Barron's*.

A Sample Newsletter

We could identify only one newsletter that follows a pure valuation strategy: the *Growth Fund Guide*, published by Walter J. Rouleau.[13] It converts the dividend yield into a price/dividend ratio so that a 5 percent yield, for example, is a 20:1 price/dividend ratio. In short, twenty dollars in price buys you one dollar in dividends.

Rouleau uses the price/dividend ratio to decide what mix of cash and stock funds you should hold. At a ratio of 34:1 (which equals a yield of less than 2.9 percent) he divides your investments half and half between money market funds and conservative mutual funds. If the price/dividend ratio drops to 20:1 (yields of 5 percent or more) he puts you 100 percent into aggressive stock funds.

Rouleau's system would adapt very easily to a timing model with CREF. Where he prescribes cash, you would use CREF's Money Market fund. Where he prescribes a conservative mutual fund, you would use CREF's Social Choice fund, since it is a balanced fund with both stocks and bonds. Where Rouleau prescribes an aggressive fund, you would put your money into CREF Growth fund or the CREF Stock, Global Equities, or Equity Index funds.

How the Valuation Model would Have Performed

Growth Fund Guide's promotional literature makes very extravagant claims for this valuation strategy. In the least successful version of the strategy, $1 invested in 1966 grew to $22 by 1991, for a 13.7 percent annual rate of return. In the most successful version, $1 grew to $365, for an extraordinary 27.7% rate of return.[14] Unfortunately, these claims are not corroborated by the *Hulbert Financial Digest*. Hulbert shows that on a timing basis the *Growth Fund Guide* underperformed the market for the one-year, three-year, and five-year periods ending in 1992. Even when Hulbert measured *Growth Fund Guide*'s model portfolio, it beat the market in only one single period, the one-year period ended in 1992.[15]

Part of the reason for *Growth Fund Guide*'s poor recent performance is clearly due to the fact that the stock market's strong bullish phase from 1982 to 1994 was punctured by only two short bear markets, the 1987 crash and the three-month drop off in 1990. Since the valuation model decreases its equity exposure as the valuations of stocks begin to exceed their historic norms, valuation strategies necessarily underperform in long, drawn-out bull markets such as the ones that have prevailed since 1982.

Advantages and Pitfalls

The lesson to investors is fairly straightforward. The biggest advantage of the valuation strategy is that it is likely to give you some downside protection when the market goes into a tailspin. As stock prices rise during bull markets, dividend yields usually fall. Even if dividend payouts increase, stock prices usually increase faster. As dividends fall, the valuation strategy slowly moves you into cash, so that you have limited market exposure when the bear market finally arrives. As the bear market progresses and dividend yields begin rising again, the valuation strategy slowly moves you back into the market. By the time the market hits rock bottom you are fully invested. If you are using mutual funds, the strategy puts you into aggressive funds and has you utilize margin so that you can use maximum leverage when prices start going back up.

This eminently reasonable strategy does have a few pitfalls. First, periods of over- or under-valuation can persist for a long time. Like the two men waiting for Godot, you can spend a lot of time sitting on the sidelines waiting for your big opportunity to arrive. Second, even if markets are overvalued, they can move back to being undervalued without a price drop. This will happen automatically if there is a big increase in dividends. Third, the valuation strategy necessarily has you selling equities as bull markets progress. This means that you don't participate fully in the bull phases of the market.

In summary, this is a strategy with considerable intuitive appeal, especially for cautious investors. The evidence from Figure 10-3 shows overwhelmingly that there is not much opportunity in CREF Stock when yields are low but there is enormous opportunity when yields are high. Using the *Growth Fund Guide* for your trading signals, you can implement the valuation strategy either with CREF or with a mutual fund family. In either case, you are not likely to suffer substantial losses. When a bear market finally shows up, a valuation strategy might well soften the blow for you. Nevertheless, it is troubling that *Growth Fund Guide*'s own claims are not corroborated by those of Hulbert.

A Seasonality Strategy

The three strategies examined to this point all had an inherent logical appeal. The trend followers are Newtonian in their belief that a trend in motion will stay in motion until it is interrupted. The interest rate strategists are confident that monetary changes are the key events driving the stock markets. The valuation strategists hold to the contrarian notion that a lot of money can be made when market trends become greatly extended.

Our last strategy, the seasonality strategy, has no inherent logic, or, if it does, it is certainly not self evident. Indeed, it almost flies in the face of logic. It says that you can make a lot of money if you simply buy the market just before the end of each month and sell it shortly after the month turns.

This strategy might not make much logical sense, but it is based on an impressive pattern. Stock market historian Norman Fosback calculated that from 1928 through 1989, the S&P 500 index grew at a 40 percent per year rate when invested at the ends of each month, but it dropped at a 4 percent per year rate during the rest of the month. He also found that the market showed an extraordinary increase just before holidays. Based on these patterns, Fosback conducted a backtest of about eight hundred hypothetical trades over these sixty-three years, and about two-thirds of them showed a profit. This pattern is so strong and is based on so many cases that it is hard to reject it as a mere statistical aberration.

Furthermore, in 1977 Fosback began trading the system in an actual mutual fund account, and that too has been profitable. His original $5,000 account grew to $40,325 from 1977 through 1990, giving it a compounded annual rate of return of 17 percent. In 1982 he began trading index futures through the seasonality system and claims to have earned a compounded rate of return of 26 percent per year over the next eight years.[16]

The Aim of the Seasonality System

The seasonality system attempts to move you into equities when the seasonally profitable period starts and move you back into the money market when that profitable period comes to an end. If the system works in the future as it did in Fosback's back testing, you can expect about two-thirds of your trades to be profitable.

A Sample Newsletter

Instructions for using the seasonality system come monthly in Fosback's *Mutual Fund Forecaster*, but if you do not want to subscribe to the newsletter, you can get the same instructions more cheaply from his book, *Stock Market Logic*[17] or from *The Stock Trader's Almanac*.[18]

If you want to experiment with the seasonality model with CREF or with mutual funds, several rules must be followed religiously. Be prepared to track your accounts carefully, because the system requires 13 to 14 round trip transactions per year.

- Buy CREF Growth (or another CREF equity fund) on the third-to-last trading day of the month, unless the next trading day is a Monday. In that case buy on that Monday.

- Transfer back into CREF Money Market on the fifth trading day of the next month, unless that day happens to be a Monday. In that case, sell on the preceding Friday.

- Buy CREF Growth on the third-to-last trading day before a holiday closing of the stock markets, unless the next trading day is a Monday. In that case, buy CREF Growth on that Monday.

- Transfer back to the CREF Money Market on the last trading day before the market closing, unless the day after the holiday is a Friday. In that case sell CREF Growth on that Friday.

When using the seasonality strategy in your SRA account, it will sometimes be advantageous to use TIAA rather than CREF Money Market for your cash holdings. In SRA accounts, TIAA offers unlimited transferability and it usually carries a higher interest rate than the Money Market fund. Do not, however, attempt this in your retirement annuity (RA) account.

Unlike most of the other trading systems we have reviewed, the seasonality system is actually easier and cheaper to implement with CREF than it is with mutual funds. With CREF you are permitted an unlimited number of no-fee transactions, whereas most no-load funds would run out of patience with anybody who tried to trade their funds fourteen times per year. You can trade no-load funds through discount brokers who will let you trade as often as you like, but they will charge you a small fee. Depending on your broker's fee structure, fees for this service may or may not cut deeply into your profits.

Although it is easier to use the seasonality system with CREF than with a mutual fund, using a mutual fund instead of CREF has two advantages. With a discount broker you might be allowed to use margin, and you can also use aggressive funds or high relative strength funds as your trading vehicle. This will bring steeper losses on your losing trades. But if two-thirds of future trades continue to be winners as the back tested trades were, trading aggressive mutual funds should produce better returns than trading in CREF. Within CREF, the preferred trading vehicles would probably be the CREF Stock, Growth or Equity Index funds.

How the Seasonality System Would Have Performed

The *Hulbert Financial Digest* confirms that the seasonality system would indeed have produced a superior return historically. Although the seasonality system did not beat a buy-and-hold approach for the three-year period ending in mid-1994, it did beat the buy-and-hold approach for the five-year, eight-year, and ten-year periods. Indeed, it is one of only three timing systems that beat a buy-and-hold approach over those time spans.[19] When this system was back tested with CREF since 1990, it also beat a buy-and-hold strategy.

Advantages and Pitfalls

The biggest advantage of the seasonality system is its historical performance. The pitfalls, however, are obvious. The system requires extraordinary discipline. You have to remember to phone in your orders at least twice a month. It is also psychologically very difficult to buy tens of thousands of dollars of stock for no other reason than a change of date on a calendar. The trained mind wants a logical and compelling reason for doing something, but, as we pointed out, it is difficult to find a compelling reason for the market to rise at the end of the month and sink in the middle of the month. Furthermore, the losing trades do not come every third time. Sometimes they bunch up, and you will get four or five losses in a row. If this happens when you have just started the system, it will be very difficult to stay with the system long enough for the winning trades to bail out your early losses.

To make the seasonality strategy work, you have to follow it persistently month in and month out over an extended time period. There will be long periods of several months during which the seasonality strategy underperforms the market, and you will be tempted to give up on it. If you try skipping a month during these periods, the odds are two-to-one that you will have skipped a winning trade, not a losing one. Every time you skip a winning trade, you dilute the ability of the system to work for you. Of course you always face the possibility that seasonality patterns in the future might be the reverse of those in the past. If that happens, the seasonality strategy could cost you a lot of money.

Multivariate Timing Systems

Unlike the timing systems discussed above, most market timers do not restrict themselves to a single variable. Most of them combine some form of fundamental and technical analysis to generate trading signals. Some combine trend-following techniques with monetary indicators. Others rely heavily on macro economic assessments of the overall U.S. economy. One even makes market predictions on the basis of planetary cycles (although he carefully avoids calling this astrology). Still another has people pay a substantial annual fee to join his organization and attend regular meetings that seem designed as much for esteem building as for investment strategizing. There are certainly some very interesting practitioners in this field!

It is not this chapter's intention to boost particular market timers, but to discuss those whose procedures exemplify coherent timing strategies. This is much more difficult to do with the newsletters that follow multivariate strategies, because the strategies are often complicated, they are frequently not explained very clearly, and we can assess only a limited number of timers. Yet some of these have much better performance records than the ones we highlighted above, so we compromise by simply listing in alphabetical order those newsletters that were found by the 1994 *Hulbert Financial Digest* to have beaten the returns of the S&P 500 over at least one of the periods presented by Hulbert. If any of these newsletters strike you as interesting, you can turn to *The Hulbert Guide to Financial Newsletters* for more information. The periods indicated by each newsletter are for the 3-year, 5-year, 8-year, and 10-year periods ending in June 1994. The inclusion of one of these indicates that the portfolio beat the S&P 500 over that time period.

- *Big Picture* Masterkey; 5 year.
  Excellent record according to Hulbert, who also charges that it has a disarming tendency to grossly overstate its performance. [20]

- *Bob Brinker's Market Timer*; 3 year, 5 year.
  Uses technical and fundamental data for timing signals and asset allocation advice.

- *Bob Nurock's Advisory*; 10 year.
  Uses a timing system called the Technical Market Index that was used by the Wall Street Week television show until 1989.

- *Cabot's Mutual Fund Navigator*; 3 year
  Uses technical and fundamental analysis. A relatively infrequent trader.

- *Chartist Mutual Fund Timer*; 5 year.
  The number-five ranked mutual fund newsletter for the 5 years through 1993.

- *Donoghue's Moneyletter*; 3 year, 5 year.
  Uses changes in the average money market rate to generate trading signals.

- *Dow Theory Forecasts*; 3 year.
  One of the oldest newsletters in continuous publication.

- *Fidelity Monitor*; 3 year, 5 year.
  The number-three ranked mutual fund newsletter over the 5-year period. Focuses on the Fidelity family of mutual funds.

- *Garside Forecast*; 3 year.
  Offers timing advice for several markets.

- *Granville Market Letter*; 5 year.
  Perhaps the most famous newsletter in the business.

- *Hussman Econometrics*; 3 year.
  Uses econometric models to make market forecasts.

- *Investor's Intelligence*; 3 year, 5 year.
  Tracks the advice of other newsletters and ranks them as bullish or bearish.

- *Marketarian Letter*; 3 year, 8 year.
  Offers several model portfolios of mutual funds.

- *Mutual Fund Forecaster* Seasonality System; 5, 8, and 10 year.

- *Professional Timing Services*; 5 year.
  Uses various technical indicators.

- *Systems and Forecast*; 5 year, 8 year, and 10 year.
  Very active timing system. Averages about 14 trades per year.

- *Wall Street Generalist*; 3 year, 5 year.
  Uses technical and fundamental data to analyze markets.

Some Guidelines

If you decide to investigate a professional timing newsletter, do it carefully. Some subscriptions can be very expensive, but it is often possible to purchase a trial subscription at a reduced rate. Be cautious in following the newsletter's recommendations. If the newsletter turns out to be wrong on the market and you follow its advice to time your movements into and out of CREF Stock, you could lose a substantial amount of money. Here are some guidelines.

- Check out the newsletter's performance with the *Hulbert Financial Digest*. It is always possible that the advisor's performance may be a random event, as the random walkers charge. But better to have a successful random walker than an unsuccessful one.

- Do not accept performance claims at face value. Hyperbole seems to be an occupational hazard among investment newsletter writers. Misrepresentation of the *Hulbert Financial Digest* rankings is so bad that Hulbert frequently complains about it.[21]

- Has the adviser ever been successfully sued? It is hard to know this, but if you see a newspaper article about it, make it a point not to subscribe to that service.

- Does the investment strategy fit your personality and your circumstances? There is no point in starting a strategy that averages less than one round trip per year if your personality drives you to be more active than that. There is also no point in starting a strategy that requires 14 round trips per year if you are so overloaded with committee assignments and other work that you might forget to make the required trades on the required days.

- Since timing is risky, don't risk any more money than you can afford to lose.

- Remember that market environments change. A timing strategy that worked last year might not work in this year's environment.

- If the part of your portfolio you are going to expose to timing is large enough to justify the subscription costs, consider following two or three strategies. Perhaps one third could follow an interest rate strategy, another third a trend-following strategy, and the last third a valuation strategy or a seasonality strategy.

- Even when you find a market timer with a good record, it is useful to remember the advice of the random walkers. No matter how good this person's record, there is a precise statistical probability that somebody would have produced such a record. And in the last analysis there is no way to know for sure whether this person's record is an exhibit of superior skill or just a random occurrence. It seems unlikely that the feat of beating the market consistently over several different time frames for a long time could be simply a random statistical event. But it is always possible.

Notes

1. *Timer Digest*. P.O. Box 1688, Greenwich, Connecticut 06836-1688. (203) 629 3503.

2.   Mark Hulbert, ed., *The Hulbert Financial Guide to Investment News-letters* (Chicago, Ill.: Dearborn Financial Publishing, Inc., 1993).

3.   Martin Zweig, *Winning on Wall Street* (New York: Warner Books, 1990), chap. 7.

4.   Using a 200-day moving average to trade the Dow Jones Industrial Average during the 1980s would have kept you on the right side of the market trend up to the crash of October 1987, for example. See William A. Remaley, "Moving Averages as Market Timing Indicators," *AAII Journal* 9, no. 9 (October 1987): 11-14.

5.   Addresses for all the newsletters cited in this chapter can be found in Hulbert, *The Hulbert Guide to Financial Newsletters*.

6.   *The Hulbert Financial Digest*, January 1993, p. 3.

7.   *Chartist Mutual Fund Timer*, June 3, 1993, p. 3.

8.   Zweig, *Winning on Wall Street*, chap. 4.

9.   *The Hulbert Financial Digest*, January 1993, p. 3.

10.   For example, a slick promotional piece dated Fall 1992 claimed Donoghue will avoid market crashes and beat the Twentieth Century Growth mutual fund by 86 percent. While it might be true that Donoghue accomplished that in the past, he may or may not be able to avoid the next crash, and the odds against his beating the Twentieth Century Growth fund by precisely 86 percent verge on the infinite. See *Mutual Fund Report* (290 Eliot Street, Box 9104 Ashland, Mass. 01721-9104) (Fall 1992), p. 8.

11.   Mark Hulbert, "Lies and Near Lies," *Forbes*, September 30, 1991, p. 193.

12.   For instructions on calculating an exponential moving average, see Norman G. Fosback, *Stock Market Logic: A Sophisticated Approach to Profits on Wall Street* (Chicago: Dearborn Financial Publishing, Inc., 1992), pp. 142-43. The key component is a so-called smoothing factor, and different methods can be used to calculate it.

13.   "The Valueratio Asset Direction Program," *Growth Fund Guide, 1991*.

14. Ibid.

15. *The Hulbert Financial Digest*, January 1993, pp. 10-11.

16. Fosback, *Stock Market Logic*, pp. 154-63.

17. Ibid.

18. Yale Hirsch, *1994 Stock Trader's Almanac* (The Hirsch Organization, Inc.; Six Dear Trail, Old Tappan, New Jersey; 07675).

19. *The Hulbert Financial Digest*, July 1994, pp. 10-11.

20. Mark Hulbert, "Computer Tricks," *Forbes*, September 13, 1993.

21. Hulbert, "Lies and Near Lies," p. 193.

Chapter 11

Doing it Yourself:
A Test of Timing Mechanisms

Can do-it-yourselfers successfully modify for use with CREF the timing strategies discussed in Chapter 11? We want to explore this question for two reasons. First, if the timing strategies of the pros amount to anything other than random good luck, then they ought to be replicable by any conscientious person equipped with nothing more than a hand calculator and a little diligence.

The second reason for exploring this question is to empower those readers who may want to try timing but feel wary of putting their fate in the hands of professional market timers. This is a world loaded with high-priced newsletters, egocentric and charismatic pitch persons, occasional charlatans, esoteric timing schemes, secret trading formulae, and ubiquitous exaggerated claims. Many more professional timers get beaten by the market than in fact outperform it.

Trading Models

With these rationales as a basis, this chapter aims to test three of the four timing strategies examined in Chapter 11: the trend-following, interest rate, and seasonality models. Given what we know about the assumptions of these strategies, it is possible to develop specific timing models for each one and to back test them over the period of CREF's existence, from 1953 through 1992.

This forty-year time span covers a wide variety of conditions that affect equity markets. It covers bull markets, bear markets, sideways markets, wartime, peacetime, economic booms, economic recessions, periods of high interest rates, periods of low interest rates, periods of

185

high inflation, and periods of low inflation. It includes periods in which the White House was controlled by Democratic liberals as well as periods when it was controlled by Republican conservatives. By back testing the models over this time span, we should gain some insight into the performance of these models under many different market conditions.

Mechanics of the Trading Models

Each model will start on January 2, 1953 with $1,000 in cash that will be transferred into the S&P 500 index (as a proxy for CREF Stock) on buy signals and back into cash on sell signals. Since all transfers into and out of CREF take place at the closing price on the day you give CREF your instructions, all of the backtests will use closing prices of the S&P 500 on the day of the transaction. The impact of dividends and interest rates have been included in the calculations. Dividend rates are those of the S&P 500 index as reported weekly in the *Federal Reserve Bulletin*. Interest income is computed from the three month Treasury Bill rate, also reported weekly in the *Federal Reserve Bulletin*. However, starting in 1981, Donoghue's average money market rates became widely available, and since many more people buy money market funds than buy T-Bills, that rate is used instead of the T-Bill rate starting in 1981.

Trading Days Make a Big Difference

Some of the models developed here will trade on a weekly, rather than a daily, basis. This is not ideal. Logically, one would expect to have a better long term performance if one executed trades on the day the signals were generated rather than waiting for a weekly buy day or sell day. In fact, however, it does not always work out this way. Furthermore, a practical aspect of following a weekly system is absent from a daily system. No busy, career-minded person has the time to follow the markets on a daily basis and make the calculations needed to follow a timing model. However, if the calculations are not onerous, it is a simple matter to make them once a week and decide what transactions to make with CREF or your equity accounts the next day.

One of the first tasks in using a weekly model is to decide which days of the week to use for generating trading signals and for actually executing your transactions. The days you use for these purposes make a great deal of difference. Keep three days in mind: a day for determining signals, a day for buying, and a day for selling. Through a process of trial and error with the trend-following model, Friday was found to be the optimal signal day. Backtesting each day of the week as a signal date over different moving average strategies for the past twenty-two years, it was discovered that Friday signals consistently did better than signals on any other day.[1] Friday also has a practicality for most of us that no other signal day possesses. It gives you the entire weekend to make the mathematical calculations and decide what transactions you will make. Busy career people are too pressed for time to do these tasks on weekday mornings. But Saturday morning is another matter, and as an added bonus, doing your calculations on Saturday gives you an excuse to put off your weekend chores.

So Friday will be the signal day with the trend-following strategy. However, you cannot trade on the signal day, because you normally will not know if you have a buy or sell signal until the market is closed. The natural inclination is to conduct one's trading the following Monday. But this does not work very well, because Monday turns out to be the worst selling day of the week. In the analysis for 1970 through 1991, the stock market suffered more declines on Monday than on any other single day. (See Table 11-1) The market closes at its lowest point of the week more frequently on Mondays than on any other day. Other analysts looking at different time periods found the same pattern.[2]

Table 11-1   **Market Ups and Downs by Days of the Week: 1970-91**

	Mon	Tues	Wed	Thurs	Fri
No. of days up	540	541	631	579	563
No. of days down	582	505	478	531	524
Ratio of up days to down days	.93	1.05	1.32	1.09	1.07
Percent of time highest day of week	24.5	12.9	16.8	13.4	32.4
Percent of time lowest day of week	33.1	18.2	11.7	12.0	25.0

The very factors that make Monday a poor selling day, however, make it an excellent buying day, since they allow you to buy CREF Stock on average at the lowest closing price of the week. On the face of it, Tuesday would seem to have an advantage over Monday, because it has the second worst ratio of up days to down days. In addition, waiting until Tuesday would give you an extra day to see if the Friday buy signal was confirmed. But tests of Tuesday as the buying day did not find it any more likely to beat the buy-and-hold. Accordingly, our tests of the timing strategies make all their purchases at the closing price on the Monday following the buy signal.

Whereas Monday emerged as the best buying day, it is more difficult to settle on the best selling day. Mondays and Tuesdays can be easily eliminated because of the factors that make them the best buying days. But choosing among Wednesday, Thursday, or Friday as the selling day is less clear-cut. Of these days, Table 11-1 shows that Friday has a slight tendency to be the best closing day of the week. For this reason, all of the backtests used in this chapter will use Friday as the selling day.

In practice, even though Friday is the best selling day on average, it is psychologically difficult to wait for an entire week before taking action on a sell signal. This is especially the case if the market drops sharply. Thus, even though the backtests in this chapter conduct their selling on Fridays, the results would not have suffered greatly if sales had been done on Wednesdays or Thursdays instead. The important thing, as made clear in Table 11-1, is not to sell consistently on Mondays or Tuesdays.

A Caveat

In conducting these back tests it is important not to assume that future results will be the same as past results. Back testing essentially looks for patterns that worked best in the past. If one looks at enough patterns, inevitably a best-performing pattern will be found eventually. One could easily jump to the conclusion that this best performing pattern has an underlying causal relationship. This is especially true with the trend-following models.

The purpose of the backtesting is much more limited in scope. If, for example, only one moving average beats buying and holding the market over the long term, you would not have much confidence in that best-performing moving average. However, if several moving averages beat the market and they were all clustered together in similar time spans, this would increase one's confidence in the moving average as a means of identifying market trends. The same is true of the interest rate models. If only one interest rate model beats the market, one would be skeptical of it. However, if the discount rate model, the prime rate model and the money market rate model all beat the market, then this would increase one's confidence that interest rate model is a reasonable bet as a market timing instrument.

A Trend-following Approach

Chapter 10 described the use of moving averages to identify market trends. To review the steps in using a moving average, the example below shows how to construct a five-week moving average of the S&P 500. You simply add up the weekly closes of that index for the past five weeks and divide that number by five to get the five-week average. To update this next Friday, as seen in column 2, just add that week's closing S&P to the total, subtract the first week's closing number, and divide the

	Week 1	Week 2	Week 3
Weekly closes	448.65		
	447.95	447.95	
of the S&P 500	448.73	448.73	448.73
	453.41	453.41	453.41
Index	454.16	454.16	454.16
		455.22	455.22
			459.17
Previous total		2252.90	2259.47
Minus first week		-448.65	-447.95
Plus most recent week		+455.22	+459.17
New total	2252.90	2259.47	2270.69
Moving average	450.58	451.89	454.14

new total by five. The task is so simple that you do not even need a computer to crunch the numbers.

There are many ways to use moving averages. Some people use moving averages of two different markets and generate trading signals only if they appear in both markets.[3] Other people use two different moving averages on the same markets and use the points where those averages cross to indicate trading signals.[4] Still others use moving averages to construct oscillators that show overbought and oversold conditions in the trend.[5] Some analysts draw bands a few percentage points above and below a moving average. When the market moves above the upper band it means the market is ripe for a correction and when it moves below the lower band the market is ripe for a rally.[6] Still other strategists use moving averages of the advance-decline line instead of a market index.[7] And many purists insist that an exponential moving average should be used instead of a simple moving average.[8]

We believe that if a trend-following system is going to work, the strategy needs to be simple enough for you to use without transforming yourself into a statistician. Accordingly, we are going to test a model that uses a simple weekly moving average of the S&P 500 since 1952. Buy signals occur when the Friday S&P 500 index closes above the moving average and sell signals, when the index falls below the moving average.

We will backtest moving averages of different lengths to discover which ones give the best performance against a strategy that buys the S&P 500 on January 2, 1953, and holds it through the end of 1992. Such a buy-and-hold strategy in the S&P 500 with dividends reinvested monthly would have turned $1,000 into $76,886, for an average annual rate of return of 11.5 percent. This is slightly better than CREF Stock's 10.8 percent rate of return which would have turned $1,000 into approximately $60,500.

Before describing the back tests, it is important to stress that we should not expect too much from the results. As Norman Fosback wrote, "Some moving average lengths may have worked best in the past, but, after all, *something* had to work best in the past and by testing everything possible, how could one help but find it?"[9] Consequently, if just one optimal moving average stands out from all the others, one will have reason to be skeptical. However, if several moving averages beat a buy-and-hold approach, and most of those moving averages are bunched together in a small cluster of time frames, we will have better grounds for believing that a moving average approach to market timing is reasonable.

Backtesting the Model

Although logically there would seem to have been a single, optimal moving average over the past forty years, discovering that optimal moving average turned out to be a tedious task. Some strategists advocate a 26-week span for the moving average, others a 39-week, some a 42-week, and still others a 52-week span. We tested all of these strategies against a buy-and-hold approach on both a pure timing basis and a basis that reinvested dividends and interest payments.

In all, nineteen different moving averages were tested for the period 1953 through 1992. These averages ranged from 30 weeks to 65 weeks. Eight of them beat the buy-and-hold return of 11.5 percent per year when dividends and interest are taken into consideration. Eight moving averages also beat the buy-and-hold strategy on a pure timing basis without the reinvestment of dividends or interest. This suggests that the moving average is indeed a valuable tool for identifying long term market trends. Furthermore, most of the winning moving average strategies were clustered together. All but one were between 51 and 60 weeks, with the best results obtained from the 53-, 54-, and 55-week moving averages.

This forty year test is not totally relevant to most CREF participants, since few of us started our CREF programs in 1953 and even fewer of us retired on December 31, 1992. Further, the market was at an all-time high when these tests ended in December 1992, but it might not be at an all time high when you choose to retire.

Table 11-2 shows the results of following the 55-week moving average over five time frames: 1953 through 1959, 1960 through 1969, 1970 through 1979, 1980 through 1989, and 1990 through 1992. These decade-long time spans are lengthy enough to be relevant to one's retirement planning and yet short enough to give us some insight into when the system works well and when it does not.

Table 11-2 is worth exploring, because it sheds light on the advantages and pitfalls of the trend-following approach. What works well in one period does not necessarily work in other periods. Although the 55-week moving average beat the buy-and-hold over the long term, most of that performance came in the post-1970 period. Prior to 1970, the 55-

Table 11-2   A Test of the 55-Week Moving Average Over Different Time Spans

	1953-59	1960-69	1970-79	1980-89	1990-92
$1,000 grew to: (Annual Rate of Return in percent)					
With Dividends and Interest Reinvested					
Moving Average	2,787 (15.8)	1,866 (6.4)	**2,613** **(10.1)**	**7,851** **(22.9)**	**1,375** **(11.2)**
Buy-&-Hold	**3,068** **(17.4)**	**2,077** **(7.6)**	1,832 (6.2)	6,883 21.3	1,336 (10.1)
Pure Timing					
Moving Average	**2,330**	1,407	**1,617**	**4,694**	**1,233**
Buy & hold	2,257	**1,567**	1,160	4,120	1,211

Winning strategies shown in bold face.

week moving average consistently lagged the market, when dividends and interest are included in the calculations.

Table 11-2 points to two differences between the pre- and post-1970 periods. First, the relationship between interest rates and dividend yields changed. Until the 1960s T-bill rates never reached 5 percent and in fact remained under 3 percent most of the time. Yields, by contrast, never fell below 3 percent and reached as high as 5.55 percent, meaning that dividend yields exceeded the T-bill rate. During the 1953-59 period, the 55-week moving average led the buy-and-hold strategy on a pure timing basis, but it lagged it after dividends and interest were calculated. This indicates that part of the success of the moving average system is due to the interest that is earned during those periods when it is out of the market. When interest rates drop below the dividend yields by a percentage point or more, as they did prior to 1965, the trend-following model falls behind the buy-and-hold strategy.

Interest rates and yields do not fully explain why the moving average lagged the market prior to 1970, however. During the 1960s, the moving average model also lagged the buy-and-hold on a pure timing basis. This points to a second difference between the pre-1970 and the post-1970 periods: the market dynamics were different. Only one prolonged bear market occurred during the earlier period, and that took place from November 1968 to May 1970 when the S&P 500 dropped 36 percent in 18 months. The other market drops in this period were relatively short-lived. Short, rapid market changes greatly increase the likelihood of opportunity losses when one sells out and then has to buy back in at a higher price. During the pre-1970 period the moving average strategy suffered several whipsaws and opportunity losses. The later period, by contrast, saw fewer of such whipsaws. That same era also had four bear markets which lasted longer than a year and dropped nineteen percent or more. (1968-70 36.1 percent; 1973-74 48.2 percent; 1976-78 19.4%; 1980-82 27.1 percent).

Pitfalls of the Model

The lesson of Table 11-2 is complex. The 55-week moving average, as well as seven other moving averages, handily beat the buy-and-hold approach. Over long periods of time, the trend-following approach appears to be a superior investment strategy and a successful method of capital conservation. If you stayed with the system for at least two years, at no point would you have lost money. Nor did the 55-week moving average involve excessive transactions. There were 51 round trips (a purchase followed by a subsequent sale), of which two-thirds were profitable. Its worst losing round trip was only 5.1 percent and the median loss was 1.4 percent. The median winning round trip, by contrast, was 5.1 percent. Even its worst loss, the 5.1 percent loss in November 1973, came on an extremely timely sale. Over the next twelve months, the market dropped nearly 40 percent, and at the end of the subsequent transaction, the model was 45 percent higher than it was before the bear market started. The buy-and-hold strategy over this period increased barely 13 percent.

The trend-following model does have some important pitfalls, however. As Table 11-2 shows, it underperformed the market prior to 1970. There can be long periods of time when you underperform the market. You are not likely to lose money during these periods, but your returns might be mediocre compared to the market as a whole.

The second pitfall occurs during narrow trading ranges, which occur occasionally. Because the 55-week moving average is fairly long, it avoids many whipsaws that undercut shorter moving averages. But it cannot avoid all whipsaws. The longer that a trading range lasts, the more susceptible the moving average model is to costly whipsaws.

A third pitfall stems from the relationship between interest rates and dividend yields. When yields exceed money market rates, it is difficult for the moving average strategy, or any trend-following strategy, to outperform the market. This was especially true in the 1950s. During those years, the moving average model beat the market on a pure timing basis but fell behind when dividends and interest were factored in. Each time the model was in cash it earned less money from T-bills than the buy-and-hold model earned from dividends.

A fourth pitfall to remember is that the moving average strategies will not always protect you from sharp market declines. None of the strategies tested here, regardless of the signal day or selling day used, was able to exit the market before its infamous 22 percent drop in October 1987. It is conceivable that a daily moving average strategy would have gotten you out of the market before that infamous day. For reasons explained earlier, however, we have confined our tests to weekly moving averages. For a moving average strategy to have avoided the Black Monday drop of 22 percent would have required such a short moving average that whatever was saved on missing that horrendous drop would have been more than eaten up by losing trades and repeated whipsaws over the years.

The trend-following strategy also presents a fifth, psychological, pitfall. While it might make you a good deal richer than the people you meet at cocktail parties, it will not give you anything to brag about in the way of dramatic exits at the top of the market or entrances at the bottom. There were eleven market drops of 15 percent or more during these forty years,[10] and the median exit point of the timing model was 9.1 percent below the market top. This is not bad. But the model does not do as well at buying near the bottom. After the eleven bear markets, the model's median re-entry point was 18.1 percent above the market bottom.

A final pitfall of the timing strategy is also psychological. Because of its long time span, the 55-week moving average rides out many small corrections. During the forty years of this test, for example, the moving average model stayed in the market many times through market corrections of 8 or 10 percent. Only a person with extraordinary discipline could stick with the strategy consistently during those frequent times when the market is correcting during a buy signal phase.

The Advantages

Despite its pitfalls, the trend-following strategy also has important advantages. If you have the mental discipline to follow it for a long time period, it gives you a very good chance of outperforming the market. All but one of the moving averages from the fifty-one through the sixty-week range beat the market over the 40 years examined. Compared with the three-fourths of mutual funds and investment newsletters that consistently fail to outperform the market, the moving average strategy looks attractive. Even during the periods when the trend-following model failed to beat the buy-and-hold approach, it did not lag greatly behind the buy-and-hold, as Table 11-2 shows.

Another advantage of this strategy is its ease of use. On average, it involves barely one round trip per year. You can make your calculations within minutes on a weekend and telephone your instructions to CREF any time of day or night. If you use a touch-tone phone, you do not even have to talk to anybody about it.

The greatest advantage of the trend-following approach, however, is that it reduces the volatility of your equity assets as compared to the buy-and-hold strategy. Not counting the 1987 Black Monday drop, the largest reduction in capital was 13.6 percent. Following a buy-and-hold approach, your CREF Stock account would have dropped that much on seventeen different occasions, approximately once every two-and-one half years.

The trend-following approach achieved slightly better long-term results than the buy-and-hold strategy with considerably less volatility. It outperformed the buy-and-hold significantly during periods containing sustained bear markets such as those of 1969-70, 1973-74, and 1981-82. It also outperformed the buy-and-hold during periods of high interest rates. However, the trend-following model lagged the buy-and-hold during two kinds of markets: (1) extended bull markets in which market corrections, such as the one in 1987 were too short to take advantage of the long term moving average and (2) long periods of a narrow trading range that subjects the moving average to repeated whipsaws.

In sum, if you use the trend-following model, historical patterns suggest that you have a decent chance to lessen your portfolio volatility, beat the buy-and-hold strategy during periods that include at least one major sustained bear market, beat the market during periods of high interest rates, and outperform the buy-and-hold strategy over long periods of time. But you must be prepared to lag the buy-and-hold strategy during trading ranges and during long, sustained bull markets.

Interest Rate Approaches

Unlike the moving average model that follows trends, the interest rate models anticipate changes in trends. They are based on the assumption, as described in Chapter 10, that stock markets will perform poorly when short-term interest rates are rising and will perform well when those rates are falling. Three interest rate strategies were backtested for this chapter. The first and simplest was to buy the market when the Federal Reserve Board's discount rate went down after having previously gone up and to sell the market when the opposite occurred. The second model followed the same strategy but as a signal used the prime rate of major banks instead of the discount rate. Neither of these strategies produced much trading. The discount rate model resulted in thirteen round trips during the 40 year period, and the prime rate model twenty-one round trips. Historical data for both rates are published in the *Federal Reserve Bulletin*, and current changes are easy to track. Because they do not occur very often, they are inevitably headlined in the business section and often on the front pages. If you miss the changes during the week, when they are announced, you can check over the weekend in *Barron's* to see if any changes have occurred.

The third interest rate model tests the Donoghue strategy discussed in Chapter 10, except that these tests use a simple moving average rather than the exponential average used by Donoghue. A buy signal is triggered when the average money market rate falls below its moving average and a sell signal when it rises above its moving average.

All three models buy the market on the Monday following the signal and sell on the Friday following the signal. Discount rate and prime rate changes can occur any day of the week, and average money market rates are printed in the *Wall Street Journal* on Thursdays as well as in the weekend *Barron's*.

Backtesting the Interest Rate Models

Table 11-3 shows the results of backtesting these models. All three models beat the buy-and-hold as well as the trend-following strategies. Under the prime rate model and the 35 week moving average model turned an initial $1,000 was turned into $125,000 over the forty year period. Even the worst performing money market model outperformed the buy-and-hold strategy.

Table 11-3   Interest Rate Models: 1953-1992

Strategy	Initial Investment of $1,000 becomes:		Rate of Return	Number of Trades		
	$	$	%	Win	Lose	Total
Discount Rate Model	20,914	95,790	12.1	13	0	13
Prime Rate Model	26,519	124,910	12.8	19	2	21
Money Market Models						
35 week (best)	22,055	125,076	12.8	42	6	48
45 week (median)	18,566	98,938	12.2	37	4	41
65 week (worst)	16,060	80,731	11.6	19	4	23
Benchmarks						
Buy-and-hold	16,417	76,886	11.5			
55-week Moving Average	17,938	86,548	11.8	34	17	51

Pitfalls of the Model

The first pitfall of the interest rate model is that the stock market frequently declines or undergoes a correction even though the interest rate environment is favorable. When this happens, the model is forced to ride out some hefty stock market corrections. The prime rate model rode out five corrections of ten percent or more including one drop of 28 percent and another of 19 percent.

The second pitfall of the interest rate model is that it sometimes keeps you on the sidelines during a market advance. The most dramatic example of this occurred in the wake of the 1987 bear market. On the positive side, the discount rate model exited the market well before the October 19 Black Monday drop of 22 percent and it eventually got back into the market at about the point where it exited. In the meantime, however, it stayed out of the market from December 1987 through September 1989 while the market advanced 60 percent. The prime rate model also missed about half of that market increase.

Advantages of the Interest Rate Model

Balanced against these pitfalls are some very important advantages of the interest rate models. All three interest rate models outperformed both the trend-following model and the buy-and-hold model. There appears to be little risk of loss in following either the discount rate or prime rate model, since the discount rate model produced no losing trades and the prime rate model produced only two losing trades out of twenty-one total trades. The larger of these was, however, a hefty 6.8 percent, and both models forced you to ride out significant market corrections.

The second advantage of the interest rate models is an important one. They tend to avoid many of the whipsaws that plague the trend-following approach. For example, there was a prolonged period of nearly three years, from August 1977 through May 1980, when the discount rate and prime rate models stayed out of a market that traded within a fairly narrow range of just 36 percent. During that same period of time, the trend-following model experienced eight round trips of which five were direct losses and six were opportunity losses in which the subsequent purchase was higher than the previous sale.

In sum, based on historical patterns, all three of the interest rate models performed well. They offer decent probabilities of outperforming the market both in the intermediate term and the long term. They reduce your portfolio volatility more than the buy-and-hold approach, but not as much as the trend-following approach. Negatively, however, you run the risk of repeated periods of frustration when the model either forces you to ride out a bear market or fails to get you back into a bull market.

Seasonality Models

A third market timing model is the seasonality model. Norman Fosback, as described in Chapter 10, constructed a seasonality strategy for trading mutual funds. His strategy produced one of the best performing portfolios tracked by the *Hulbert Financial Digest*, beating the market in most of the time frames since Hulbert began following it. Can Fosback's seasonality system be utilized with the S&P 500 as a proxy for CREF? And, since this chapter demonstrated earlier that the 55-week moving average model can be enhanced by making purchases on Monday and sales on Friday, will this Monday-Friday trading sequence enhance the seasonality model as well?

Our tests of the straight seasonality system follows Fosback's rules as they were outlined in Chapter 10 (p. 176). For our enhanced model we will adapt the seasonality trading rules as follows.

- Buy on the Monday before the third to last trading day of the month, or on that day if it is a Monday.

- Sell on the Friday after the fifth trading day of the month, or on that day if it is a Friday.

- Buy on the Monday before a holiday closing of the market.

- Sell on the day before the holiday closing or on the day after the closing if it is a Friday.

- Do not sell on any Friday if the following Monday is scheduled to be a purchase day.

Table 11-4   **A Test of the Seasonality Models**

Strategy	Initial Investment of $1,000 becomes:		Rate of Return	Number of Trades		
	$	$	%	Win	Lose	Total
Straight Seasonality	28,726	217,553	14.4	415	176	194
Enhanced Seasonality	73,893	514,101	16.9	344	140	484
Benchmarks						
Buy-and-hold	16,417	76,886	11.5			
55-week Moving Average	17,938	86,548	11.8	34	17	54
Prime Rate model	26,519	124,910	12.8	19	2	21
Money Market 35 week model	22,055	125,076	12.8	42	6	48

- In following the holiday rules, do not buy if the impact of the trades would be to keep you in the market for the entire month. This may occur with President's Day and Good Friday.

The necessary result of this enhancement of the seasonality system is to increase the amount of time spent in the market and consequently increase your market risk. Counterbalanced against this, however, is a significant reduction in the number of trades you need to make.

Backtesting the Seasonality Models

Table 11-4 shows that both the straight seasonality model and the enhanced seasonality model beat the previous bench marks by a sizable margin. The enhanced seasonality model added 2.5 percentage points to the annual rate of return of the model, giving it an annual rate of return nearly 50 percent greater than the straight buy-and-hold.

Pitfalls

The seasonality model also has several pitfalls. If you are trading this model with any substantial amounts of money (one-third of your assets, for example), it is difficult to put that money at risk just because the calendar has turned to the last Monday of the month. If you are in a strong bull market, it is also difficult to sell just because it is the first or second Friday of the month. Even though this model produced superior results over the past forty years, the mind nevertheless rebels at using it because it lacks a convincing, logical rationale.

The model is also difficult to implement because of the large number of trades that it requires--almost fifteen per year following the straight seasonality model. It is easy to miss trading dates with this system. Even though you can call CREF's toll free number any time of day or night, it is very easy to forget to do so or to find yourself in a position where it is inconvenient. You may have forgotten to place your transaction Thursday evening and find yourself in meetings all Friday afternoon.

In theory this model would work even better with high-relative strength mutual funds than it would with CREF. But no-load mutual fund families or discount brokers might resist making the necessary twenty-five to thirty transactions per year without a transaction fee.

Finally, unless this model were being applied in a tax deferred account, it would pose a cumbersome tax problem. The more trades you make in a taxable account, the more complicated your income tax return becomes. And the inability to defer taxes on your winning transactions eats into the performance you will gain from the model.

Advantages of the Model

Despite these pitfalls, the seasonality models offer two important advantages. First, they offer the possibility of superior performance. Second, they lessen your portfolio volatility below that of any of the other models. The biggest decline in market value of the model was eight percent in 1987.

Combining the Models

None of the systems works perfectly, and following any one of them exposes you to considerable market risk in event it fails to give you a good exit point or entry point. The trend-following model, as seen, not only failed to avoid the 1987 Black Monday drop of 22 percent but it also did not move investors back into the market until their re-entry point was considerably higher than their exit point had been. The interest rate model rode out a drop of 28 percent in 1962. To date the seasonality model has suffered no more than an 8 percent loss, but nothing guarantees that the next Black Monday will take place in the middle of the month, rather than at month's end when the seasonality system would have you fully invested.

Prudence, then, would dictate that you combine the three models. The simplest approach is the tripartite model which divides your timing portfolio into three groups. The first group invests in a trend-following strategy, the second group in an interest rate strategy, and the last group in the enhanced seasonality strategy. This amalgam approach would have roughly averaged out the returns you would have gotten from each of the three approaches.

A second and slightly more complicated approach would be to combine the multiple strategies in the same model. There are several different ways that this might be done, and Table 11-5 explores three of them. The first way follows the 55-week moving average strategy when it is on a buy signal and shifts to the enhanced seasonality model when the moving average model generates a sell signal. This model compounds an original $1,000 to $260,756 over the forty years. The second way follows the same approach but uses the prime rate model instead of the moving average. It grows to $247,598. The third, and most successful, way to integrate the models is to follow the same strategy but using the discount rate model. This approach grows to $617,404 for a 17.4 percent annual rate of return. This is an extraordinary achievement over a period as long as forty years. It would take a rare money manager or mutual fund to have surpassed this growth.

Pitfalls of the Combination Model

The major pitfall of the combination model is that it is more complicated than any of the others. Being more complicated, it is easy to miss trades that should have been made. There also is no guarantee that the seasonality model will continue to avoid the worst periods in future bear markets as it has over the past 40 years.

Advantages of the Combination Model

It is unlikely that the model's superior performance over the past forty years occurred totally by accident or at random. During the time you are following the seasonality portion of the combination model, you will incur a fair number of losing trades, but if historical patterns hold for the future, you are unlikely to suffer a major erosion of capital. Because you use the seasonality model in the late stages of the bear market, you begin moving into the new bull market earlier than you would if you followed the trend-following model, and possibly earlier than if you followed an interest rate model. You also do not run the risk of entirely missing a bull market as you would with a pure interest rate model. Finally, although this combination model has a large number of trades, it has only 40 percent of the trades of the straight seasonality model.

Why did the combined seasonality-discount rate model work so well? Negatively, we could charge that it simply exemplifies the principle that if you test enough combinations of mechanical trading rules, you will eventually come up with the best performing set of rules. This criticism would be plausible, over a short time span. But it loses plausibility when we consider that this combination beat the buy-and-hold strategy over a forty-year period and in all the individual decades within those forty years. Each of the individual components of the combination model also beat the buy-and-hold, so it is not unreasonable that the combined model would also beat the buy-and-hold.

A more plausible response is that these models have indeed tapped into some recurring market patterns. Recognizing that the discount rate model keeps you in cash during a portion of bull markets, the seasonality approach enables you to minimize those portions. This is especially the case during bear market recoveries and during those periods when the discount rate model rides through a bear market. During these periods, the seasonality model adds value to the discount rate model. On the other hand, it is very difficult for the seasonality system by itself to beat the buy-and-hold during a strong bull market. During these periods the discount rate model adds value to the seasonality strategy by keeping you

Table 11-5   **Combining the Timing Approaches**

Strategy	Initial Investment of $1,000 becomes:		Rate of Return	Number of Trades		
	$	$	%	Win	Lose	Total
Enhanced seasonality and the discount rate	121,479	617,404	17.4	188	78	266
Enhanced seasonality and the 55-week average	63,321	260,756	14.9			
Enhanced seasonality and the prime rate	54,494	247,598	14.8			
Benchmarks						
Buy-and-hold	16,417	76,886	11.5			
55-week Moving Average	17,938	86,548	11.8	34	17	54
Prime Rate model	26,519	124,910	12.8	19	2	21
Money Market 35 week model	22,055	125,076	12.8	42	6	48
Straight seasonality	28,726	217,553	14.4	415	176	194
Enhanced seasonality	73,893	514,101	16.9	344	140	484

fully invested in the market for a longer period of time. It also adds value to the seasonality model by reducing the number of trades. And it is probably the small number of transactions that enables the discount rate model to add value to the seasonality model in a way in which the more frequently trading prime rate model or moving average models fail to add value. For these reasons, combining the discount rate model with the seasonality model makes for a potent combination. Whether this combination will be as potent in the future as it was in the past, of course, is the important issue.

Conclusion

In summary, based on backtests since 1953, there is reason to believe that a timing strategy based on the moving average, interest rate, or seasonality systems will outperform the buy-and-hold strategy over the long run and the intermediate term. The risk associated with trying to time the market can be reduced by dividing your timing portfolio into thirds and applying one of the three models to each third. It seems unlikely that all three models would suffer extensive losses at the same time. It is also possible that your overall returns can be bolstered by combining the enhanced seasonality model with the discount rate model.

No doubt other timing strategies will outperform the ones reviewed here, but these models have several advantages for the individual TIAA-CREF participant. They are economical; do not require a $300 subscription to a newsletter or frequent hot line telephone calls; are easy to use; and are adaptable to CREF as well as mutual fund families, index funds, and no-load funds through discount brokers. If you are really venturesome, you can even trade the futures indexes with margin.

Finally, it is important to remember that market timing is inherently more risky than a more traditional diversification of your holdings through asset allocation. The random walkers might be correct. The past patterns we've found here might merely be random and accidental patterns with no predictive power. The next twenty or forty years may be totally unlike the previous years, in which case the market strategies of the past may no longer work.

Notes

1.   John J. Harrigan, "Finding the Optimal Moving Average Strategy," *AAII Journal* 14, no. 1 (January 1992): 9-15.

2.   Yale Hirsch, *1993 Stock Trader's Almanac* (Old Tappan, N. J.: The Hirsch Organization, 1992), pp. 118-19. Another study examined Over the Counter prices from 1983 through 1989 and found Thursday and Friday to be optimal selling dates. Monday, Tuesday, or Wednesday

were found to be optimal buying dates. Richard D. Fortrin and O. Maurice Joy, "Buying and Selling OTC Stocks: Fine-Tuning Your Trade Date," *AAII Journal* 15, no. 3 (March 1993): 8-10.

3. This appears to be the strategy followed by the *Chartist Mutual Fund Timer* that we examined in Chapter 10.

4. See Curtis M. Arnold and Dan Rahfeldt, *Timing the Market: How to Profit in Bull and Bear Markets With Technical Analysis* (Chicago: Probus Publishing, 1986), pp. 70-71.

5. An oscillator fluctuates between two numbers, a plus 1 and a minus 1, for example. Typically, an overbought condition is signaled when the indicator moves toward plus 1 and an oversold condition when it moves toward minus one. The most famous oscillator is probably the McClellan Oscillator, which is shown several times an hour on the CNBC ticker tape. For a description, see Arnold and Rahfeldt, *Timing the Market*, pp. 92-93.

6. See *John Bollinger's Capital Growth Letter*, Manhattan Beach, California. Bollinger uses standard deviations instead of percentages.

7. Edward P. Nicoski, "A Fresh Look at Old Lore," *AAII Journal* 9, no. 5 (May 1987): 22-24.

8. Norman G. Fosback, *Stock Market Logic* (Dearborn: Financial Publishing, Inc., 1992), pp. 139-143.

9. Ibid., p. 145.

10. Two of these was 15 percent only if the numbers were rounded. These were the January to September 1953 drop of 14.8 percent and the August 1956 to February 1957 drop of 14.8 percent.

Chapter 12

Should You Transfer Out of TIAA-CREF?

The last several chapters have examined capital management strategies such as asset allocation and market timing for which TIAA-CREF may or may not be the ideal vehicle. On the plus side, SRA accounts and CREF funds in RA accounts work very nicely for asset allocation and market timing strategies, because you can transfer funds between accounts with a simple telephone call at no cost. These funds also have very low expense ratios, respectable performance records, and the absence of commission costs, 12(b)-1 charges, and redemption fees that are popular among mutual funds.

Balanced against these positive features, however, is the fact that TIAA in your RA accounts has too rigid of a withdrawal policy to make it optimally useful for either asset allocation or market timing. If you annuitize upon retirement you are frozen into the asset mix you choose at that particular moment regardless of whatever changes occur in the rest of your life. And during your early career years of capital accumulation, CREF does not offer a small company stock fund, an aggressive capital appreciation fund, or several other types of funds that are easily obtainable from mutual fund families and that would be admirable vehicles for dollar cost averaging strategies.

Until 1990, most TIAA-CREF participants had no option other than TIAA-CREF as their main retirement vehicle. Fewer than 600 colleges permitted their employees any other choice.[1] This changed in 1990 because of an agreement between TIAA-CREF and the Securities and Exchange Commission that let colleges offer their employees other retirement accumulation vehicles in addition to TIAA-CREF. Many of these college employees are now being approached by a growing army of financial planners and sales representatives who are more than happy to point out the limitations of TIAA-CREF. The salesperson pushes some combination of load or no-load mutual funds that he or she promises will outperform CREF at less cost to the individual.

How does one evaluate these pitches? How do you fit TIAA-CREF into a systematic retirement plan? Should you consider switching some or all of your TIAA-CREF holdings to an independent financial adviser? One way to approach these questions is to take a deeper look at the advantages and drawbacks of TIAA-CREF for the individual and develop a set of guidelines for assessing the options. This chapter proposes some ideas for doing this.

Advantages of TIAA-CREF

When confronted by a financial adviser, it is important to remember that TIAA-CREF has some very important advantages that your adviser might or might not be able to duplicate. The most important of these concern historical performance, expenses, annuitization, services, and ease of timing.

Historical Performance

Over the long term, CREF Stock has roughly tracked the performance of the overall U.S. markets. The Money Market account has historically carried a better yield than the average money market fund. And the other CREF accounts have also performed credibly in comparison to comparable types of mutual funds. In using historical performance data to make judgments about CREF's record, the critical account to examine is CREF Stock, since its records go back to 1952.

Can the CREF Stock account's long term performance be beaten? Yes, but doing so is not as easy as it looks. The first argument sales representatives make is that CREF's long term performance can be beaten by switching into a mixture of no-load mutual funds or stocks selected by the adviser. How likely is this?

Not very, suggest Tables 12-1 and 12-2. Table 12-1 compares the CREF Stock fund with the S&P 500 Index over ten-year periods extending from 1970 to 1993. CREF lagged the S&P 500 in the ten year periods up to 1985, outperformed the S&P for the balance of the 1980s, and then lagged the S&P after 1990. Since the early 1980s, however, there

Table 12-1   CREF Stock Performance Compared to the S&P 500 Index

| Period | Annual rate of return | | $1,000 grows to: | |
	CREF	S&P	CREF	S&P
1970-79	3.8%	5.8%	1,451	**1,759**
1971-80	6.6	8.4	1,898	**2,241**
1972-81	4.5	6.4	1,556	**1,865**
1973-82	4.9	6.7	1,619	**1,906**
1974-83	9.5	10.6	2,475	**2,740**
1975-84	14.1	14.7	3,752	**3,958**
1976-85	14.2	14.3	3,770	**3,798**
1977-86	14.2	13.8	**3,789**	3,644
1978-87	15.6	15.3	**4,258**	4,134
1979-88	16.5	16.3	**4,602**	4,522
1980-89	17.7	17.5	**5,084**	5,017
1981-90	14.3	13.9	**3,794**	3,667
1982-91	17.5	17.5	5,008	**5,030**
1983-92	15.9	16.1	4,369	**4,453**
1984-93	14.8	14.9	3,978	**3,994**

Source: CREF data are from *Charting TIAA and the CREF Accounts: Winter 1993-1994* (New York: TIAA-CREF, 1993), p. 38. S&P 500 results are calculated from publicly available data and are compounded monthly. The better performing indicator is shown in boldface.

have been only minor differences between the results of CREF and the S&P. For all practical purposes, CREF's performance mirrored that of the S&P 500. This is not surprising, because two-thirds of CREF's portfolio was indexed to the S&P 500 over much of this time frame.

Table 12-2 shows how difficult it was for professional investors to keep up with CREF and the S&P over this period. According to *Forbes* magazine's 1992 mutual fund survey, three-fourths of professionally managed mutual funds failed to match the S&P's performance over the previous ten years. Past patterns may well not continue, but in recent history, the person who transferred his or her CREF account to a randomly selected mutual fund stood a three to one chance of doing worse than CREF, not better.

Not a fair comparison, the financial planner will charge. Most mutual funds are not designed to beat the overall market, and the planner will claim, "I won't choose your mutual funds randomly. I will select the ones that do in fact beat the market over time." Unfortunately, no comprehensive statistics compare the abilities of financial advisers to beat the market and to beat it with less risk. But the *Hulbert Financial Digest* has collected extensive data on the category of investment advisers that write investment newsletters. As Table 12-2 indicates, the performance of the typical newsletter writer does not appear to be any better than that of the typical mutual fund manager. Whether one examines *all* investment newsletter portfolios or just those specializing in mutual funds, it is evident from Table 12-2 that the record of most is dismal. Most newsletter portfolios fail to beat the market, and the record for mutual fund newsletters is worse than that of newsletters in general. Considering that a mutual fund package is the most likely vehicle that your financial planner will use for the funds you transfer out of CREF, these data are sobering.

CREF's performance can be topped. About a fourth of mutual fund managers and investment newsletters have consistently beaten CREF over time, with some beating it by a substantial margin. A good investment adviser might also be able to beat CREF Stock with funds that are less risky. Before you switch to another vehicle solely on the basis of promised performance, however, examine the long term record of the mutual fund family or the investment adviser under consideration.

Low Expenses

If the individual investor is greatly concerned about expenses, it is hard to see how CREF's expense ratio is going to be beaten. The CREF Stock Account in 1991 had 36 cents of expenses for every one hundred dollars invested; the comparable figure for the typical mutual fund in the

Table 12-2   Mutual Fund and Newsletter Writer Performance

The Percent of mutual funds or investment advisers that beat the S&P 500's 14.1 percent annual rate of return for the period November 1980 through June 1992.

Stock mutual funds	25.3
Balanced mutual funds	25.0
Investment newsletter stock portfolios	
1988 through 1992 (5 years)	27.3
1990 through 1992 (3 years)	37.6
Investment newsletter mutual fund portfolios	
1988 through 1992 (5 years)	10.5
1990 through 1992 (3 years)	26.0

Mutual fund results are tabulated from *Forbes*, August 31, 1992. p. 123. Annual Survey of Mutual Funds. Investment newsletter results are calculated from "Long Term Performance Ratings: Model Portfolios," *The Hulbert Financial Digest* (January 1993): 2.

Forbes annual survey was $1.27, and only 9 of the 1836 funds surveyed had an expense ratio lower than CREF's 36 cents.[2] Furthermore, CREF has no sales charge, no redemption fees, no annual account maintenance fees, and no 12b-1 charges to cover marketing costs that are typical of many no-load mutual funds.

In buying mutual funds for the long term, you especially want to watch for the expense ratio of the fund and the existence of any 12b-1 charges. The 12b-1 charge is usually used by the mutual fund to reimburse sales representatives, and thus is little more than a hidden load. Expense ratios are listed in the fund prospectus and in many of the magazines and publications that rate mutual funds. If CREF has an annual expense ratio of .36 percent and you are considering the purchase of a fund whose expense ratio is 1.36 percent, that fund's investments have to outperform CREF's investments by one percent per year on a long term basis to make you more money.

The individual investor who relies on a financial planner or investment adviser to select and monitor his or her portfolio will, naturally, have to pay additional fees for those services. The issue boils down to one of whether value is added. If the financial planner or the mutual fund adds value to your investments above and beyond CREF's returns while keeping you at the same risk level, then the advice is well worth paying for. If not, then you might as well stick with CREF.

Some TIAA-CREF participants have expressed frustration at the sizable TIAA-CREF bureaucracy that has to be paid for and the fact that TIAA-CREF executives draw very high salaries. Considering that two-thirds of the CREF Stock fund portfolio involves no investment decisions whatsoever, since it is indexed to the overall U.S. market, complaints about the high salaries may have some justification. However, it is unlikely that the executives of the mutual funds you buy are going to be paid any less than those at TIAA-CREF. At the bottom line, CREF's expenses compare very favorably with typical mutual funds.

Annuitization

TIAA-CREF also allows you to annuitize your holdings once you retire. This is the process of distributing a population's retirement assets into monthly payments at a rate based on the life expectancy of all the people in the population. If you transfer your TIAA-CREF assets to a mutual fund family and you underestimate how long you are going to live when you begin making your withdrawals, you may well outlive your retirement fund. To TIAA-CREF, however, it does not matter how long any specific annuitant lives, since the annuities are based on the collective life expectancy of the entire population of annuitants. For this reason, TIAA-CREF can confidently issue an annuity that will always assure you an income that you cannot outlive. If you set up your own annuitized program based on your personal investments, you have to assume that you or your spouse will live for a very long time--perhaps to 90 or 100--just to be sure. Obviously, the longer you plan to live, the less annual income you will be able to withdraw from your retirement accounts.

Annuitization is not the only way to take your withdrawals out of TIAA-CREF, however, and for many people, it might not even be the best way. Chapters 13 and 14 examine the pros and cons of annuitization. If you do decide to annuitize, TIAA-CREF is a very good vehicle. It offers monthly annuitization income that compares favorably with other large insurance companies.

TIAA-CREF Services

For its relatively meager administrative costs, TIAA-CREF provides a wide array of services: unlimited telephone transfers between CREF accounts, a staff of knowledgeable people ready and willing to answer questions, calculations of how much can be contributed to SRAs, representatives who travel to campuses to explain TIAA-CREF products and options, and a plethora of publications of varying quality. TIAA-CREF also has full time retirement counselors who can give individual help to people as they enter retirement and are forced to make difficult choices from a complicated array of annuity options.

These services are also available from financial planners and financial institutions such as banks and mutual funds. The Stein Roe mutual fund family, for example, establishes an asset allocation service that gives each client a personal representative to give advice on his or her personal asset allocation strategy. You receive a monthly statement showing how your portfolio has done since it was started, since the year began, and over the previous twelve months.[3] Although Stein Roe does not charge a fee for this service, most other financial institutions do. The T. Rowe Price mutual fund family will give you software for your personal computer that you can use to estimate your financial needs in retirement.[4] Individual financial planners will also help you estimate your retirement needs, tailor their advice to your specific goals, and be happy to help you invest your retirement funds.

One key characteristic about TIAA-CREF services, however, makes them different from the services you are offered by the average financial planner or mutual fund family. The TIAA-CREF retirement counselors you meet are not sales representatives. They are not totally disinterested observers, since they are certainly not going to recommend that you transfer out of CREF, and most of their pre-retirement advice is going to focus on simply annuitizing your accounts. They are not likely to stress other ways of withdrawing your TIAA-CREF accumulations, even if you might be better served by not annuitizing. Nevertheless, they do not earn a commission or a fee from your investment decisions, which makes them fundamentally different from financial planners or mutual fund sales representatives.

Each participant must decide for him or herself whether this is an advantage. Like some participants, you might prefer the idea of receiving advice from TIAA-CREF counselors who have no financial stake in the decisions you make. Or, like others, you might prefer receiving advice from an adviser who stands to benefit if your accounts grow and prosper.

A second key difference between TIAA-CREF counselors and financial advisers is that the TIAA-CREF counselors are much more oriented toward educating you rather than making decisions for you. People who sign up for personal counseling sessions with TIAA-CREF representatives frequently come away saying that the representatives are very helpful at clarifying issues and explaining conditions under which one strategy makes more sense than another. But the representatives usually stop short of actually urging you to take a specific course of action.

Again, this may or may not be an advantage. Whether you get more from TIAA-CREF counseling services or those of an individual financial planner may depend on your own personal style. If you are independently minded about your finances, TIAA-CREF's educational style of counseling may be more comfortable. On the other hand, if you are so strongly focused on your career and personal life that you do not want to invest a lot of energy into finances, then you might be well advised to seek out a good financial planner who will give you advice or even make your investment decisions for you.

In the last analysis, TIAA-CREF provides its participants with a valuable array of services. Before cutting ties with TIAA-CREF it would be useful to ensure that comparable services are offered by whatever planner or financial institution you are going to use.

Ease of Adjusting to Market Changes

It is unlikely that many CREF participants systematically try to move into and out of the CREF funds with changes in the market cycle. For those who do, however, CREF is a suitable vehicle. You can move into and out of CREF funds with a single telephone call. With a touch tone phone you do not even have to talk to anybody. You just need to push the right buttons. There are no fees for such transfers or any limits to the number of such transfers. Most investment analysts advise against trying to time the market in this fashion, but if you are determined to try market timing, you can probably do it easier through CREF than through the average mutual fund.

Drawbacks to TIAA-CREF

Balanced against these advantages are a number of drawbacks to concentrating your retirement assets in TIAA-CREF. The most important of these involve the rigidity of TIAA, the difficult of asset allocation, and the potential vulnerability of CREF's indexing to changing market conditions.

TIAA Rigidity

Perhaps the biggest drawback of TIAA-CREF is the rigidity of TIAA, as discussed in Chapter 4. Having a fair portion of one's retirement dollars in fixed income assets makes sense during the retirement years. However, young people in their early careers can look forward to many years of growth from the equity markets and have the time to ride out periodic bear markets. Nor did it make much sense to have huge sums of money tied up in TIAA during the great bull market of the 1980s when, as Table 12-1 (p. 209) shows, CREF quintupled your money. Until recently, money invested in TIAA's fixed annuities was stuck there forever. Even today, you can transfer only 10 percent of TIAA holdings per year to CREF in your RA account. As recommended earlier, TIAA should adopt a Plan B fund that would permit unlimited transfers.

Like everything else in the financial world, this rigidity of TIAA is a two-edged sword. Extremely cautious investors might take comfort in the fact that the difficulties of cashing out of TIAA protects TIAA from a rash of redemptions.[5] This in turn gives TIAA great staying power to wait out the periods when real estate prices sag and bond prices decline. Aggressive investors, however, might be frustrated by this long wait.

Difficulty of Asset Allocation

A second major drawback of CREF is that it is not an optimal vehicle for strategic asset allocation as discussed in Chapter 8. Several roadblocks hinder the use of TIAA-CREF in a systematic asset allocation plan. For example, few TIAA-CREF funds are distinct enough to fit neatly into most asset allocation categories. CREF will not permit you to use its Bond fund once you retire and begin your retirement annuity. This violates a fundamental principal of asset allocation, since almost all financial planners advise that bonds be included in a person's retirement portfolio.

Bonds, of course, are included in the Social Choice fund which is available for annuitization. But, as Chapter 8 showed, it takes a fair amount of mathematical computation to calculate how they fit into one's asset allocation system.

In theory, TIAA could be substituted for bonds in the allocation scheme, since it is a fixed asset investment and it does not have the volatility of the Bond fund. The cumbersome restrictions that TIAA imposes on transfers become a huge problem when it comes time to rebalance after one category of assets has dramatically out-performed or under-performed the others. One can certainly allocate assets between TIAA and the seven CREF funds, but figuring out how these funds break down into asset categories demands a fair amount of spreadsheet wizardry. As showed in Chapter 8, allocating assets effectively almost requires using TIAA/CREF in tandem with some mutual fund family.

Although you could use a mutual fund family in tandem with TIAA-CREF to implement an asset allocation strategy, this poses the logical question whether one might not just as well transfer out of CREF to a mutual fund family. The bottom line is that TIAA-CREF does not facilitate systematic asset allocation.

Vulnerability of Indexing

While it is not possible to know what CREF's future performance will be like, CREF participants should understand the implications of CREF's investment philosophy. The CREF Stock fund has outperformed three-quarters of mutual funds over the past decade in no small measure because of the indexation of two-thirds of its portfolio to the overall U.S. markets, and the earmarking of another one-seventh to foreign stocks. The sustained bull market of the 1980s was one of the most lucrative periods in stock market history. As Table 12-1 shows, CREF averaged 17.7 percent per year during that decade, compared to an historical return of about 10.9 percent per year. When the market eventually reverts to its mean or goes to an extreme in the other direction, some financial analysts fear that indexed portfolios will underperform the market.[6] Professional money managers tend to dump stocks like hot potatoes when bear markets erupt. There is no reason to think that they will behave differently the next time around. With its $55 billion portfolio, the CREF Stock fund is too big and unwieldy to shift with market sentiment.

No one can predict the future, but CREF's size and its reliance on indexation would seem to make it do better relative to the S&P in prolonged bull markets (1982-87) than in bear markets (1973-74) or sideways markets (1976-78). If the bull market continues over the next decade, the CREF Stock fund should do well. If foreign stock markets outperform American markets and the dollar weakens in relation to other currencies, CREF's international exposure will give it a boost. But if the great bull market is nearing its end, then individuals who construct a portfolio based on the principles of asset allocation will most likely do better than individuals whose portfolios are indexed to the overall U.S. market.

Some Guidelines

Given these advantages and drawbacks of TIAA-CREF, how does the typical person decide whether to stay or to switch? Although each person must evaluate the stay-or-switch decision in light of his or her own situation, some guidelines might help clarify those situations.

- People fifteen or more years from retirement should begin transferring from TIAA to CREF. A division of your assets among the seven CREF funds will probably outperform TIAA at only a moderately greater risk. You can always transfer your CREF funds back to TIAA at retirement if you want TIAA's fixed annuity.

- CREF holdings should be viewed in the context of one's total retirement assets. Given the importance that financial research currently attributes to asset allocation, prevailing financial wisdom would have you divide your holdings among at least three or four different asset classes that do not move in tandem with each other. If you have no retirement assets outside of TIAA-CREF, it would make sense to transfer a portion of your CREF account to another carrier, just in case CREF's investment style fails to work as well in the balance of the 1990s as it worked in the 1980s.

- If you choose to put your money into a mutual fund family, it should be a no-load family or at least a low-load family with no annual maintenance fees or redemption charges. The funds should also have reasonably low administrative expenses, permit telephone switches between accounts, have a variety of funds, and be free of a 12b-1 charge. The funds should have distinct investment philosophies that you can understand, and several funds in this family should also have excellent historical performance records.

- If your own investment record is superior CREF's, and if your circumstances are such that CREF will permit it, consider transferring a portion of your CREF funds into a self-directed IRA or better yet a 403-(b) account with a discount brokerage house. This can usually be done when you leave an employer with whom you made CREF contributions.

- As you approach the retirement years, you will want to investigate whether a systematic cash withdrawal or a variable annuity is better for you. TIAA-CREF offers a competitive annuity in comparison to other life insurance companies. If you opt for a cash withdrawal plan, most mutual funds would make it easier for you to set up a systematic program of cash withdrawals.

- As you advance into your retirement years, it is also important to remember that you will eventually reach a point where you lack the energy to manage your own investments. There may then be an advantage to having your retirement funds managed by a non-profit organization such as TIAA-CREF rather than a profit-seeking organization.

- Staying or switching is not an all-or-nothing decision. You could switch part of your CREF portfolio to another vehicle and compare the performance of the two over time. If you become displeased with that the results of that experiment, you can later on transfer eligible funds back into TIAA-CREF.

- At some point you will probably also consider contracting with a financial planner to guide you through these many decisions. Chapter 13 gives some tips on selecting a financial planner.

Notes

1. Maggie Maher, "Still in an Ivory Tower," *Barron's*, October 15, 1990, p. 16.

2. See Jason Zweig and Mary Beth Grover, "Fee Madness," *Forbes*, February 15, 1993, pp. 159-63.

3. *Investor's Business Daily*, June 18, 1993, p. 21.

4. *T. Rowe Price Retirement Planning Kit*, a software package. (T. Rowe Price, Inc., 1992).

5. For example, TIAA-CREF's publication *Life Stages* touts TIAA as the vehicle for people who want "safety and security," for people who are "risk averse" and want "maximum safety." TIAA-CREF, *Life Stages: Lifestage Investing and Financial Education*: 1992), pp. B7, B15.

6. A. Gary Shilling, "Indexing is Injurious," *Forbes*, March 29, 1993, p. 127.

Chapter 13

Selecting a Financial Planner

Most of us are focused on our careers and personal lives to the extent that we do not want to invest huge amounts of energy managing our investments. Enter the financial planner. For a fee, he or she will offer to guide you through the maze of finances and retirement planning. If such a person is competent, the fee might be money well spent.

How do you find a financial planner?

You might not really need to go out and look for one. The odds are fairly good that one or more people calling themselves financial planners have already found you and have offered their services. Your task might simply be to weed through the potential financial planners in your area to find one that is right for you.

As financial affairs became more complicated in the past two decades, the number of people calling themselves financial planners exploded from just a few thousand to more than 250,000 today. Some of them are not very good at what they do, a few of them are outright shysters, and a great many of them lack minimal certification in their field. Barely a fifth of people who call themselves financial planners carry either of the two major planner certifications--CFP or ChFc.[1] Fewer than half are registered with the federal Securities and Exchange Commission[2] (SEC) even though they are legally obliged to be registered if they offer investment advice. When *Money* magazine sent reporters to ask thirty-two planners in Santa Rosa, California, a dozen questions about financial affairs, not a single planner answered all twelve questions correctly. Half of them got at least a third of the answers wrong, and almost a third of the planners could not state within four percentage points the historical average annual return on stocks.[3] This glaring knowledge gap should not appear in someone who aims to advise you about risk levels and expected returns on investments.

We live in a world where good advice is critical to our well being, but a lot of incompetents and a few hucksters have invaded the field of financial planning. How do you separate the good from the bad? There are no how-to-do-it manuals on selecting a financial planner, but there are four steps you can take to gauge whether the planners vying for your business might be good choices. These four steps form a simplified Guttman scale.[4] If the candidate passes the criteria for step two, then he or she has met all the criteria for step one. Conversely, if the candidate does not meet all the criteria for step one, then you need not bother going on to step two in your evaluation. This is not like a final examination where you feel obliged to read a student's blue book even though that student has already failed every test up to that point. To help you work you way through these steps, Appendix 4 provides a series of guideline questions.

Step 1: The Bare Minimum

At bare minimum you do not want to deal with a crook. Call the National Association of Securities Dealers disclosure hot line (800 289 9999) to find out if any of your candidates have been subject to any complaints or disciplinary actions. Typical actions that would draw a complaint would be churning a client's account, selling investments that were unsuitable for a client, or even making unauthorized trades. Then, check your state regulatory body to see if it has have any negative information on the planner. One or two minor complaints may not mean that a candidate is a bad planner any more than one or two bad student evaluations mean that an applicant for a faculty position in your department is a bad teacher. But, if the applicant has a pattern of bad evaluations you probably would not hire him or her for the teaching slot. The same principle applies to financial planners. The bad ones tend to have repeated violations.

Once you are satisfied that the person is not a known crook, you want to find out whether he or she has appropriate certification and registration. Candidates for your financial planner position should be registered with the SEC and with your state regulatory body. If you meet the planners for an interview, ask them to present a copy of Parts I and II of the ADV form that they filed with the SEC when they registered. This material will give you important information about the planners' education and experience.

You also want your potential planners to have at least one of these certifications: Certified Financial Planner (CFP), Chartered Financial Consultant (ChFc), or Personal Financial Specialist (PFS). The CFP certificate is earned by completing a one-and-one-half to two-year study program (usually through the mail) and passing a two-day examination conducted by the International Board of Standards and Practices for Certified Financial Planners. There are currently about 25,000 CFPs.

The ChFc is awarded by the American College in Bryn Mawr, Pennsylvania after the candidate completes a three to four-year program and passes an examination. There are about 24,000 ChFcs. The PFS is awarded by the American Institute of Certified Public Accountants. The CFP is probably the most broad based of these three certifications. The ChFc has more of an insurance orientation and the PFS an accounting orientation.

You want your planner to have one of these certificates for the very same reason that you want your new faculty to have the expected degrees for their teaching positions, or for the same reason that you want your lawyer to be a member of the state bar association. Certification and degrees do not guarantee competence, but they do indicate that somewhere along the line the person has met some minimal knowledge requirements. So, if the person applying for the job of your financial planner lacks one of these certifications, there has to be a very good reason for it.

Step 2: Compensation

You want to retain a planner who is completely open about his or her method of compensation. Ask your prospective planners if they will disclose their compensation structure in advance and if you will receive regular statements itemizing all compensation the planners receive from your account. Lawyers can explain their fee structures in advance and stock-brokers can give you monthly statements listing the commissions earned from your account activity, so financial planners ought to be able to do the same.

Especially ask if the planners are compensated by fee, by commission, or by fee and commission. The ideal situation is to hire a fee-only planner, because there is less chance of a conflict of interest in dealing with a fee-only planner.

By contrast, commission-based planners, present an inherent possibility for conflicts of interest. You may want to give tax-free gifts to your children or set up trusts or shift income or buy term life insurance, none of which generate much in the way of commissions. To expect a commission based planner to recommend these noncommission-type products when he or she could be selling you something earning a hefty commission is to expect a lot from human nature.

One major product that planners are likely to recommend to you is a mutual fund. No-load mutual funds and load funds have comparable performance returns based on their net asset value. However, a commission-compensated planner can earn a commission by putting you into a load fund, whereas there is no commission in the no-load fund. The commission comes directly out of your investment, meaning that for every $1,000 you invest, less of it actually goes to work in a load fund than does in a no-load fund. The load fund necessarily has to outperform the no-load fund just to achieve the same result. To expect commission-based planners to put you into no-load funds rather than load funds is to expect a lot from human nature.

Skepticism should also surface if the planner invests in funds with 12b-1 charges, and also receives a payment from the fund you buy. Most no-load funds do not levy 12b-1 charges and planners who limited themselves only to 12b-1 funds would be eliminating some of the most important fund families in existence.

Mutual funds are not the only commission-based products planners can recommend. Cash value life insurance carries a higher commission than does term life insurance. Mutual fund companies frequently promote incentives such as vacations in Hawaii to sales representatives who sell enough of their funds. In 1988, the Securities and Exchange Commission (SEC) studied sixty-nine planning firms and found that only half of them sold U.S. government securities (such as T-bills and bonds) that produced a $50 commission. Eighty percent of the firms sold limited partnerships with an 8 percent commission.[5]

We cannot blame sales representatives for trying to sell the products that generate the most commissions. After all, that is how they make their livelihood. But we also should not confuse such salesmanship with disinterested financial advice.

For these reasons most critics advise confining yourself to fee-only planners. With fee-only planners, you need to ask if they charge a flat fee, an hourly one, or one based on a percent of assets under management. The fee as a percent of total assets is common among money managers and generally provides them with a powerful incentive to make your assets grow rather than shrink. This is what you want, of course, but the approach does present some dangers as you near retirement age or as you get to an age where your risk tolerance is lower. You may calculate, for example, that you can achieve your retirement savings goal in an acceptable time frame with only an 8 percent return, which means you really do not need to make risky investments. Your planner's interest in maximizing your assets, however, may lead him or her to put you in higher risk investments than you need in the hope of gaining a higher return.[6] A frank discussion of your goals and the risk levels acceptable to you can eliminate this situation.

In theory, the best arrangement is to consult a financial planner who charges an hourly fee. In practice, this seldom works. Most people hesitate at spending $1,000 or $2,000 upfront for a plan and financial advice. Most planners find that they cannot earn the type of income they want on a fee-only basis.

For these reasons, a fee of about 1 percent of assets under management (with declining rates for larger portfolios) might be a reasonable compromise. The arrangement must be accompanied by frank discussions about your financial circumstances and a written contract stipulating the fee arrangement as well as such issues as whether the planner has discretion to trade in your account without informing you.

Step 3: Matching Your Needs

If your prospective planners meet the bare minimum and will be fee-only planners, it becomes important to evaluate whether the planners' expertise matches your needs.

Determine what experience the financial planner has in working with people like you. If your estate has grown to a million dollars, you probably do not want a planner whose experience has been limited to estates one-tenth that size. Also, does the planner have experience in the areas where you have particular needs? These could include disability coverage, retirement savings, college savings, life insurance, estate planning, charitable giving, health care planning, and taxes. If your major concern is accumulating your retirement savings and the person before you is basically an insurance salesperson, you have not yet found a very good match.

Another significant factor in choosing a planner is the length of time he or she has been in business in your community. It is a good sign if they have been there five or ten years and are still in business.

Step 4: Judgment Calls

You could resolve the questions raised in steps one through three with a short telephone call. The more probing questions of Step four require a face-to-face interview with your prospective planners. The first test, according to one financial adviser, is to ask prospective planners what to do with $100,000 that has just come into your possession.[7] A planner fails this test if he or she suggests how you should invest this money without first finding out something about your financial circumstances and your goals.

For those who have passed this hurdle, you want to pose several other questions. What types of products do they sell? Do they receive special remuneration for promoting some types of products rather than others? Insurance salespersons who call themselves financial planners may have a bias toward insurance programs and annuities. Mutual fund sales representatives who call themselves financial planners may have a bias toward those products.

Does the planner devote full time to the job or is this a part-time avocation? At first glance it may not seem objectionable that someone is working part-time at the job. But you are hiring this person for professional advice, not part-time musings. You would not want a part-time surgeon or a part-time lawyer, and you probably do not want a part-time financial planner. Does this planner regularly attend conferences and continuing education seminars that will keep him or her abreast of fast breaking changes in the field of finance?

What level of risk do these planners suggest for their clients? They need not adhere to the risk levels outlined in Table 8-2, but they should certainly recommend a lower risk level for a seventy-five year old than for a fifty year old. You hope to be seventy-five yourself some day, and you probably do not want a planner to put you into a risky limited partnership at that age.[8]

To gauge client satisfaction, ask what percent of their clients have been with them for more than three years. While it would be unreasonable to expect an answer of 100 percent, a high level of client turnover would be a negative sign. You can also ask if the planners themselves ever terminated relations with a client. Answering yes would be a good sign. It shows potential integrity to sever ties with someone who is too demanding or whose needs no longer mesh with the planner's expertise.

Of course, the best way to gauge client satisfaction is to ask for the names of three or four clients you can interview. Find out if the clients are satisfied with the planner. More importantly, find out if the clients are sophisticated enough to know whether they *should* be satisfied. So ask how the planner helps them meet their needs for disability coverage, retirement, college savings, life insurance, and estate planning. Then ask each client to give the planner a grade from A to F.[9]

The most difficult character aspect to judge is how open and honest the planner will be with you and how open you will be able to be with the planner. A planner who does not inspire you to be frank about your own circumstances is probably not a good match. The planner also needs to be perceptive of your needs. It is a good sign if the planner listens to your descriptions of your life style and asks questions about your financial and goals. The planner may need to lead you into some unfamilear financial terrain, but it is a bad sign if the planner simply pushes a product on you before ascertaining your circumstances.[10] Even if that product makes sense in the abstract, it won't leave you satisfied if it is totally inconsistent with your value system and the lifestyle you want to lead.

As suggested, it if very important to find out if the prospective planners are biased toward certain investments. If they seem to specialize in complicated schemes such as limited partnerships or collateralized mortgage obligations, be wary. These can be legitimate investments for some people, but often in the past they were marketed to people who neither understood the risks nor were in a good position to incur them A traditional rule of thumb among investors has been, "If you don't understand it, don't buy it."

When you finally settle on a planner to manage your assets, you should agree on benchmarks against which your account will be measured. For example, if the planner is putting you into a mix of stock funds and bond funds, CREF Social Choice would serve as a reasonable benchmark. If your account is to be totally in stock funds, the CREF Equity Index fund would be a reasonable benchmark. On the day that you make the transfer of funds to the financial planner, phone TIAA-CREF (1 800 842 2252) to get the unit values for these funds. By comparing percentage changes in the funds over the coming years with the changes in your account value, you will be able to compare your financial planner's performance to that of relevant CREF accounts.

Is the planner across the desk from you going to be the one handling your account, or are you conferring with just a sales representative? If it is the actual person who will work with you, try to learn how much time will be spent working on accounts as compared to drumming up business to get new accounts. Be reasonable in your expectations. If the planner fails to spend some time drumming up new business, pretty soon he or she will be out of business. Planners are like athletic coaches in that respect. To build winning teams, they not only have to train their current athletes, but they also have to recruit new ones constantly.

Conclusion

In sum, these four steps give you some straightforward guidelines for the extremely difficult task of assessing the financial planners who may seek to manage your affairs. Each step furthers a weeding-out process. If any prospective planners cannot pass the criteria at one step, there is no need to waste your time going on to the next step with them. The questions in Appendix 4 will help you work your way through these steps.

At step 1, determine if the planner is certified by one of the appropriate certification bodies, registered with the SEC, and free of any violations or substantial complaints.

At step 2, learn if the planner is willing to work on a fee-only basis or a percentage-of-assets basis and to give written disclosure of all compensation received for services. Avoid planners whose compensation is tied to commissions on products they sell you.

At step 3, ascertain if the planner's expertise matches up with your needs.

At step 4, decide whether you feel confident about the planner's competence and integrity.

This four-step process does not guarantee that you will end up with a competent and honest planner, but it increases the odds of a successful search. Finally, if you decide to use a planner, do not turn all your assets over at once. Turn over a portion, compare your account's performance with that of the CREF funds. Evaluate after a year whether you account's performance meets your goals and whether the planner gives sufficient attention to your concerns.

Notes

1. Earl C. Gottschalk, Jr., "Ten Things Your Financial Planner Won't Tell You," *Smart Money* (June 1993): 71-72.

2. Ruth Simon, "The Broken Promise of Financial Planning," *Money* (November 1992): 133-149.

3. Ibid., p.

4. This is a scale in which each level of attainment rests on the attainment of all the levels below it. The simplest example would be a young child's proficiency at mathematics. Level 1 might be the ability to count, level 2 the ability to add, level 3 to do multiplication, and level 4 to do division. Any child who reached level 4 could easily do the tasks at the lower levels. And there would be no point in trying to make a child perform at level 4 until he or she had already mastered the lower levels.

5. Simon, "The Broken Promise of Financial Planning."

6. James D. Schwartz, "Picking a Financial Planner: A Baker's Dozen of Questions to Pose to Candidates," *Barron's*, January 11, 1993, p. 19.

7. Ibid.

8. For some real life illustrations of inappropriate advice by financial planners, see Simon, "The Broken Promise of Financial Planning."

9. Schwartz, "Picking a Financial Planner."

10. William Giese, "What to Expect from a Financial Planner," *Kiplinger's Personal Finance Magazine*, August 1994, pp. 73-74.

PART IV

THE PAYOUT PHASE

After years of paying into TIAA-CREF's retirement plan, one day you will start drawing benefits out of the system. TIAA-CREF calls this the payout phase. The payout options you choose for retirement are just as critical to your financial well being as were the investment options you chose during the years of accumulations. Chapter 14 outlines the payout options offered by TIAA-CREF and indicates the circumstances under which each would be desirable. Chapter 15 grapples with the fundamental question whether or not you should annuitize your TIAA-CREF accumulations. Chapter 16 shows how to estimate your income needs in retirement, and Chapter 17 shows how to calculate how large a kitty of assets you will need to generate that income. Chapter 18 examines the impact of Social Security on your retirement and addresses two other important issues as well: health care and taxes. Finally, Chapter 19 summarizes the main arguments of this book.

Chapter 14

Your Payout Options

After years of paying in, you eventually enter what TIAA-CREF calls "the payout phase." Many people find their payout options to be a confusing part of TIAA-CREF, but it need not be so. The options are simple, in general, but if you relish complexity, there is no end to the fun you can have studying all the choices at your disposal. This chapter will outline the TIAA-CREF payout options as simply as possible.

The TIAA-CREF Payout Options

TIAA-CREF offers you three different ways to receive your benefits: (1) annuitizing the benefits, (2) setting up a plan of cash withdrawals without annuitizing, or (3) postponing the choice between annuitizing or taking cash withdrawals. This deferral of choice is done by using some other option such as IPRO (Interest Payment Retirement Option) or MDO (Minimum Distribution Option). For purposes of illustration, this chapter discusses the choice between annuitizing or setting up a cash withdrawal program as an either-or choice. In reality, however, you are not forced into an exclusive choice. You can use some of your TIAA-CREF accumulations to set up an annuity, while you take the balance in the form of cash withdrawals. Or you can start out with cash withdrawals when you retire and postpone the annuitizing decision until later.

Annuitizing Your TIAA-CREF Payouts

Annuities are investment contracts that provide one with a certain amount of income for life or for a specified number of years. These contracts help you resolve the problem of not knowing how much of your retirement savings you can safely spend each year. For example, if person A has a life expectancy of ten more years and $100,000 in assets invested at a 9 percent annual rate of return, how much can she withdraw each year? Mathematically, this is a very simple problem. A few moments with pen and paper confirm that she can withdraw exactly $15,582 each January 1 and without exhausting her savings until the end of her life expectancy.

This simple mathematical problem becomes complicated in real life by the fact that A does not how long she will live. If she lives more than ten years, this plan will put her in deep financial trouble. Consequently, she has to assume a very long life and take a much smaller withdrawal.

If, however, instead of dealing with this problem in isolation, she belongs to a group of 1,000 people in the same kind of circumstances, the problem disappears. The number of people who live beyond the ten-year life expectancy will be counterbalanced by the number who die earlier. The group as a whole could establish a fixed annuity giving each person an annual payment of precisely $15,582 and probably not exhaust the group's collective savings until the last person had died. We say probably not, because with a fixed group of only 1,000 people it is possible that some revolutionary medical discovery could extend the average life of this group beyond its life expectancy. With TIAA-CREF that possibility becomes infinitesimally small, because the group of potential annuitants numbers 1.7 million and thousands of new annuitants are added each year.

How TIAA-CREF Calculates Your Annuity Payments

TIAA-CREF's annuities differ from this simple example in that while the returns of TIAA-CREF fluctuate, this example posed a fixed annuity earning a fixed rate of return. Additionally TIAA and CREF each calculate your annuity payout in a slightly different fashion.

TIAA's Annuity

As shown earlier, TIAA invests primarily in securities that pay a fixed rate of return. Consequently, its earnings are much steadier and more predictable than those of the CREF accounts, which fluctuate with the stock markets and the short-term money markets. This enables TIAA to function more like a traditional annuity and guarantee you a minimum payout each year. Currently that guarantee is 3 percent. Any earnings above the guaranteed 3 percent are distributed to the annuitants in their monthly benefit checks. TIAA recalculates its payout rate each spring, and each May your TIAA check is adjusted accordingly. The new rate then stays in effect through the following April.

It is important to realize that even though you receive a 3 percent guaranteed payout, your total payment fluctuates with TIAA's total investment experience. Over the long run, TIAA has been able to raise its monthly payments. But TIAA annuitants received a rude shock in the early 1990s when their benefit payments began dropping instead of going up. This was because of the decline in long-term interest rates that took place in those years. As TIAA's interest earnings declined, it had less money to pay out to annuitants. Unfortunately, many of these annuitants did not see a commensurate increase in their benefit payments when interest rates subsequently began to rise. The structure of TIAA's portfolio and its practice of tying its own interest payouts to the periods when the money was put into TIAA mean that TIAA payouts will not rise as dramatically as the interest rates that TIAA gains on its new investments.

CREF's Annuity

In contrast to TIAA, which calls itself a traditional annuity, CREF is a variable annuity. Its investment earnings vary with the stock, bond, and short-term money markets. Let us focus on CREF Stock to illustrate how CREF calculates its annuity payouts. During the accumulation phase, you purchase accumulation units each time you make a contribution to CREF. When you start your annuity, CREF converts these accumulation units to a fixed number of annuity units, and this number stays the same for the rest of your life.[1] As the price of CREF Stock goes up, your annuity units are worth more; as the price of CREF Stock goes down, your units are worth less. Once per year, CREF adjusts the value of its annuity unit. This adjustment is reflected in your May 1 check, and the amount stays the same through the following April.

Converting your accumulation units to annuity units is a three-step process. First, CREF calculates the dollar value of your accumulation units on the day you annuitize. Second, it then calculates a monthly amount that would be payable for life if these dollars bought a traditional annuity earning 4 percent per year. Third, it finally converts that monthly amount to a number of annuity units based on an actuarial tool called an annuity factor. This is the amount of principal that would be needed to pay $1 per month for life. CREF's use of an assumed investment return of 4 percent rather than its historical return of 10.9 percent does not cheat you out of the 6.9 percentage point difference. You will still receive whatever percentage change occurred the previous year. But using the lower figure smooths out the variations in annual payments to CREF annuitants. For example, using an assumed investment return of 4 percent means that CREF payout checks would rise 5 percent if the CREF unit value increased by 9 percent (9-4=5) and drop by 13 percent if the CREF unit dropped 9 percent (-9-4=-13). But if an assumed investment rate of 8 percent were used, than CREF payout checks would rise by only 1 percent on a 9 percent market rise and drop by 17 percent on a market loss of that amount.

TIAA-CREF Annuity Choices

For many people, the great attraction of choosing an annuity over cash withdrawal is that the annuity can guarantee an income for life. However, if you decide that you want an annuity, you must also make some other decisions. Do you want the annuity to cover only yourself (a one-life annuity) or do you want your spouse covered as well (a two-life annuity).

One-life Annuity Options

If you have no spouse, or if your spouse already has an adequate retirement income and is willing to forego receiving part of yours, you may be attracted to the one-life annuity. This will give you a stream of income for life, and all payouts will stop when you die.

Suppose, however, that you have dependent children who would have no other income if you died. One way to protect them is to choose a 10-, 15-, or 20-year guaranteed period. If you have a two-year old child it would make sense to opt for the 20-year guaranteed period. This choice would reduce your monthly check, but you would still receive it for life. If you died two months after signing up, your child would receive that same monthly check until the 20-year period was up. To take another example, someone with a twelve year old child might opt for the 10-year guaranteed period to ensure that if the child were orphaned, he or she would receive an income roughly through the college years. If you had no dependents, you probably would not want to choose any guaranteed periods. Also, if you are already past age 66 or if your life expectancy is short, these guaranteed periods might not be available to you.

Two-life Annuity Options

The two-life annuity will seem most attractive if you have a spouse or other dependent who lacks an adequate source of retirement income. In TIAA terminology, you are called the annuitant if the policy is in your name, and your annuitant partner is called the second annuitant. Normally, the second annuitant will be your spouse and this chapter will refer to the second annuitant as your spouse, but the second annuitant could also be some other relative or a nonmarried domestic partner. Under the two-life annuity, you and your annuity partner will receive a monthly check for life. The dollar amount of those checks will be depend on which one of the following 3 options you select: (1) a full benefit to the survivor, (2) one-half benefit to the second annuitant, or (3) two-thirds benefit to the survivor.

Full Benefit to Survivor

If you select this payout method, the monthly check stays the same after the death of either you or your spouse. This option is likely to be attractive under two conditions: (1) your spouse has no separate income and/or (2) the survivor's expenses are likely to remain the same after the other dies.

One-Half Benefit to Second Annuitant

If you die, the second annuitant receives one-half of the monthly payout check. But if your spouse dies, you receive the full paycheck. This option would be attractive if you would need the full check in event your spouse died first, but your spouse would need only half of it if you died first. This situation could occur if your spouse had a separate retirement income source that would terminate with his or her death.

Two-Thirds Benefit to the Survivor

Regardless whether you or your spouse die first, the survivor gets two-thirds of the benefit. This would be attractive if the survivor's expenses would drop substantially in event that either of you died, but neither of you would be eligible for an outside source of income.

Before choosing among these options you need to explore a TIAA-CREF booklet *Comparing TIAA-CREF Income Options*[2]. You should also talk with a TIAA-CREF planning consultant, your own financial adviser, and, above all, your spouse. To gain the maximum benefit from your retirement annuity, you need to integrate it with your spouse's retirement income. Under federal law, once you designate your spouse as beneficiary you cannot change beneficiary without his or her approval.

Fixed Period Annuity

In addition to a life annuity, TIAA-CREF will also write an annuity that will guarantee you an income for a fixed number of years. For example, suppose you took out a 20-year mortgage on a vacation condo in Hilton Head, South Carolina, that required monthly payments of $450. By setting up some of your RA or SRA accounts into a 20-year fixed period annuity you would be assured enough income over those years to make the payments on that mortgage.

Payout Features: Standard vs. Graded

If any part of your accumulations are with TIAA, you will also need to decide whether you want to take your TIAA payments in the standard method or the graded method. The graded method is TIAA's attempt to cope with inflation. You get the guaranteed 3 percent each year, but some of the earnings above the 3 percent are plowed back into your TIAA account to increase your principal and thus give you higher monthly payouts in future years. Under the standard method, all of the dividends are paid out to you annually and nothing is reinvested to cope with inflation.

Does the graded plan in fact give you adequate protection against inflation? Chapter 15 will address this question.

Setting Up a Cash Withdrawal Plan

An alternative to establishing an annuity with your TIAA-CREF accounts is to set up a systematic plan for cashing them out. TIAA-CREF does not make this as easy to do as a large mutual fund family would, but you can set up your own plan nonetheless.

If your employer permits, your RA CREF account can be cashed out or rolled over into an IRA any time after you leave your employer. Your RA CREF accounts, if permitted by your employer, can be transferred to a financial planner or a mutual fund family that will manage your 403-(b) account. At retirement time, these RA CREF funds can be fully or partially cashed out as you wish. Thus, when you leave your employer, you may continue to let CREF manage your money and take cash withdrawals on a regular basis. Or you can roll your CREF accounts into another tax deferred account managed by a financial adviser or by a mutual fund family and take monthly cash payments from that source. You could also take the entire sum in cash at once, but it would not be wise to do this without the advice of an experienced tax expert. You would could easily be pushed up into a higher tax bracket in the year in which you cashed out. Immediate taxes would sharply reduce your principal, and the remaining balance would not compound tax deferred. If you keep the funds in CREF or some other deferred compensation account, however, you must begin making a minimum withdrawal by April 1 after you reach age 70 1/2.

TIAA funds in your SRA can be cashed out at any time, but cashing out TIAA funds in your RA account is more complicated. You can cash out 10 percent immediately by transferring it to CREF. The balance can be put in a Transfer Payout Annuity that will shift your TIAA funds to CREF over a 10-year period. Once in CREF, of course, those monies can be cashed out under the same terms as your other RA account CREF holdings.

In theory, you could set up a monthly cash withdrawal plan, but CREF does not make it easy for you to do this, since you have to fill out a form for each withdrawal. More likely, you would make a withdrawal once a year, transfer the cash to a money market fund with a check-writing provision, reserve enough to cover your income taxes, and write yourself a monthly check for one-twelfth of the balance. Even less cumbersome would be to transfer your CREF holdings to a 403(b) plan with a mutual fund or financial planner and set up a monthly withdrawal plan that would automatically send you the checks. Most mutual fund families would made a monthly schedule of cash withdrawals much easier than TIAA-CREF makes it.

Intermediary Options

Many people at the point of retirement might find themselves not quite ready to bind themselves for life into an annuity. Yet they are skeptical of cashing out their TIAA-CREF accounts and turning them over to the management of a fee based financial planner. If you are in this position, TIAA-CREF offers you two other options that enable you to tap into your TIAA-CREF accounts and leave open the chance of annuitizing later on.

IPRO: Interest Payment Retirement Option

First is TIAA's IPRO, the Interest Payment Retirement Option. Under this option, TIAA sends you a monthly payout equal to the interest earned on your TIAA account without tapping into the principal. This gives you current income but leaves the principal intact so that it can later be annuitized, transferred to CREF under a Transfer Payout Annuity, or passed on to a beneficiary.

IPRO involves your TIAA Retirement Annuity or a Group Retirement Annuity. It does not apply to CREF or to your TIAA SRA, because you already have the right to withdraw any amount from those accounts.

If you choose IPRO as an option, it is important to remember that your IPRO payout check will vary each year as TIAA's dividend rates change and that by taking IPRO you will not be reinvesting your dividends. Thus, your principal will not grow, and if you annuitize later on, your annuity payments will be less than they would have been been if you had been reinvesting the interest dividends.

MDO: Minimum Distribution Option

The second alternative to annuitizing or cashing out is the MDO, the Minimum Distribution Option. Federal law requires that you begin taking payouts from your pension plan and other tax deferred accounts by April after you turn age 70 1/2. If you fail to do so, the Internal Revenue Service (IRS) will charge you a 50 percent tax on the amount of payout that should have been made. Under MDO, TIAA-CREF will calculate the minimum you need to withdraw each year to avoid this tax and will then send you an annual check for that amount.

The rules on MDO are complicated and vary with age, employment status, and the type of tax deferral plan you own. For these reasons, it is very important to touch base with TIAA-CREF as you approach age 70.

The great advantage of MDO is that you are not bound into an annuity and thus your account can be passed on to your beneficiaries. The great disadvantage is that your TIAA-CREF accounts might well be used up before you die. To use a simplistic example, if your MDO paid out one-twentieth of your accumulation the first year, one-nineteenth the second year, and so on, you would eventually draw down your assets. At the end of twenty years, there would not be very much money left in your TIAA-CREF accounts. If you had not reinvested some of those payouts and had the financial bad luck to live another five or ten years, you could be left in a desperate situation.

The MDO is very attractive to people who, for whatever reasons, want to delay setting up an annuity or who have enough other income that they do not need to set up an annuity. For people in either of these situations, the MDO gives them greater opportunity than the annuity to pass assets on to their heirs.

The MDO could also be integrated with a cash withdrawal plan. Say, for example, that you were withdrawing $40,000 each January and using that money to cover your regular living expenses. However, on April 1 after you reach age 70 1/2, the IRS minimum distribution requirements call for you to withdraw $50,000 that year or incur a 50 percent tax on the $10,000 difference. You could use CREF's MDO to withdraw $50,000, put $40,000 into your regular budget, and invest what is left of the $10,000 after taxes in a balanced mutual fund that would allow you to continue to get the growth you need to sustain your cash withdrawal plan.

Conclusion

When you become ready to start withdrawing your TIAA-CREF accumulations, you have three choices. You can annuitize all or part of your holdings. You can forego annuitization and set up a plan of cash withdrawals. Or, you can postpone the decision and use either the Minimum Distribution Option or the Interest Payout Retirement Option until you have made up your mind. TIAA-CREF strongly urges you to annuitize. But before you do so, it would be useful to examine the pros and cons of annuitization with us in Chapter 15.

Notes

1. See TIAA-CREF, *Understanding How CREF Units Work*, The Library Series, No. 4 (New York: TIAA-CREF: 1992), pp. 9-14.

2. TIAA-CREF, *Comparing TIAA-CREF Income Options*, The Library Series, No. 6 (New York: TIAA-CREF, 1992), p. 36.

Chapter 15

Should You Annuitize?
The Pros and Cons

At retirement you can annuitize your TIAA-CREF accumulations, or you can set up some other method of cash withdrawals for giving yourself a monthly retirement check. The vast majority of retirees have chosen to annuitize, making it the most ppular way of taking TIAA-CREF payments. Prior to 1990, TIAA-CREF retirees had no choice; they were forced to annuitize their RA accounts. Since 1990, however, you do have a choice, and this makes it imperative for you to examine whether annuitization is the best way for you to withdraw your accumulations. To help you in that task, this chapter begins by outlining the advantages and disadvantages of annuitizing.

Annuitization: The Advantages

In general, annuitizing has some indisputable advantages. It can give you and your spouse a guaranteed income for life from a reputable firm. TIAA and CREF will not be the hottest money managers in any given year, but their track record over the intermediate and long-term is very good. They will most likely still be in business throughout the period of your retirement, and it is not clear how confidently that statement can be made by many of the fee-based financial planners who would like the chance to guide your financial affairs.

Annuitization also provides for your spouse and dependents in case you die an early death. Through the two-life annuities with a guaranteed option you can ensure that your surviving spouse has a lifetime income and that your children have income up to and through their college years.

No matter how much you enjoy financial planning, the day will come when neither you nor your spouse will have the energy and alertness to manage your financial affairs effectively. Having a regular monthly annuity check is simpler and easier than reassessing your financial situation each year to see what adjustments you have to make. Having an annuity protects you from making disastrous financial errors when your strength and judgment wane. If you do not annuitize, you or your widow will at some point need to find an adviser to help manage your accumulations. A good adviser may well do this better than TIAA-CREF. But many con-artists posing as advisers have been known to defraud the elderly of their life savings. With your life savings tied up in an annuity, there is less chance of this happening.

In some cases, you might garner an additional legal advantage in not having access to the large pool of cash that would be available under any system of cash withdrawals that you might set up. For example, if your life savings were in cash, those savings could easily be wiped out and your spouse left unprotected if you had huge medical expenses or nursing home fees. The same thing could happen if you were sued by somebody who had a large claim against you. By contrast, with a two-life annuity, your spouse's benefit checks would probably be safer.

Finally, unless you can manage your cash accumulation better than TIAA-CREF does, your initial monthly payout checks will probably be larger if you annuitize than they will if you set up your own cash withdrawal plan. A corollary of this principle is that you probably do not have to accumulate as many dollars to annuitize as you do under your self-created cash withdrawal plan to provide for any given amount of monthly income. The word "probably" in these two sentences serves as an important reminder that many variables go into determining what your monthly withdrawals could be, and analysts have honest disagreements about the issue. Some financial planners think that your payments would be substantially higher if you did not annuitize. TIAA-CREF publications suggest the exact opposite.

Annuitization: The Drawbacks

Despite its advantages, annuitization is not the best option for everybody. TIAA-CREF illustrates this with the extreme example of a person with a terminal illness who has only a few years to live and has no spouse or other dependents. Even TIAA-CREF admits that in these circumstances, annuitization is probably not the best choice.[1] Better that this person spend and enjoy as much of the life savings as possible rather than simply let it disappear into the pockets of other TIAA-CREF annuitants who have been blessed with a longer life expectancy.

By illustrating the case for non-annuitization with such an extreme example, however, TIAA-CREF makes it appear that cashing out is a sensible option only if you, too, have an extremely unfortunate situation. The question is not whether cashing out is better for someone in dire circumstances but whether it is better for you in your particular circumstances.

Let us pursue this argument with a more moderate example. Suppose, for example, that you and your spouse were both 65 and had accumulated $500,000 dollars (in 1994 dollars), with half of that in CREF and the rest in other investments or savings. You can include in that amount any equity in your home beyond $100,000 on the assumption that you could purchase an acceptable dwelling in a reasonable location for $100,000 and use the balance of your equity to generate spendable income. Because $500,000 is a lot of money, it will seem beyond the reach of most people on an assistant professor's salary. In fact, it is quite realistic, and it is almost certainly achievable by anybody who follows the investment practices suggested earlier in this book.

If the couple in this example had followed the asset allocation advice in Table 8-3 for a 65-year old (p. 123), they could expect to start with approximately $41,000 annual income per year, increase that amount by 4.1 percent each year for inflation, and never exhaust their assets.[2] More precisely, their assets would not be exhausted until they reached age 105, which is probably long enough for most of us, since the longevity record for TIAA-CREF annuitants is 110 years.[3]

Does this seem farfetched?   Examine Table 15-1. This couple would withdraw the equivalent of $21,850 per year from their accumulations and about $18,000 in Social Security benefits. If they wanted to invest the funds more conservatively than advocated in Table 8-3, they would, of course, have to withdraw slightly less. This example depends on the continued inflation indexing of Social Security benefits. But that is not an unreasonable assumption, considering that aging baby-boomers will be the biggest age cohort in the voting public throughout this period.

With $500,000 in assets, therefore, this couple has no financial need to annuitize its assets. They can live off the earnings of their accumulations and in all probability leave a substantial inheritance for their children or some worthy cause. This recommendation flies in the face of

Table 15-1   First Year Income Projections for a 65-Year-Old Couple

Income Category	Income
Social Security for the First Spouse	$12,000
Spousal Social Security for the Other Spouse	6,000
Withdrawal from CREF and Other Accumulations	23,150
Total Income	$41,150

Assumptions include an initial starting capital of $500,000, an average 8 percent annual rate of return and withdrawals increasing at 4.1 percent per year. At these rates, the capital will be exhausted in 40 years.

TIAA-CREF's advice: "We think a lifetime annuity is the best form of payment for most people."[4]   The fact of the matter is that you do not need to annuitize your assets to assure yourself a lifetime income and still have plenty of money left over to bequeath to your dependents or to some cause. You yourself may need more or less than $500,000. If you want to live more luxuriously at the $60,000 level, of course, you will need more assets, probably $900,000, even if you and your spouse are eligible for a combined $18,000 in Social Security benefits. If you are willing to settle for a $30,000 income you only need $252,000 in total assets. Think that option over carefully, however, because after one of you dies, the Social Security benefits will decrease.

There is no guarantee that the asset allocation plan for 65-year olds will return 8 percent per year or that some financial catastrophe will not wipe out their assets. But, as TIAA annuitants sadly learned in the early 1990s, there is also no guarantee that TIAA's payments will increase rather than decrease each year.

Several arguments can be made for setting up your own TIAA-CREF cash withdrawal plan rather than annuitizing.

Inflation Devastates Your TIAA Payments

Table 15-2 shows that by TIAA's own data, both the standard and the graded benefit methods failed to keep pace with inflation through every time period illustrated through mid-1992. The standard method

Table 15-2 **TIAA Monthly Benefits in Inflation-Adjusted Dollars**

Period	Standard Method		Graded Method	
	Starting Amount $	Ending Amount $	Starting Amount $	Ending Amount $
1968-92	750	250	700	600
1973-92	900	350	650	700
1978-92	1,000	500	600	800
1983-92	1,100	750	650	950

Source: TIAA-CREF, *Comparing TIAA-CREF Income Options*, The Library Series, No. 6 (New York: TIAA-CREF, 1992), p. 49.

fared the worst. Anybody taking TIAA benefits under the standard method would have suffered a devastating erosion of purchasing power. A retiree who started receiving $900 per month in 1973 would have seen its purchasing power erode by almost two-thirds over the next two decades. Even the youngest retirees, those in the 1983-92 period, saw their purchasing power drop by more than 30 percent. Considering that half of today's 65 year olds can expect to live longer than twenty years, these statistics are chilling.

To compensate for inflation, TIAA introduced the graded method for taking monthly payouts. Even under this method, Table 15-2 shows that the 1968 retiree saw an erosion of purchasing power. The benefits started at $700 per month and declined to the equivalent of $600 per month by 1992. The retirees of the other periods seem to have kept ahead of inflation. However, this is true only if the ending graded amount is compared to the starting graded amount, not the starting standard amount. At first glance the 1983 retiree seems to have done best. The inflation-adjusted starting benefit of $650 per month grew to $950 in 1992. But, to get that growth, this person had to take almost a 50 percent reduction from what he or she could have received under the standard method. The standard method would have started with $1,100 per month, not $650. So the most relevant figure to compare to the ending figure of $950 is not $650, but $1,100. By this comparison, the person ended up receiving fewer inflation adjusted dollars than what he or she could have started with ten years earlier.

In fact, the person could have set up his or her own graded plan by taking the standard payment of $1,100, spending only $650, and plowing the other $450 into a no-load indexed mutual fund. Assume that this plan was started in the first year of the person's retirement. In the second year, only $400 per month was reinvested into the fund and the other $50 was used to increase take-home pay. Each succeeding year, the reinvested amount is decreased by $50 per month. After doing this for ten years, the fund grew to over $73,000 (given an index growth fund appreciation rate of about 15 percent during that period), which itself would generate income of about $306 per month (at a 5 percent withdrawal rate) and continue growing. This scenario easily shields the person from inflation better than following TIAA's graded method, and it leaves that person with an extra $73,000 in assets. Admittedly, it would take extraordinary discipline to implement this scenario, and it would require making your re-investments in an equity portfolio that has some chance of beating inflation. There are easier ways of setting up a retirement program to beat inflation.

The bottom line is that your TIAA retirement savings will be eroded by inflation over the long run. The graded payout method offers some protection from this, but it comes at the cost of reducing your starting payouts by such a huge amount that most people probably could not afford them and those who could afford them, could find easier ways of protecting themselves from inflation.

Accepting TIAA's standard method of payout will devastate the purchasing power of your benefit payments as time goes on, but the graded method is highly overrated. Many people would be better off getting the bulk of their money out of TIAA and setting up an asset allocation plan as discussed in Chapter 8.

You Might Get Better Returns
Outside of TIAA-CREF

You might want to transfer your CREF accumulations to the care of a private financial planner or a mutual fund family, if you think they could give you better long-term performance. Certainly, any financial planner will make this argument to you. Before signing up, however, it would be useful to re-read Chapters 12 and 13.

The key to a successful return is asset allocation. For reasons discussed in Chapter 8, CREF has its drawbacks. If you can tolerate the psychological risk, you might be better off setting up an asset allocation plan with a good mutual fund family and having those funds send you a monthly withdrawal check.

Annuitization Reduces the Size of Your Legacy

If you set up your own cash withdrawal plan as advocated here, on the assumption of living to 105, you have at least a 99 percent chance of passing on a substantial inheritance to your heirs. This is because your assets will not be exhausted until age 105.

Whether you want to pass a substantial inheritance to your heirs, is of, course, a question of personal values. Many people are philosophically opposed to the idea. Some believe, on egalitarian grounds, that no child should start life with an undue financial advantage. Others believe that large inheritances corrupt the recipients, and the sorry escapades of many rich people certainly provide anecdotal evidence to confirm this judgment. Still others, like legendary Detroit Lions quarterback Bobby Lane, want to pass out of this world with their financial balance sheet at zero. Having made good money as a top ranked football player, he wanted to enjoy as much of that money as he could. History records that Bobby Lane more than achieved his goal. When he finally died he was not only broke but deeply in debt.

However, some people relish the idea of leaving an inheritance to their children, their grandchildren or some cause that has been important throughout their lives.[5] Maybe you would like to have a class room or an art gallery named after you. After all, you've spent your entire career in buildings named after other people. Or maybe you want to help your children because you fear that the economic opportunities that were available for you will not be there for them. Whatever the motive, the idea of leaving an inheritance appeals to some people.

If you set up a system of cash withdrawals, you at least determine who gets endowed with the unspent balance of your accumulations. If you opt for an annuity plan, the odds are 50 percent that you will die before your accumulations and earnings are spent, meaning that the balance goes to subsidize the annuities of the other half of TIAA-CREF annuitants who happened to live longer than you did. If you are going to live to age 81, why would you want to leave the balance of your assets to that small number of people who will go on until age 91? We don't hear of many people who deliberately leave an inheritance intended solely for the strangers who outlived them. Yet this is precisely what happens to half the people who annuitize.

If you annuitize, you have a 50 percent chance of endowing those who live longer. If you set up a plan of cash withdrawals, you have a 100 percent chance of either spending all the money yourself or at least deciding who is going to get the balance.

Annuitizers May Lose Some Benefits of CREF Growth

It is not absolutely clear that annuitizers receive the full benefit of CREF performance. As was explained in Chapter 14, the CREF annuity unit value is adjusted each May to reflect the prior year's performance of the fund's portfolio. In the forty years from 1953 to 1992, for example, the CREF Stock accumulation unit value multiplied by a factor of 57.5 from $.98 to $56.31. During the same period, the CREF Stock annuity unit value multiplied much more slowly by a factor of only 11.2 from $9.46 to $105.49.[6] If your CREF holdings are annuitized and grow in proportion to the annuity unit value, it seems apparent that they will not grow as fast as they will if they are not annuitized. Non-annuitized CREF holdings grow in proportion to the faster growing accumulation unit value.

Other Arguments against Annuitizing Your Assets

There are other arguments against annuitizing your assets as well. First, the decision is irreversible. No matter what happens in the real world of investments, you are locked into the allocation scheme you set up at the moment of annuitization. If you annuitize at a moment of high interest rates and put the bulk of your funds into TIAA, you cannot change that investment later on when interest rates decline. Or, if you annuitize at the height of a bullish U.S. stock market and put the bulk of your funds into CREF Stock, you cannot change that later on if it looks like you should have put a larger portion into the Global Equities or the Social Choice funds.

As teachers, most of us warn our students that they are entering a fast-changing world, that they must learn to be flexible, that they must be prepared to change careers several times, and that one of the biggest detriments to their future well being is locking themselves into a rigid mindset that cannot adapt to social and economic changes. Ironically, many of us give this advice to our students and then turn around and lock ourselves into an annuity plan that will be irreversible for the rest of our lives.

Second, you cannot stop your monthly payments, even if it were to your advantage to do so. For example, in a given year you might receive an inheritance or other windfall that would push you into a higher tax bracket. In such a case, tax advisers suggest that you postpone any discretionary income until the following year when your tax rate will drop. This would be easily accomplished if you had set up a cash withdrawal plan through a mutual fund, but it would be impossible to do with any contractual annuity payments.

Third, an annuity plan also opens you to the possibility of spending the rest of your life paying for a benefit that nobody will receive. Suppose, for example, you choose a one-life annuity with a twenty-year guaranteed payment period to cover your spouse. To gain that protection, your monthly benefits will be reduced from the maximum by 13 percent.[7] If you have a $2,000 per month benefit, in effect you are paying approximately $260 per month for this protection. If that protection is needed, of course, your spouse will consider it money well spent. But if, heaven forbid, your spouse dies in an automobile accident, nobody will ever receive the benefit, and you will be paying out the equivalent of that $260 per month for the rest of your life.[8] Furthermore, the $260 per month cost will go up each year as your annuity payout check goes up. Under a plan of cash withdrawals, these potential problems do not exist.

Certainly, you need some form of protection if you still have dependents. Unless you have other assets or adequate life insurance, one of the guaranteed periods might be a good choice for you. Advocates of the cash withdrawal plan, however, would argue that the best way to protect your dependents would be to *not annuitize*. Their argument would be that a properly structured cash withdrawal plan will leave your estate with a substantial lump sum that would probably serve your dependents better than either a guaranteed annuity period or a term life insurance policy.

Fourth, if you sign up for any of the guaranteed benefit periods and name your children as beneficiaries, your children will receive those benefits for a given specific, finite period of time, regardless of how well TIAA-CREF performs. If, for example, you sign up for a ten-year guaranteed period, you die, and CREF enjoys another rip-roaring bull market like that of the 1980s, the value of your CREF annuity will have exploded to an amount that would easily provide income beyond the guaranteed period. But your beneficiaries will not receive these extra benefits. Under a cash withdrawal plan your beneficiaries would not have to stop enjoying the fruits of this successful investment experience once the ten year period stopped.

Fifth, by annuitizing you give up control over an asset that took you a life time to acquire. Someone else will now control the investment decisions, the allocation of investment portfolios, and the disposition of your assets.

Comparison Shop

After considering the pros and cons of setting up a cash withdrawal plan, you might still decide you want to annuitize part of your retirement savings. If so, it is important to do some comparison shopping, especially for the TIAA portion of your savings. One study examined the benefits offered by fifteeen different insurers for a 50 percent joint and survivor annuity for a 65-year-old man with a 60-year-old wife. For each $100,000 in the annuity, benefit payments differed by $257 per month from the most generous to the stingiest plan.[9] Once you find out what your TIAA annuity payments will be, a little research could tell you whether TIAA's benefits could be beaten by another insurer with a comparable safety rating.[10]

Monthly Benefit Levels

For many people, the decision on whether to annuitize might well boil down to two key questions: How much accumulation would I need in order to receive a respectable benefit level without annuitizing? Will my benefit levels be higher if I annuitize or if I forgo annuitizing? Let us address the second question here and defer the first question to Chapters 16 and 17.

Much of the answer to the question about how much assets you will need depends upon the time frame and the performance of your investments over that time frame. Using CREF Stock as an example, for the decade from 1983 through 1992, a person would have been much better off not annuitizing. Published TIAA-CREF data show that a one-life ten-year guaranteed annuity based on $100,000 in accumulations would have started this period with a $604 monthly benefit and would have grown over the ten years to $1498 per month.[11] Over the ten-year period, a total of $126,435 in benefits was distributed. At the end of period, of course, there was no cash balance that could be withdrawn, willed to an heir, or donated to a worthy cause.

By contrast, if the original $100,000 had not been annuitized, the same $126,435 could have been taken out at the same rate through cash withdrawals, and, as Figure 15-1 shows, at the end of the period there

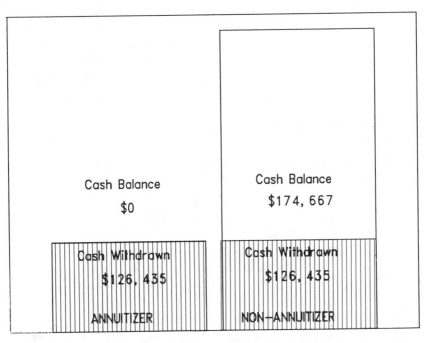

Results for 1983—1992 starting with $100, 000 in CREF Stock

**Figure 15-1 Withdrawal Results for Annuitizers and
Non-Annuitizers: A Best Case Scenario**

would have been a cash balance of $174,667, which the retiree could have used any way he or she saw fit. Alternatively, the retiree could have chosen to pay himself or herself larger monthly payments and be satisfied with a smaller cash balance. For example, although it would not be a very good idea, the retiree could have doubled the starting payments to $1200 per month and increased them at a 4.1 percent annual rate in order to compensate for inflation. This retiree would end up withdrawing a total of $176,268 but would have only $76,395 left as a cash balance.

It turns out, however, that the wild bull market of the 1980s made the 1983 through 1992 period a best case for the nonannuitizer. The worst case for the nonannuitizer was probably the 1973 through 1992 twenty-year period. The period started with a two-year bear market that drove down the CREF unit value by nearly 50 percent. According to TIAA-CREF data, the annuitizer started this period with a $100,000 accumulation and a monthly withdrawal of $710. This shrunk almost in half over the next two years but eventually grew to $2,403 per month by 1992. Over the twenty year period, the retiree received $278,268 in distributions. If the nonannuitizer stuck to the same payout schedule, his or her holdings would have been exhausted by 1989. To maintain a substantial cash balance, the nonannuitizer would have had either to take a smaller initial payout or else reduce the payout level during the 1973-74 bear market until the CREF unit recovered.

Most time periods, of course, are neither best case nor worst case situations, and no prudent person would have left all of his or her holdings in CREF Stock throughout his or her retirement. So we do not want to read too much into these two extreme examples. They do, nevertheless, serve to reinforce four ideas. First, it is important to follow the principles of asset allocation outlined in Table 8-3 (p. 123). This should give you some downside protection when bear markets appear. Second, because the nonannuitizer has flexibility to rebalance after a bear market and to adapt the payout schedule to the experience of his or her account, the nonannuitizer seems better positioned than the annuitizer to profit from the subsequent bull market. Third, although these two extreme cases show that it is not always clear who is going to have the larger monthly payment, prudence dictates that the nonannuitizers keep their withdrawals small enough that their cash balance does not get depleted prematurely. This probably means that the initial payments will be higher for the annuitizers than for the nonannuitizers. However, if the nonannuitizers become dissatisfied with their system of cash withdrawals, they can always decide to annuitize at a later date. For any given amount of assets, the monthly benefit checks would be even higher if one annuitized at age seventy than at age sixty-five. Finally, there would be an advantage in not annuitizing if you were a whiz at investing or had a financial adviser who could generate better returns than TIAA-CREF at the same levels of risk.

Conclusion

Annuitizing is the traditional way to receive TIAA-CREF benefits, but many participants might find it worthwhile to consider the non-annuitizing options before binding themselves irrevocably into an annuity. You need to view your TIAA-CREF assets in combination with all your other assets.

Whether you annuitize is equally a question of values and a question of how much in assets you have managed to accumulate by the time retire. If you have enough assets, as Table 15-1 hints and as Chapter 17 will show, you may not need to annuitize.

- If you follow none of the advice in the earlier parts of this book and fail to build up sufficient assets and savings, then you really may have no choice but to annuitize. Nobody can afford the risk that they and/or their spouse will outlive their assets. If you accumulate only $200,000, the only way you can cash out enough money to live on each year will be to exhaust your accumulation in ten or fifteen years, and the chances are pretty good that you or your spouse will live beyond that. On the other hand, if you take out only enough money each month so that your assets will last until age 105 (as in Table 15-1), that amount is going to be very small. In this case, you have no choice but to annuitize, because that will give you a somewhat higher monthly benefit payment and guarantee it for life.

- However, the question of whether to annuitize is also a question of values. Setting up a cash withdrawal plan gives you a 100 percent chance of either using up all the cash yourself or bequeathing it to some person or cause of your choice. Setting up an annuity plan gives you no chance to decide who will inherit the unspent accumulations and only a 50 percent chance of drawing the accumulations down to zero.

- If you have enough cash accumulated, you may not have to annuitize.

- To set up a cash plan and leave a nest egg for your child or your cause might require sacrifice. It might mean that you may have to start with lower initial monthly withdrawals than under an annuity plan.

- To not annuitize you have to take the risk that you can manage your assets as well as TIAA-CREF can.

- The goal of your accumulation years should be to accumulate enough assets so that you are not bound into annuitizing if you do not want to be.

- Stated this way, the key question then becomes: How much do I need to provide for myself and my spouse without annuitizing? We will explore this in Chapters 16 and 17.

Notes

1. TIAA-CREF, *Annuities: The Lifetime Choice* (New York: TIAA-CREF, 1991), p. 6.

2. Following the allocation advice in Table 8-2 we assumed a portfolio halfway between that of a 65 year old and a 75 year old. market. Such an allocation in TIAA-CREF would have produced an historical return of 8.1 percent per year.

3. Ibid., p. 8. The longest payout period for a TIAA-CREF annuity was fifty-eight years.

4. TIAA-CREF, *Comparing TIAA-CREF Income Options*, The Library Series, No. 6 (New York: TIAA-CREF, 1992). p. 29.

5. A study of 1,064 TIAA-CREF annuitants found that roughly one-half of them had altruistic beliefs that it was important to leave an estate for relatives or for a cause. John Laitner and F. Thomas Juster, "New Evidence on Altruism: A Study of TIAA-CREF Retirees," Institute for Empirical Macro-econmics, Discussion Paper 86. (Minneapolis: Federal Reserve Bank, May 1993), p. 2.

6. Calculated from TIAA-CREF, *Comparing TIAA-CREF Income Options*, p. 56 and TIAA-CREF, *Charting TIAA and the CREF Accounts*, Winter 1993-94 (New York: TIAA-CREF, 1994), p. 50.

7. TIAA-CREF, *Comparing TIAA-CREF Income Options*, p. 45.

8. This example is not as far fetched as it may seem at first glance. One pension benefit consultant said this complaint is common. See Malynda Dovel Wilcox, "How to Take Your Pension Payments," *Kiplinger's Personal Finance Magazine*, August, 1994, p. 56.

9. Melynda Dovel Wilcox, "Why *Not* to Take the Company Pension," *Kiplinger's Personal Finance Magazine*, January 1994, p. 78.

10. Any competent financial planner could generate these comparisons for you. Some sources that you could use to make the comparisons yourself are *Annuity and Life Insurance Shopper* (800 872 6684) and *A. M. Best Retirement Income Guide* which should be available at the nearest financial library.

11. TIAA-CREF, *Comparing TIAA-CREF Income Options*, pp. 25, 48.

Chapter 16

How Much Retirement Income Will You Need?

Whether you annuitize or not, how much annual income will you need when you start your retirement? And how large a kitty of assets will you need to generate that income? We will address the first of these questions in this chapter and the second in Chapter 17.

The Importance of Estimating Your Retirement Income Needs

Estimating your income needs ten or twenty years from now is not an easy task and can easily strike one as tedious and useless. Tedious because of the detailed financial data you feel you must come up with. Useless because it is all based on uncertain assumptions about the future. By the time we become old enough to start worrying about predicting our retirement needs we have enough experience to remember how frequently the future has eluded our many predictions in the past. Maybe money is like sex; no matter how much you have you can still use more. If so, there is no point in predicting how much you will need.

Nevertheless, it is important to estimate our retirement income needs. Except for the infinitesimally small number of people who will win the lottery or market a best selling rock song, the only way that most of us will accumulate substantial assets is through hard work, sensible investment decisions, and deferring some pleasures today to provide some comfort for tomorrow. If it is true that the only way you can provide some comfort for tomorrow is by deferring pleasures today, then it is important to make some estimate of how much you will need in the future. If you provide for too much retirement income, you will make more sacrifices today than are really necessary. On the other hand, grossly underestimating your future income needs is also shortsighted. If you fail to defer enough pleasures and undershoot your goal, your golden years might end up being tarnished by the financial inability to do what you would like.

This chapter aims to help you estimate your future income needs in a way that is simple enough to get you started. This will make your task easier when you sit down with a financial planner who can help you fine-tune your estimates and consider their ramifications.

Variables that Affect Your Retirement Income Needs

There is no established way to calculate your future income needs. Financial planners talk in terms of a replacement ratio.[1] This is the percent of your current income that needs to be replaced by your annuities and investment earnings. Some planners say that this replacement ratio should be 60 percent of your current income, others say 80 percent, and still others 100 percent. In most cases, this ratio is directly related to your income level. The higher your income, the lower the ratio. Someone at a $20,000 income level before retirement will probably need the same amount after retirement. A person at the $100,000 level, however, might need only $60,000 in retirement.

Rather than guessing at your replacement ratio, it is more useful to start by examining the variables that will affect your replacement ratio. Many of these variables will induce you to spend less money when you retire than you spend now. It is very likely that your children will be finished with college, your mortgage will be paid off, and you won't have to make any more contributions to your SRA and other retirement vehicles. Additionally, as people age they tend to spend less money acquiring gadgets and things in general. Powerboats, sailboats, pianos, art collections, expensive mementos from places travelled to or lived in, no longer seem so urgent. Indeed, many elderly begin divesting themselves of much of the stuff that they have spent a life time accumulating. Many retirees reduce their expenses even further by moving from a large home to a smaller condominium or town home. You will certainly need to replace your automobiles and VCRs every so often, but you will probably spend considerably less on buying things than you spend now.

Because you are unlikely to take out a larger mortgage or buy as many expensive items (other than automobiles) as you did before, it is also likely that most of your expenses in retirement will be less affected by inflation than they are now. Counterbalanced against the variables reducing your retirement expenses are two in particular that will increase. And, unfortunately, they will be highly vulnerable to inflation. These are travel and health care. Many people travel more in retirement than they did while working. They travel to see their children, to attend elder hostels, to revisit the fond places of their youth, and simply to visit places they've never been able to see before.

The biggest question mark in future expenses is health care costs.[2] There is no way to know if or when you will have to enter a nursing home. But if you do enter one, it could easily cost $35,000 per year (in 1994 dollars). Your direct health costs will also rise. Many employers are backing away from paying the health insurance premiums of their retirees. The nation is generally moving toward a philosophy that charges the individual with paying a larger portion of his or her health costs directly. Even if Congress passes a national health insurance plan in the next few years, you must anticipate that your health costs will inflate much faster than the overall inflation rate.[3]

Calculating Your Retirement Income Needs

Calculating your income needs can be as complex a process as you want to make it. TIAA-CREF, for example, publishes an excellent guide, *Life Stages: Getting Ready to Retire*[4] that walks you through copious worksheets for retirement income, disability insurance review, life insurance review, estate planning, estate settlement, net worth calculation, cash flow analysis, goal setting, retirement expenses, inflation planning, risk tolerance, and income tax projection.

The more detail the better, no doubt, but the demand for excessive detail can easily lead one to put off doing this critical task. A good way to get started is to reduce the demand for detail and calculate a ball park estimate of what your retirement income needs will be. There is a fairly simple way to do this. Assuming that all your current income goes to taxes, savings, or spending, subtract from your current, regular, pre-tax income any expenses (including savings) that you do not expect to have in retirement. Add in new expenses that are likely, and adjust that figure for the impact of inflation between today and the day you plan to retire.

**Table 16-1   Retirement Income Estimates of
Mr. and Mrs. Far Seer**

Current Age	55
Anticipated Retirement Age	65
Current Pre-tax Income	$52,000
Expenses to be Eliminated in Retirement	
Social Security FICA Tax	3,928
SRA Contribution	9,000
College Expenses for Children	3,000
Other Unneeded Expenses	2,000
Subtotal	$17,928
New Expenses Expected in Retirement	
Increased Travel	3,000
Increased Health Costs	4,000
Net Retirement Income Needed	$41,072
Inflation Adjustment to Income Needs	
Years to retirement	10
Inflation factor from Appendix I	1.50
Inflation Adjusted Income	$61,608

This will give you a good, general estimate of your pre-tax income needs both in today's dollars (which are easier for making comparisons) and inflated dollars. This process is not as elegant as the one that a financial planner can provide, but the net result will probably not be that different.

As practice, let us make a rough estimate of the retirement needs of Mr. and Mrs. Far Seer who are both 55 years old and live on his salary of $52,000 per year. They hope to retire in ten years at age 65. Table 16-1 outlines their situation. Although they earn $52,000 per year, they actually live on much less. They contribute $9,000 to his

CREF SRA account which they will no longer need to do after retirement. They spend $3,000 per year on college loans for their children that will be paid off shortly. They also pay a $3,928 FICA payroll tax for Social Security and Medicare that they will not have to pay from their retirement income. Their spending money on other savings, lunches, clothes, and miscellaneous items could easily be reduced by $2,000 per year. The net result is that their direct expenses could be reduced by $17,928 per year if they retired in the near future. If their retirement income is low enough to drop them into a lower income tax bracket, that will also bring a further reduction in expenses, but the Far Seers prefer not to speculate on that possibility.

Balanced against these income reductions, however, is the fact that they plan to increase their travel budget by $3,000 per year. They do not know how much their health costs will increase, but they estimate an additional $4,000 per year. They plan to put this amount into a separate money market account from which they will write checks for health expenses. If the first year's health expenses do not add up to $4,000, which seems likely, they will let the account grow. If the first year's health expenses unexpectedly exceed this amount, they have enough flexibility in their other budget items to be able to increase their health care budget. After adding in these increased expenditures, they estimate that they would need $41,072 per year in pre-tax income if they retired tomorrow.

Since the Far Seers do not plan to retire for ten more years, they need to estimate the impact of inflation. Using the second column of Appendix I, they calculate that it will probably take $61,068 in ten years to buy what $41,072 buys for them today.

Having walked through this exercise with the Far Seers, you can use the space provided in Table 16-2 to estimate your own retirement income needs. As noted, any financial planner worth his or her salt will find Table 16-2 much too simple. If you want a more sophisticated model, TIAA-CREF's book *Life Stages* provides one that will give you hours of fun pouring over old check books, income tax returns, and paycheck stubs.[5] In the meantime, fifteen minutes spent with Table 16-2 will give you a rough idea of where you stand.

In filling out Table 16-2, make sure to include all of your income sources, except for one-time extraordinary items and investment income that you save. Also, be realistic about your subtractions. Although you might not be paying off your children's college loans, you will quite likely continue to spend some money on them. Also, be realistic about

Table 16-2   Estimating Your Own Retirement Needs

Current Ages (You) (Spouse)   ___ ___

Anticipated Retirement Age   ___

Current Pre-tax Income   _____

Expenses to be Eliminated in Retirement
     Social Security FICA Tax   _____
     SRA Contribution   _____
     College Expenses for Children   _____
     Other Unneeded Expenses   _____
     Subtotal   _____

New Expenses Expected in Retirement
     Increased Travel   _____
     Increased Health Costs   _____

Net Retirement Income Needed   _____

Inflation Adjustment to Income Needs
     Years to retirement   ___
     Inflation factor from Appendix I   ___

Inflation Adjusted Income   _____

---

your additions. If you decide to take up a new hobby, such as becoming an airplane pilot, for example, you have to add in the expenses for that.

Finally, if you are married, your estimates are more complicated than if you are single. If you are single, you only need to calculate your own retirement income needs. If you are married, you could calculate your own and your spouse's income needs separately. Or you could make one calculation for the entire family.

Notes

1. TIAA-CREF, *Looking Ahead to Retirement*, The Library Series, No. 3 (New York: TIAA-CREF, 1993), p. 12.

2. See TIAA-CREF, *Planning for Health Coverage in Retirement*, The Library Series, No. 8 (New York: TIAA-CREF, 1993).

3. From 1960 through 1990, total national health expenditures grew at an annual rate of 10.9 percent per year. Calculated from Bureau of the Census, *Statistical Abstract of the United States: 1992* (Washington, D.C.: United States Government Printing Office, 1992), p. 97.

4. TIAA-CREF, *Life Stages: Getting Ready to Retire* (New York: TIAA-CREF, 1992).

5. Ibid., p. 3.

Chapter 17

How Large a Kitty of Assets Will You Need?

Having established your income needs, you now have a base for calculating the amount of assets it will require to generate that income. The amount of assets varies greatly depending on whether you annuitize or whether set up your own plan for withdrawing your TIAA-CREF accumulations.

Initial Benefits of Annuitizing

Chapter 15 examined several pros and cons of annuitizing versus not annuitizing. Here we want to focus solely on the financial consequences of annuitizing versus not annuitizing. TIAA-CREF's advice is very clear: for most people, annuitizing is the better course of action.

If you annuitize, you probably do not need to accumulate as much in assets to generate a dollar in monthly income as you would if you were not annuitizing. TIAA-CREF can calculate an annuity for a single man, age 65 as though he were going to run out of money at age 84, which is his life expectancy. Any given man, however, would have to add an extra five or ten years just in case he lived longer than he planned. For the money to last those extra years there either has to be a larger initial accumulation, a smaller monthly withdrawal, or a better rate of return than you would get from TIAA-CREF at comparable risk levels.

In its booklet *Annuitizing: The Lifetime Choice*, TIAA-CREF makes the case for annuitizing by comparing two 65 year olds, each with a $100,000 accumulation that earns an 8.5 percent rate of return. The first annuitizes and receives a monthly check for $874.62 (or $10,495 per year) which will last the rest of his life.[1] The second person chooses not to annuitize, but if he withdraws $874.62 per month, he will run out of money in nineteen years. According to TIAA-CREF, for the nonannuitizer not to exhaust his principal, he can withdraw only $677.53 per month.

Table 17-1 illustrates TIAA-CREF's point very clearly. But the argument still has several flaws. First, by saying that the nonannuitizers could withdraw only $677 per month to have their money last a lifetime, TIAA-CREF has grossly underestimated what they could withdraw. By our calculations, at the same 8.5 percent return, they could withdraw $727 per month and their money would last until age 105, which is probably long enough for most of us.

Second, TIAA-CREF's assumptions about the future might not turn out any more realistic than yours. TIAA is not earning 8.5% per year in the 1990s, and TIAA annuitants have seen their monthly payments decline. CREF annuitants also see their payments decline each time the stock market suffers an annual loss, but that loss is counter balanced by the fact that CREF has historically had three up years for every down year.

Third, although the nonannuitizers start out withdrawing $148 less per month, they retain enormous flexibility. They can shift their investments as investment climates change. And they still retain the option of annuitizing at a later date, if they want to. If they do choose to annuitize at a later date, their annuity payments are likely to be higher, because they will have to cover fewer years.

Fourth, the nonannuitizers also possess a huge principal at every point along the way. Unless there is some pending threat to this pool of cash, such as a lawsuit or entrance into a nursing home, it is probably better to have control over those assets than not to have control over them.

A Question of Income Needs

By using this example, TIAA-CREF is really looking at the issue from the wrong end. Instead of asking how much can be withdrawn from a given amount of assets before the money runs out, a person ought to ask: How much in assets do I need to have in order to live at the level of lifestyle I want? Given the assumptions behind Table 17-1, for example,

Table 17-1 Annuitizing vs. Nonannuitizing

	With Annuity	Cash Withdrawals Without Annuity			
Monthly (in $)	874.62	874.62	799	727	703
Annually (in $)	10,495	10,495	9,588	8,724	8,440
Principal Gone at Age	Never	84	90	105	Never

Source: Data for annuitizing taken from TIAA-CREF, *Annuitizing: The Lifetime Choice* (New York: TIAA-CREF, 1991), pp. 6-9.

Based on $100,000 invested at 8.5 percent.

the nonannuitizers can withdraw just as much as the annuitizer ($10,495 yearly) if they will just let their accumulations grow a little more before they begin withdrawals. With $110,000 in assets the withdrawals will last until age 90, and with $120,000 in assets the withdrawals will last until age 105.

We obviously have no control over how long we will live. But we do have a great deal of influence over how many assets we accumulate before we begin drawing on them. This is because we can choose when to stop working and start living off of our accumulations. Given the 8.5 percent growth rate assumption in Table 17-1, a person's $100,000 retirement savings would grow to $120,000 in less than a year if that person taught for just two more semesters and made the maximum contribution into an SRA. In all probability, any 65 year old who had made the maximum SRA contributions over the years would have seen his or her SRA and RA funds grow well in excess of $120,000.

Accumulation NeedsIf You Do Not Annuitize

To repeat, rather than ask how much I can withdraw from my assets, it is more useful to ask how much in assets I need in order to live at the level I want. The critical issue is whether one has enough assets to sidestep the need for annuitizing. The nonannuitizer usually needs more assets to retire at a given income level than does the annuitizer. So how do you calculate how much is enough?

Let us use Tables 17-2 and Appendix II to calculate the asset requirements for Mr. and Mrs. Far Seer, whom we met in Chapter 16. First, to determine how well they want to live, we transfer from Table 16-1 (p. 260), the $41,072 that the Far Seers estimated that they would need to retire today. Second, we subtract from that all of the non-investment income sources they would have if they retired today. Having requested and received a Benefit Estimate Statement from the Social Security Administration, the Far Seers determine that in today's dollars, Mr. Far Seer will receive a monthly benefit of $14,000 at age 65, and Mrs. Far Seer a spousal benefit of $7,000. So they subtract that from their income needs and discover that they need to generate $20,072 per year from their investments if they do not annuitize.

How large a kitty will it take to generate $20,072 annually for life and allow the Far Seers to increase their income by 4.1 percent each year to combat inflation? The answer is contained in Appendix II, but it depends upon two key assumptions. What growth rate do they think their money will earn and how long do they plan to live? Knowing that life expectancy at age 65 is 15.2 years for men and 19.0 years for women,[2] the Far Seers start out by deciding that they do not want to run out of money before age 95, which gives them a 10-year margin of safety. Even this is a little risky, however, because they belong to an upper socio-economic background that undoubtedly has better medical care, health habits, and a longer life expectancy than the average person. TIAA-CREF estimates that 21 percent of its participants who make it to age 65 will also make it to age 95.[3] So, after talking with their financial planner the Far Seers raise their target to age 100, or 35 years beyond age 65. If they are still alive at that point, they do not think they will be alert enough to spend the equivalent of $41,000 per year anyway, and they are willing to live on their Social Security checks for whatever time they have left after age 100.

As for their investments, they plan to keep their funds in the TIAA-CREF system and allocate them according to the Early Retirement portfolio shown in Table 8-3 in Chapter 8. That is, they will keep 30 percent in CREF Stock, 45 percent in TIAA, and 25 percent in CREF Money Market. Based on historical precedent they hope that this will give them an annual rate of return of 7.6 percent.

Looking across the row for 35 years in Appendix II, $10,000 in real dollar income can be generated for 35 years if $233,000 is invested

Table 17-2   Asset Calculation for Mr. Far Seer

Years until anticipated retirement		10
Income needs if retiring today (from Table 16-1).		$41,072
Income Sources in Today's Dollars		
Social Security	14,000	
Spousal SS	7,000	
Other	none	
Subtotal		$21,000
Income That Must be Generated from Retirement Accumulations		$20,072
Using Appendix 2, these assets are needed today to generate this income for 35 years.		$432,752
Adjusting this for the inflation factor shown in Appendix 1, this is the amount that will be needed to start retirement in 10 years.		$649,128

at 7 percent or if $204,000 is invested at 8 percent. Since 7.6 percent is 0.6 of the distance between 7 and 8 percent, they make the extrapolation that $215,600 will produce $10,000 in income at a 7.6 percent rate of return. They need to generate $20,072 in income, so they multiply $215,600 times 2.0072 and calculate that they will need $432,752.[4] Since they won't start retirement for another 10 years, they adjust this by the appropriate inflation factor of 1.5 shown in Appendix I and arrive at $649,128.

This estimate also has a large margin of safety built into it, since they have used a generous estimate of their income needs and it is unlikely that either Far Seer will live till age 100. Consequently, even if they have overestimated their rate of return or underestimated inflation, they probably will not suffer too much damage. They could probably retire comfortably with considerably less, but being the financial conservatives that they are they set their ten year target on reaching $655,150 in financial assets.

Accumulating $649,128 sounds formidable. But the Far Seer's position is not quite so difficult as it seems. Having contributed the maximum to their SRA over the years, it is not unreasonable to assume that by age 55 the Far Seerers already possess $200,000 in their TIAA-CREF RA and SRA accounts plus $40,000 in IRA accounts that they had opened in the early 1980s. This gives them a total of $240,000. Additionally, Mr. Far Seer is contributing $9,000 to his SRA and another $5,000 is going to his RA, which will increase as his salary increases. If they allocate their assets according to the Late-Career Portfolio in Chapter 8, Table 8-3, they can expect an 8.5 percent annual growth rate which would easily enable them to reach their $649,128 target in ten years. As a cushion, it is likely that the Far Seers have additional funds in CDs, Keogh accounts, savings, and stock brokerage accounts. They probably also own a house that will have an equity that they could tap to generate further income if it were needed.

With any luck at all, the Far Seers will be in a position to retire long before their 65th birthdays. And their situation conveys a powerful lesson. If you contribute regularly to your SRA and build up some other savings, you will slowly build up a substantial accumulation. Once you reach the $250,000 to $300,000 range you do not need to take extraordinary risks or receive large rates of return to generate the kind of growth rates you need to retire without annuitizing.

Calculating Your Own Asset Needs

To estimate your own asset needs, you can follow the same exercise that the Far Seers did. Appendices II and III will be help you do this. Suppose you calculated that you would need an income of $40,000 to retire tomorrow and Social Security would contribute $10,000 of that. Unlike the Far Seers, however, you cannot imagine living to age 100. Age 90 is sufficient, and you are 60 now, so your savings need to last for 30 years. You also want to increase your income by 4.1 percent each year to counter inflation, and you are fairly confident that you can earn an 8 percent rate of return on your investments. Appendix II shows that you need $567,000 ($189,000 x 3) in today's money to retire on these terms. If, however, you are only 35 years old and your early retirement is twenty-five years away, you multiply this by an inflation factor of 2.63 (see Appendix I) and arrive at $1,491,210,. This sum is not at all out of reach for a thirty-five year old who follows the advice of this book, puts the maximum into his or her SRA, and allocates those funds aggressively.

Let us examine one more way to look at the retirement needs of the nonannuitizer. Suppose you currently have $645,000, have just had a difficult spat with the dean, and decide that you want to retire tomorrow morning. You think you could easily earn 8 percent per year with your investments, want to increase your income by 4.1 percent each year for inflation, and do not want to exhaust your assets for forty years. How much could you safely withdraw without annuitizing? Appendix III shows that the answer is precisely $29,864 the first year. Looking down to the cell where the 8 percent column intersects with the 40 year row, Appendix III shows that you can withdraw 4.63 percent or $29,864 the first year.

Accumulation Needs for the Annuitizer

All the illustrations to this point have been for the nonannuitizer. The annuitizer is in a more favorable position only in the respect that he or she does not need to accumulate as much capital to make an equal initial withdrawal. The nonannuitizer calculations have also factored in a realistic inflation rate. TIAA-CREF's annuity calculations do not, unless you take the graded payout plan that Chapter 15 argued, was not a good way to protect yourself from inflation.

Estimating the accumulation needs for the annuitizer is much simpler, because TIAA-CREF sends you an annual benefits report (ABR) each year that itemizes your year-end accumulations and the annuity payment that it would buy you at age 65 under various scenarios and assumed rates of return. It is important to remember, however, that these projected annuities are given in today's dollars, not the inflated dollars you will require several years from now. Consequently, you need to use Appendix I to calculate what that income will be worth at the time you start drawing the annuity.

If the vagueness of your Annual Benefits Report leaves you unsatisfied about where you stand, TIAA-CREF will make a very precise calculation for you. You can phone TIAA-CREF, give the anticipated date of starting the benefits, state whether you will make further contributions until that date, indicate how you plan to allocate your premiums between the TIAA-CREF accounts, and tell what payout option you want. You will soon receive a report indicating just what your annuity payments will be under those circumstances.

If you enjoy developing these types of scenarios yourself, you can ask whether your personnel office has TIAA-CREF's personal computer software program. It will estimate payments from virtually any set of assumptions you feed into it.

Integrating Annuitization Plans with Cash Withdrawal Plans

For purposes of illustrating we have been treating annuitizing vs. nonannuitizing as an either-or situation choice. In reality, it is not such a situation. Some persons might, for example, use the TIAA-CREF annuity and Social Security to establish a minimally acceptable comfort level that will last for life. With this minimum comfort level assured, they have less need to worry about making the balance of their assets last well beyond their life expectancy, and they can set up a very generous cash withdrawal plan.

How might this work? Let us assume that a person estimated a minimum comfort level would cost $25,000 in today's dollars. Social Security would provide $10,000 of that amount. This person could then have TIAA-CREF annuitize enough of his or her accumulations to provide the other $15,000. The nonannuitized balance plus all other savings could be used to set up a cash withdrawal plan or spend-down plan in any other manner that the person chose. If you follow this strategy, however, it is important to remember that TIAA-CREF's annuity projections do not adjust for inflation (unless you use the graded plan). For that reason, you need to make some provision to reinvest enough of your $15,000 annuity to compensate for inflation.

Conclusion

- When calculating your asset needs make fairly conservative estimates of your investment return and how long you plan to live. This gives you a margin of safety in case things do not work out as well as you hope.

- Once you have calculated your asset needs, you are in a good position to decide whether you need to annuitize. Appendices I through III are helpful in making these calculations.

- If retirement is imminent, use Appendix III to calculate how much you can start withdrawing without annuitizing. If this amount will provide the standard of life you want for enough years, then you may not need to set up an annuity.

- If retirement is several years off, use Appendices I and II to calculate how big a kitty you will need at the future date when you hope to retire.

- You will probably find that annuitizing will bring you a higher initial monthly benefit than will a cash withdrawal plan. But remember that the TIAA portions of your annuity are not a good hedge against inflation. By contrast this book's tables for calculating your asset needs have a 4.1 percent inflation factor built into them.

Notes

1. TIAA-CREF, *Annuitizing: The Lifetime Choice* (New York: TIAA-CREF, 1991), pp. 6-7.

2. U.S. Bureau of the Census, *Statistical Abstract of the United States: 1992* (Washington, D.C.: U.S. Government Printing Office, 1992), p. 77. Expectancy is for the year 1989. TIAA-CREF publications cite a higher life expectancy of 21 years for men and 24 for women. TIAA-CREF, *Comparing TIAA-CREF Income Options*, The Library Series, No. 6 (New York: TIAA-CREF, 1992), p. 22.

3. TIAA-CREF, *Annuities, the LifeTime Choice*, p. 8.

4. They actually need slightly more, but rounding the numbers in Table 17-3 to the nearest thousands necessarily leads to a small discrepancy in the outcome.

Chapter 18

Social Security, Health Care, and Taxes

As you fit TIAA-CREF into your retirement plans, several related matters need consideration, but we can touch them only briefly here. Three of the most important of these are Social Security, health care, and taxes. Let us conclude this excursion through retirement planning by examining each of these issues.

Social Security and Its Impact

There are four major issues involving Social Security. What benefits will you be eligible for? Should you start those benefits at age 65, start them earlier, or defer them until later? If you decide to teach or earn other income, how will that income affect your Social Security benefits? And how much of your Social Security benefits will be subject to taxes.

Eligibility for Benefits

The simplest and most accurate way to determine your eligibility for benefits is to fill out and mail to the Social Security Administration the "Request for Earnings and Benefits Estimate Statement." (Call 800 772 1213 to order a copy). For any retirement date you choose, the Social Security Administration will calculate your estimated benefits as of that date. Even if you are several years from retirement, it is still a good idea to make this request every few years because it gives you a handy checklist to ensure that you have been given the proper credit for all the contributions you made into the system.

In general, you are eligible for Social Security retirement benefits if you have worked for at least ten years in covered employment. Your precise level of benefits will depend on how much you earned over the years, how much you paid in FICA taxes, and how many years you worked. Based on this information, the Social Security Administration calculates a Primary Insurance Amount (PIA), that is the basic amount upon which all of your benefits are predicated.

Your spouse and dependent children might also be eligible for Social Security benefits. Your spouse may take the greater of his or her own Social Security benefits or the spousal benefit that is one-half of your benefits. Thus, if you are eligible for $14,000 per year at age sixty 65, you and your spouse together will be eligible for $21,000 at that age.

Should You Start Your Benefits Early?

The minimum age for receiving full Social Security retirement benefits is currently age 65, but this minimum will gradually increase until it reaches age 67 in the year 2007. The earliest you can begin receiving your Social Security retirement benefits is age 62.

If you take benefits early, they will be reduced by 5/9 of 1 percent for each month before your sixty-fifth birthday. Thus, your benefits will be reduced by 20 percent if you start them at age 62, by approximately 13 percent if you start at age sixty-three, and by slightly less than 7 percent if you start at age sixty-four. On the other hand, if you delay receiving benefits until after age 65, your benefits will be increased at the rate of 4.5 percent per year for each year of delay until age 70. This rate of increase will be gradually pushed up until by the year 2009 benefits will be increased by 8 percent for each year that benefits are put off. The Social Security Administration is obviously giving people an enormous incentive to stay in the work force and delay the taking of benefits.

One big issue for early retirees is whether they should begin taking their reduced benefits early or whether they should wait until their normal retirement age so they can receive full benefits. If they live long enough, they will always end up getting to spend more Social Security money if they postpone benefits to age 65. When stated this way, the critical questions then become: How long do you plan to live? What will

Table 18-1   Three Strategies for Social Security Benefits

	Cumulative Amounts Spent: (in $)		
Age	Strategy 1	Strategy 2	Strategy 3
62	8,000		
63	16,000		
64	24,000		
65	32,000	10,000	10,500
78	128,000	130,000	136,500
86		220,000	217,805

Strategy 1:   Start receiving benefits at age 62 and start spending them immediately.

Strategy 2:   Start receiving benefits at age 65 and start spending them immediately.

Strategy 3:   Start receiving benefits at age 62, but invest the benefits at 6 percent. At age 65 start spending $2,500 per year of that investment until the amount is exhausted.

Note: This table does not account for the indexing of Social Security benefits.

you do with the reduced benefits that you begin receiving at age 62? A good financial planner can help you calculate the breakeven points under various estimates.[1] If you do not have a good financial planner to do the calculations, Table 18-1 makes some estimates for three strategies for a person who would be eligible for $10,000 in Social Security benefits at age 65 or $8,000 at age 62. Under Strategy 1, the person takes $8,000 per year starting at age 62 and spends it. Under Strategy 2, the person starts taking benefits at age 65 and receives $10,000 per year. At approximately age 77, Strategy 2 reaches a break even point compared with Strategy 1. Up to that age, Strategy 1 was receiving more in cumulative benefits. But from that age on, Strategy 2 receives more in cumulative benefits.

Strategy 3 also starts receiving benefits at age 62, but instead of spending them immediately, it reinvests them at 6 percent. Starting at age 65, it then spends all the Social Security benefits plus $2,500 per year from the invested funds. At this rate that fund will be exhausted in twenty years. Strategy 3 outperforms Strategy 2 until age 86. Up to this age, Strategy 3 receives more money, but beyond that age, Strategy 2 receives more money.

Although these calculations are approximations and do not take into account the impact of inflation or the indexing of Social Security benefits, they do help clarify the situation for the early retiree. Strategy 3 seems to be best for a person with a normal life expectancy who does not need the $8,000 immediately but would rather have larger sums of money at ages 65 to 70 than at ages 86 to 90. Strategy 1, on the other hand, seems to be better for a person with a very short life expectancy or for a person who was forced to retire early but did not have enough other assets to get along without spending the $8,000 Social Security benefit immediately. This strategy would also appeal to the person who, regardless of immediate need, thought better use could be made of that $8,000 per year between ages 62 and 65 than between ages 77 and 80. He or she might prefer to spend $8,000 per year traveling abroad from ages 62 to 64 rather than receive an extra $2,000 per year from age 65 on. Strategy 2 would seem best for the person who expected to live for a very long time, and who also expected to be just as alert and able to enjoy spending an extra $2,000 per year for several years after age 77 as he or she could enjoy spending an extra $8,000 per year for the three years between ages 62 to 64.

How Will Social Security Affect Your Earned Income?

Many college people are able to continue earning income from royalties, consulting contracts, teaching occasional courses, or other endeavors. If their earnings from these endeavors exceed certain limits, their Social Security benefits will be reduced. Because these limits change annually, it is important to keep track of them for every year in which you expect to have earned income. As of 1994, the 1994 limits on earned income were as follows:

Persons under age 65 could earn up to $8,040 without suffering any reduction in Social Security benefits. Above that amount, $1 in benefits was forfeited for each $2 of earned income.

Persons aged 65 to 69 could earn up to $11,160 and receive no benefit reduction. Above that amount $1 in benefits was forfeited for each $3 of earned income.

Persons over age 70 have no limit on earned income.

Will Your Social Security Benefits be Taxed?

In recent years, Congress has begun applying the federal income tax to the Social Security benefits of higher income people. Notwithstanding this development, a fair portion of your benefits will remain untaxed.

For single persons whose adjusted gross income (including one-half of Social Security benefits) is less than $34,000 (in 1994), there is no tax on Social Security benefits. Taxes on Social Security benefits begin above that trigger point. Up to 85 percent of the excess will be subject to taxes, with the precise percentage depending upon income levels and benefit levels. For married couples filing joint returns, the trigger point is $44,000.

The Cost of Health Care in Retirement

This may be the biggest threat to a financially comfortable retirement. For the past three decades, health care costs have increased more than 10 percent per year. Although the rate of increase has begun to slow in recent years, there is no possibility of it dropping under the overall inflation rate. In addition, nursing home costs have the potential to drive most of us into poverty. For these reasons, if for no others, it is imperative to understand the issues involved in health care and to discuss them with your institution's benefits officer well before you commit yourself to retirement. TIAA-CREF offers an excellent booklet, *Planning for Health Coverage in Retirement*[2] which would be useful to read before you talk to your benefits officer.

Three of the most critical issues to understand are Medicare, Medigap Insurance, and long-term care needs.

Medicare

This federal program began under President Lyndon Johnson in 1965. Since then it has become the central health insurance plan for most people over age 65. Its rules, premium levels, and coverages are extremely complex and change frequently, which complicates the task of keeping yourself up to date on the program.

Medicare is divided into Part A, which covers hospitals and Part B, which is a supplemental insurance plan to cover services by physicians and other health care providers. Everyone over age 65 is eligible for Part A's hospital coverage, and there is no premium to pay if you are eligible for Social Security. Persons not eligible for Social Security pay a monthly premium, which in 1993 was $221. Everyone over age 65 is also eligible for Part B and, if they select it, must pay a monthly premium that in 1993 was $36.60. In most cases this amount is deducted from your Social Security benefit check, so you do not have to worry about forgetting to pay it.

Since Medicare does not begin until age 65, it is vital that early retirees do not surrender their existing employer's insurance until that age.

Medigap Coverage

While Medicare has helped improve health care for the elderly in a major way, the program does not cover everything, and there are limits to how much it will pay for the services that it does cover. Excluded from coverage, for example, are annual physical examinations, dental care, eyeglasses or hearing aids, prescriptions you take at home, and medical care you receive while traveling abroad.

You need to cover the gaps left by these exclusions. For most people, the best Medigap coverage is to stay on their employer's plan, which is permitted at 61 percent of TIAA-CREF institutions.[3] Even if you have to pay a larger share of the premiums than you did while working, you usually end up with better benefits than if you dropped out of the plan.

If you cannot stay with your employer's plan, it is usually possible to convert it to an individual policy. This is less desirable than staying with your current plan, because the individual plans usually have more exclusions, premiums are likely to be higher, there is greater risk of extraordinary premium increases if you develop an expensive illness, and there may be problems covering pre-existing conditions.

Another possibility is enrollment in an HMO. Many HMOs have dovetailed their plans with Medicare so that you receive a wide range of covered services, but you are not burdened with the voluminous paperwork for which Medicare is so famous. If none of these options is available to you, you can purchase a Medigap policy from an insurance company.

Because of Medicare's complexity, it is extremely important to understand the coverages and costs involved in the program, the gaps in coverage, and how you can plug those gaps. Your benefits office should be willing to help you clarify these matters.

Long-term Care

The third major health care issue casting a shadow over retirement is the dreaded possibility of needing long-term care. About 5 percent of people over age 65 live in nursing homes, and another 5 percent receive some degree of long-term care at home. Although your chances of ending up in a nursing home may be small, the fact of it happening would threaten your financial well being as well as that of your spouse, children, and other dependents you may have. In the early 1990s nursing homes frequently cost $35,000 per year or more. Of all married couples who are obliged to put one partner in a nursing home, 29 percent are reduced to a poverty-level income within one year and 49 percent within two years. Single people show even worse statistics: 36 percent and 53 percent, respectively, fall into poverty.[4] It can also be expensive to provide long-term care at home for persons who can no longer bathe themselves, feed themselves, or carry out some of the other activities of daily living.

Unfortunately Medicare will cover almost none of your nursing home care if that is needed and will cover very little of your long-term care at home. Another federal program, Medicaid, can help on these expenses, but to get that help you must "spend down" your assets. This is a euphemism for driving yourself into poverty so you can qualify for Medicaid. In theory you probably do not quibble about having to be impoverished before receiving Medicaid. If people are going to spend their last few years in a nursing home, it hardly seems unfair to ask them to spend their own money before turning to the taxpayers for help. But you probably are less willing to drive your spouse into poverty. In 1993 your spouse needed to reduce his or her nonresidential assets to $14,148 in order for you to qualify for Medicaid, and his or her income had to be under $1,149 per month. Presumably this meant that if you and your spouse received a TIAA-CREF annuity check, any amount more than $1,149 per month had to be turned over to the nursing home or the Medicaid program.

One response to the threat of long-term care is to purchase a long-term care policy. TIAA-CREF offers such a policy as do many other insurers.

Tax Considerations

Like health coverage, retirement tax issues are so complicated and change so frequently that it is imperative to consult a tax adviser. TIAA-CREF's booklet *Taxes and Your Retirement Annuities*[5] is extremely helpful as is the chapter on pensions in *Tax Guide for College Teachers*[6].

Your RA and SRA payout benefits are termed "distributions" by the Internal Revenue Service. These and other tax deferred programs such as your IRA or your Keogh account will be subject to federal income tax when you receive them as distributions. One of the great assumptions behind making tax deferred contributions to a plan such as TIAA-CREF is that you will end up in a lower income tax bracket when you retire and begin taking the distributions. Whether that assumption is borne out depends, of course, on whether future Congresses change the income tax brackets. It also depends on how well you have managed your financial affairs. If you currently earn a salary that keeps you in the 15 percent income tax bracket, but you follow the investment advice offered earlier in this book, the chances are good that you will end up in a higher income tax bracket by the time you take your distributions. So you could conceivably end up making tax deferred contributions today that are taxable at the 15 percent rate only to end up withdrawing them later on when you are fortunate enough to be in the 31 percent or 39.5 percent tax bracket. This is not the best of all worlds, but it is not necessarily as bad as it may seem. As demonstrated in Chapter 4, the tax deferred program may have trained you in the discipline of saving. Since your savings were compounding on a tax-free basis all those years, you probably would still be better off even if you ended up in a higher tax bracket.

Aside from whether you will be in a higher or lower tax bracket when retired, several key issues may require some decision on your part. Simply making a list of them brings home the need to consult a tax specialist before you make major decisions in these areas.

- Do not exceed the limit on your SRA contributions. TIAA-CREF will calculate this limit for you.

- If you receive more than $150,000 from your combined tax deferred plans in a year, you may be liable for a 15 percent income tax penalty for excess benefits. If receiving this amount is a possibility, you need a tax consultant to advise you on how to avoid or minimize this penalty.

- If your tax deferred accumulations grow to more than $750,000, you may be liable for a 15 percent income tax penalty for excess accumulations. As you approach this figure, you need a tax consultant to advise you on how to avoid or minimize this penalty.

- Usually, the tax deferred status of your IRA or 403(b) plan dies with you and your annuity partner, but it is possible to structure your affairs to bequeath assets to your children or other beneficiaries so that the earnings will continue to compound tax free.[7]

- A surviving spouse can roll over a TIAA-CREF single-sum settlement to an IRA within 60 days of the participant's death.

- Any cash withdrawals that are not rolled into another tax deferred account will be subject to a federal withholding tax.

- Your annuity payments can also have taxes deducted, and you can fill out an IRS form W-4P to determine how much that deduction will be. If you do not withhold taxes, you need to file a quarterly estimated tax statement with the IRS. Failure to pay an adequate amount of taxes through either withholding or estimated tax payments could result in a penalty when you file your income tax return the following April.

- If you are an annuity partner and a beneficiary, most of your benefits will be taxed on the same terms as those for your spouse.

But $600,000 of an estate can be passed through tax free, so some of your benefits may be tax free if they are considered part of the estate. Do not automatically assume that every bit of your check is taxable.

- Different ages serve as breakpoints for key decisions. Generally, you cannot withdraw from a tax deferred annuity before age 59 1/2 without penalty. Generally, you must begin payouts from your TIAA-CREF account by April 1 after reaching age 70 1/2.

- Finally, state tax rates affect your net payouts as well. Some states have no income tax, and other states do not tax pension income. If you were planning to flee upon retirement to a state like Nevada with no income tax, it would be useful to check your own state's tax provisions carefully. You may not save as much by moving as it would appear.

Conclusion

Effective retirement planning demands that you keep tabs on several complicated and frequently changing issues involving health care, taxes, and Social Security. A good financial planner would be invaluable in sorting through these issues. Resist the temptation to sign on with the first planner who comes along, however. Use the criteria outlined in the book to sift through the potential planners in your region. Make certain that the planner you choose has some experience and qualifications to help you on your health care, tax, and Social Security problems as well as your investment problems.

Can you dispense with the planner and learn how to do these things for yourself? Of course. Since you will be retired, you will have more time to devote to the task.

Notes

1.   See Michael E. Leonetti, "When Should You Start Social Security? Revisited," *AAII Journal* 15, no. 6 (July 1993): 17-20.

2. TIAA-CREF, *Planning for Health Coverage in Retirement*, The Library Series No. 8 (New York: TIAA-CREF, 1993).

3. Ibid., p. 18.

4. Ibid., p. 32.

5. TIAA-CREF, *Taxes and Your Retirement Annuities*, Library Series No. 9 (New York: TIAA-CREF, 1992).

6. *1993 Tax Guide for College Teachers and Other College Personnel* (College Park, MD: Academic Information Service, Inc., 1992. This book is updated annually to keep apace of changes in the tax codes.

7. Laura Saunders, "Eternal IRAs," *Forbes* (June 21, 1993): 158. Saunders argues that naming a grandchild as beneficiary on your IRA would allow you to compute your minimum withdrawal rate on the joint life expectancy rate of both you and the child. If the grandchild were five years old and the joint life expectancy were set at the child's 65th birthday, only a minimal amount would be withdrawn each year and the child would have a substantial retirement nest egg throughout his lifetime.

Chapter 19

Summary and Concluding Thoughts

The following pages summarize the major conclusions drawn from this examination of retirement planning and TIAA-CREF.

Four Costly Mistakes

The four costliest mistakes made by TIAA-CREF participants are:

1. They fail to pay themselves first by opening an SRA. Or, if they have opened one, they fail to bring their contributions up to their maximum.

2. In their early years, they allocate premiums into TIAA that would do a better job for them if dollar cost averaged or value averaged into CREF equity funds.

3. In their middle-career and late-career years, they do not develop a systematic plan of asset allocation that is commensurate with their risk level.

4. Upon retirement, they annuitize too quickly without making a critical examination of other options.

Fifteen Points for a Better Retirement

Participants who want to get more out of TIAA-CREF should consider the following points:

1. Make some effort to understand TIAA-CREF, its advantages and disadvantages, as well as alternative means of saving for a retirement nest egg.

2. Pay yourself first. Do this by opening an SRA or a comparable deferred compensation plan.

3. Gradually increase your SRA contributions each year until you reach the maximum contribution level.

4. In your early years, dollar cost average all of your premiums to the CREF equity accounts. Put nothing in TIAA.

5. Consider using value averaging in place of dollar cost averaging. Although the back tests are not conclusive, it might give you a better result.

6. As your assets begin to accumulate, remember that preserving those assets becomes more important than gaining high rates of return.

7. Follow the principles of asset allocation to tailor your portfolio to your objective level of risk tolerance.

8. If you experiment with market timing, do so with only a small portion of your assets. Select three different timing strategies, and use each strategy for one-third of your timing portfolio. It is unlikely that all three strategies would underperform the market at the same time. Strategies backtested here that beat a buy-and-hold approach since 1952 included the 55 week moving average, interest rate strategies, and the seasonality strategy. There is, however, no assurance that real money timing strategies in the future will work as well as hypothetical backtests worked in the past.

9. If you are frustrated with the difficulties of following a strategic asset allocation plan through TIAA-CREF, consider moving some of your assets into a mutual fund family that offers the type of funds you would like to include in your asset allocation plan.

10. If you want to engage in market timing and are frustrated with the absence of small company funds or maximum capital appreciation funds in CREF, consider moving some of your of your assets to a discount broker or a mutual fund family where those choices exist.

11. If you want to hire the services of a financial planner, define for yourself what your goals are and carefully review the guidelines of Chapter 13 on selecting a financial planner.

12. As you approach the moment of retirement, do not be too hasty to follow TIAA-CREF's advice to annuitize your accumulations. Your situation might be one that would do better by setting up a systematic plan of cash withdrawals. Analyze this issue carefully.

13. Using the guidelines of Chapters 16 and 17, estimate how much retirement income you will need and how large a kitty of assets you will need to generate that income.

14. Remember that Social Security has a significant impact on your retirement years. Ascertain your estimated benefits *before* you retire, determine whether you are better off starting your benefits at age 65 or some other age, and understand the impact that earned income will have on your retirement benefits.

15. Financing health care is a major issue for most retirees. Before retiring, make sure you understand how your situation is affected by Medicare, Medicaid, and the insurance policies of your employing institution.

Ten Prescriptions for TIAA-CREF

Until 1990, TIAA-CREF had a monopoly on the retirement plans of most of its participants. Because of changes made that year, TIAA-CREF's $125 billion in pension fund assets are now up for grabs.

Participants are literally sitting on a gold mine ripe for prospecting by financial planners, mutual fund companies, mutual fund sales persons, insurance sales persons, and investment advisers who could make a nice living if they could only manage some of those funds. Furthermore, some of these advisers are more sophisticated about investments than are the retirement counselors hired by TIAA-CREF and have a wider array of products to offer. Unless TIAA-CREF takes preemptive action to make its products more competitive with what now exists in the market place, TIAA-CREF faces a growing assault on its asset base.

The following ten prescriptions for TIAA-CREF would protect its asset base and help it provide better service to its 1.7 million participants. In fairness to TIAA-CREF, three of these prescriptions (7, 8, and 9) are already being planned. They had not yet been implemented at the time of going to press, however, and it is impossible to predict what the details of these plans might be when they are announced. For these reasons, points 7, 8, and 9 are kept as prescriptions even though some variation of them might be in place by the time many readers receive this book.

1. Create several new CREF funds.

In comparison to a large mutual fund family, CREF does not offer a full array of funds for setting up a systematic strategic asset allocation plan. As argued in Chapter 8, CREF should create several discrete portfolios that members can use for their asset allocation plans. These portfolios would include a small company fund, a maximum capital appreciation fund, a value fund, an equity income fund, a pure international equity fund, and a pure international bond fund.

2. Create a new asset allocation fund with five portfolios.

Following the principles outlined in Chapter 8, there should be a portfolio for each career stage: early career, mid-career, late career, early retirement, and late retirement. Each asset allocation portfolio would be a fund-of-funds that allocates its assets among CREF's discrete portfolio funds in accord with allocation formulas such as those offered in Table 8-2.

3.   Create a Plan B alternative fixed income plan within TIAA.

Although many CREF participants might occasionally like to take some of their equity or bond profits off the table, the Retirement Annuity account (RA) offers only one place to park them--the Money Market fund. But this will not be very attractive during periods of low interest rates.

This is not a problem in the Supplemental Retirement Annuity (SRA) accounts, because in SRA accounts, transfers can be made into and out of TIAA at will and still receive TIAA's current return.

What is sorely needed is a Plan B for RA accounts. This would allow new TIAA contributions to be placed in a Plan B account where they would be subject to the same terms as TIAA contributions in SRAs. Existing TIAA accumulations in RA accounts or contributions to the traditional TIAA would not be covered by Plan B.

4.   Permit monthly rather than annual TPA transfers.

Currently, transfers to CREF from a Transfer Payout Annuity (TPA) are made annually on the anniversary of the date the TPA was established. If these transfers were made monthly rather than annually, they would constitute a dollar cost averaging plan. One principle of dollar cost averaging is that monthly investments provide higher returns than annual investments. Since the transfers would be handled automatically by computers, TIAA-CREF could provide a valuable benefit to its participants at no increased administrative cost to itself.

5.   Within annuitized accounts, permit an annual rebalancing of portfolios.

Life expectancy calculations used by TIAA-CREF assume that the average 65-year-old retiree will live another 22 years. But the 87 year old does not have the same ideal asset allocation as does the 65 year old. Unless retirees are permitted to rebalance their portfolios, they are stuck forever with whatever allocation formula they settled on at the moment of annuitizing. If they make too conservative an allocation, they risk falling behind the pace of inflation before they reach their eighties. If they make too venturesome an allocation, they risk significant declines in assets when they no longer have the time to ride out such declines. Annuitizers would be much better served if they could rebalance their assets periodically.

6.   Permit the use of the CREF Bond fund in annuitized accounts.

Although the CREF Bond fund has a higher risk level than TIAA, TIAA is not an adequate substitute for a bond fund. TIAA's holdings are not marked to the market as are the CREF Bond fund's holdings and for that reason TIAA cannot fluctuate with the market. Most investment advisers urge that some bonds be included in a retirement portfolio. TIAA-CREF should permit the use of its bond fund in annuity accounts.

7.   Create a systematic monthly withdrawal plan.

The vast majority of mutual funds enable offer you a systematic monthly withdrawal plan under which you can take out a specific amount each month. Under TIAA-CREF you can only do that if you annuitize your assets or follow the MDO or IPRO choices. If you want to with- draw your TIAA-CREF assets without annuitizing or if you want to delay annuitizing, you cannot set up a systematic monthly withdrawal plan of an amount of your choice.

8.   Create an automatic dollar cost averaging plan to make transfers from the Money Market fund to other CREF funds.

With the equity markets near all-time highs as of this writing and grossly overvalued by traditional measures, many people might like to take some of their stock earnings off the table and systematically feed them back into the equity funds on a monthly basis. This would enable these individuals to gain the protection of dollar cost averaging in event the markets suffered a sharp correction yet participate if the bull market continues. The only way this can now be done is to make a monthly telephone transfer from the Money Market fund (or from TIAA if in an SRA). Human nature being as it is, one would have to have an almost compulsive personality to do this on the same day each month regardless of all the other pressures in one's life and endure the emotional turbulence that would result from having to watch the ups and downs of the market so religiously.

What would serve everybody better would be a mechanism under which one could, for example, set up an automatic transfer of a fixed sum to selected CREF funds on the 25th of each month for a specified number of months. With this arrangement handled automatically by computers, it would be even easier for TIAA-CREF to administer than the current procedure of telephone transfers. Such a system would also give TIAA-CREF participants an option not available from most mutual fund families or independent advisers.

9.   Offer a personal computer software retirement planning kit.

Similar software kits are already available from the Vanguard, Fidelity, and T. Rowe Price fund families, and TIAA-CREF should also make one available. Some TIAA-CREF publications include worksheets that would be much more useful if they were complemented with PC retirement software.

10.   Broaden the quality of advice offered by TIAA-CREF counselors.

Some no-load mutual fund families provide individual planning advice and services for shareholders whose accounts exceed $250,000. As TIAA-CREF participants see their assets grow beyond that figure, they, too, could profit from the assistance of an individual planner. Current TIAA-CREF representatives are helpful when it comes to deciphering the various annuity options, but most participants either have or will have planning needs that go far beyond this issue.

TIAA-CREF should contract with teams of Certified Financial Planners who would be available to participants. These planners would function as fee-based financial planners, but they would receive their fees directly from TIAA-CREF. The costs would be divided equally between TIAA-CREF and the individual participant, with the individual's share being deducted from the individual's account. Each of these TIAA-CREF sponsored planners could provide many useful services for participants: develop a financial profile of the individual, offer asset allocation advice, help that person assess annuitization versus nonannuitization options, answer questions on Social Security, health care coverage, and the tax consequences of different withdrawal programs, give guidance on estate planning, and perform the same services that individual participants currently seek from independent financial planners.

This move on the part of TIAA-CREF would not only provide a valuable service for TIAA-CREF participants, it would give a much needed shot in the arm to the movement for fee-based financial planning. And it would put TIAA-CREF in the forefront of the drive to educate investors about retirement planning.

Appendix I

The Estimated Impact of Inflation

Years into the future	Value then of one dollar today.	Dollars needed then to equal one dollar today.
0	1.00	1.00
1	.96	1.04
2	.92	1.08
3	.88	1.13
4	.85	1.17
5	.81	1.22
6	.78	1.27
7	.75	1.33
8	.71	1.38
9	.69	1.44
10	.66	1.50
11	.63	1.56
12	.60	1.62
13	.58	1.69
14	.56	1.76
15	.53	1.83
16	.51	1.90
17	.49	1.88
18	.47	2.06
19	.45	2.15
20	.43	2.24
25	.35	2.63
30	.28	3.35
35	.23	4.09
40	.19	5.00

The inflation rate of 4.108 percent is calculated from the decline in purchasing power of the dollar from $4.151 in 1950 to .713 in 1952.

Source: *Statistical Abstract of the United States: 1993* (Washington, D.C.: United States Government Printing Office, 1993), p. 481.

Appendix II

Assets Needed to Generate Each $10,000 in Income

The amount of principal in thousand of dollars invested at a given growth rate that will permit a withdrawal of $10,000 of income the first year and allow the withdrawal to be increased at 4.1 percent per year for inflation. The account will be exhausted in the number of years indicated.

Year   Growth Rate of the Principal

Year	6%	7%	8%	9%	10%	11%	12%
5	58	57	55	54	53	52	51
10	101	97	93	89	85	82	79
15	141	132	124	116	110	104	98
20	177	162	150	138	128	120	112
25	210	189	171	156	143	131	121
30	240	212	189	170	153	139	128
35	268	233	204	181	161	146	132
40	293	250	216	189	168	150	135
45	316	266	227	196	172	153	137
50	337	279	235	202	176	155	139
55	356	291	242	206	179	157	140
58*	367	297	246	208	180	158	141

*This is the longest period yet for an annuity with TIAA-CREF.

Example: Someone wants to withdraw $50,000 per year, increase that by 4.1 percent each year for inflation, and have the funds last twenty-five years.   At an 8 percent rate of return, he or she will need assets of $855,000.

Appendix III

Maximum Withdrawal of Principal

The maximum percent that can be withdrawn from principal in the first year and increased at 4.1 percent per year thereafter, without exhausting the principal until the end of the number of years shown.

Annual Growth Rate of the Principal (%)

Yr	6%	7%	8%	9%	10%	11%	12%
5	17.42	17.82	18.23	18.62	19.04	19.44	19.85
10	9.93	10.38	10.84	11.31	11.79	12.27	12.75
15	7.12	7.61	8.11	8.62	9.14	9.68	10.22
20	5.66	6.17	6.70	7.25	7.81	8.39	8.98
25	4.77	5.30	5.86	6.43	7.03	7.65	8.28
30	4.17	4.72	5.30	5.91	6.54	7.19	7.86
35	3.74	4.31	4.91	5.56	6.21	6.89	7.41
40	3.41	4.00	4.63	5.29	5.98	6.69	7.41
45	3.16	3.77	4.42	5.10	5.81	6.55	7.30
50	2.97	3.59	4.25	4.96	5.70	6.45	7.22
55	2.80	3.44	4.13	4.85	5.61	6.38	7.16

Example: Someone with $100,000 in principal does not want to exhaust that principal for 30 years and expects to earn a 7 percent rate of return over those thirty years. He or she can withdraw $4,720 (4.72%) the first year, increase that amount by 4.1% each year, and have the money last for thirty years.

Appendix IV

Questions to Ask Prospective Financial Planners

Step 1:   Background Information

1.   Does this planner appear to have a good record
     after checking with the NASD (800 289 9991)?   _____

2.   Does this planner appear to have a good record
     after checking with your state regulatory agency?   _____

3.   Does your prospective planner have one of the three
     planner certifications?   _____

4.   Does the ADV form suggest adequate experience and
     training?   _____

Step 2:   Compensation

1.   Does the planner present a clear explanation of the
     fee structure?   _____

2.   Is this a fee-only planner?   _____

3.   If the compensation is based on a percent of assets
     under management, is the annual fee less than 1.25%   _____

4.   Does the planner promise not to sell you load funds
     or funds with 12(b)-1 charges from which he or
     she receives compensation?   _____

Step 3:   Meeting Your Needs

1.   Does this planner have experience with clients whose
     asset levels and needs are similar to yours?   _____

2. Does this planner have experience with estate planning for people with situations similar to yours? _____

3. Has this planner been in business in this community for at least 5 years? _____

4. Are half of the clients this planner had 5 years ago still with him or her? _____

Step 4: Judgment Calls

1. Does the planner pass the $100,000 test? _____

2. Does the planner avoid selling products that remunerate him or her for pushing those products rather than other types of products? _____

3. Does the planner work full time at the job? _____

4. Does the planner attend at least one professional conference or continuing education seminar each year? _____

5. After talking to at least two of the planner's clients, do they give the planner a passing grade? _____

6. Does the planner adjust his or her investment recommendations to a risk level appropriate for you? _____

7. Has the planner ever terminated relations with a client? _____

8. Can you and the planner agree on a relevant benchmark for evaluating the planner's future permformance? _____

9. Does the planner spend less than half of his or her time drumming up new business? _____

10. Does the planner put you sufficiently at east that you are willing to speak frankly and openly about your aspirations, finances, and life style? _____

Index

305